Software Architecture for Product Families

Software Architecture for Product Families

Principles and Practice

Mehdi Jazayeri

Alexander Ran

Frank van der Linden

▲ **ADDISON–WESLEY**

Boston • San Francisco • New York • Toronto • Montreal
London • Munich • Paris • Madrid
Capetown • Sydney • Tokyo • Singapore • Mexico City

Many of the designations used by manufacturers and sellers to distinguish their products are claimed as trademarks. Where those designations appear in this book, and we were aware of a trademark claim, the designations have been printed with initial capital letters or in all capitals.

The authors and publisher have taken care in the preparation of this book, but make no expressed or implied warranty of any kind and assume no responsibility for errors or omissions. No liability is assumed for incidental or consequential damages in connection with or arising out of the use of the information or programs contained herein.

The publisher offers discounts on this book when ordered in quantity for special sales. For more information, please contact:

Pearson Education Corporate Sales Division
One Lake Street
Upper Saddle River, NJ 07458
(800) 382-3419
corpsales@pearsontechgroup.com

Visit AW on the Web: www.awl.com/cseng/

Library of Congress Cataloging-in-Publication Data
Jazayeri, Mehdi.
    Software architecture for product families : principles and practice / Mehdi
Jazayeri, Alexander Ran, Frank van der Linden.
        p.   cm.
    Includes bibliographical references and index.
    ISBN 0-201-69967-2
    1. Application software.   2. Computer architecture.   I. Ran, Alexander, 1956–,
van der Linden, Frank, 1954–   III. Title.
QA76.76.A65 J65 2000
005.1—dc21   00-029326

ISBN 0-201-69967-2
Text printed on recycled paper
1 2 3 4 5 6 7 8 9 10—MA—0403020100
First printing, May 2000

Contents

Preface

This book presents a view of software architecture for product families. It is addressed to researchers, engineers, and managers involved in the development of software-intensive products. The book is based primarily on the experience gained in the project ARES (Architectural Reasoning for Embedded Systems), carried out by six partners, funded by the European Commission. The project was concerned with the application of software architecture research results to practical problems faced by the industrial partners.

The three industrial partners shared similar problems in coping with the management of software product evolution in the presence of increasing feature requirements and decreasing time-to-market requirements. Software architecture, particularly applied to product families, appeared to offer some solutions, but there were many approaches and methodologies from which to choose. The goal of the project was to evaluate promising software architecture research results by applying them to some typical software evolution problems in industrial settings. One of the mottos of the project was "industry as laboratory."

The project was carried out by three industrial and three university partners: Nokia Research Center, Philips Corporate Research, Asea Brown Boveri (ABB) Corporate Research, Technical University of Vienna, Imperial College of Science and Technology (London), and Polytechnic University of Madrid. During the project, we produced many results that had impact on the industrial partners (in terms of practice) and the university partners (in terms of curriculum development), as well as a large number of publications and presentations in scientific conferences and journals. Rather than collecting the many results already presented in journals and conferences reporting on progress in the ARES project, we decided to integrate the results gained in the project and present a comprehensive view of the approaches we followed, of what worked and what didn't.

The purpose of this book is to bring some of the salient results together to make the big picture accessible to a wider audience. In short, the book attempts to give the reader the perspective gained by the project partners after three years of experience in applying research results to practical problems of software architecture for software-intensive systems. All chapters have been written specifically for this book.

The Introduction introduces the background of the project and the case study–based approach that we chose for running the project. It explains how the project came about and how we decided on the particular foci for the project.

Chapter 1 presents a conceptual framework for software architecture. One of the problems the field of software architecture faces is the lack of a widely accepted terminology or even a set of concepts. In this chapter we present the major concepts and define supporting terminology that allows us to discuss the problems and solutions in a uniform way. Chapters 2 through 4 are the "technology" chapters, each dealing with one major aspect of software architecture for product families: architecture description, architecture assessment, and architecture recovery.

Then follow three "experience" chapters. Chapter 5 presents the experience of Philips in applying software architecture in consumer electronics. Chapter 6 presents several experiments carried out at Nokia to deal with the documentation and assessment of software architecture. Chapter 7 describes ABB's experience in developing a software architecture for a family of train control systems, starting with three existing systems. The experience chapters describe the case studies in detail. Each chapter describes the state of the art at the start of the project in the particular area, the problems we observed and tried to address in that area, and some of the ARES results.

Software architecture, product lines, and product families are all active areas of research and the subject of intense interest in industry. There are already several good books available that present different views of software architecture both for practitioners and researchers. Some present specific methodologies, some present research approaches, some present practical experiences. Our book may best be characterized as describing the application of research results to practice. Its aim is to show the reader how current research results may be applied and how to overcome the inevitable shortcomings of research results in practice.

For example, Chapter 2 introduces the concepts and approaches in software architecture description and concentrates mostly on the language Darwin, which was invented at Imperial College, one of the academic partners in the project. Chapter 5 describes how Darwin was applied at Philips and why the engineers at Philips had to modify Darwin to use it in practice. Indeed, they ended up developing their own tool, Koala, borrowing many of the concepts of Darwin but not the language itself. Chapter 7 describes what happened when ABB tried to use Darwin in architecture recovery. It worked for some things but not for others. ABB also had to do its own customization. We expect these kinds of results to be of interest to people concerned with software architecture both in academia and in industry.

Chapter 8 concludes the book by providing a high-level summary of the results and an outlook for future developments in the area of software architecture. It also discusses the critical issue of technology transfer in such a rapidly evolving field.

This is not the definitive work on software architecture families. No such book exists and will not exist for several years to come. But we need different views of the problem until eventually there will be enough understanding to have a textbook. This book is a modest step in that direction.

How to Read This Book

The project ARES started in December 1995 and was completed in February 1999. During this time, many people from all the partners worked on the project—some for a limited period of time and others during the whole period. The focus of the project was to produce results that could be exploited immediately by the partners.

For example, we at the Technical University of Vienna started a software architecture course relying heavily on the case studies from the ARES project. At Philips, engineers developed new tools for documenting software architectures and automatically generating code for module interconnection. At Nokia, engineers developed Web-based tools for organizing the documentation of complex systems. At ABB, the results of some of the ARES work drove the design of a new family architecture for train control systems. At Imperial College, the feedback from engineers in the three companies led to improvements in the Darwin tool set. At the Polytechnic University of Madrid, the researchers developed techniques for architecture assessment and response-time analysis that were used by the different industrial partners.

Although such results of the ARES project were useful and beneficial to the partners, the goal of the project was much larger. As a research project, we wanted to communicate our results to the larger research and industrial community. This we did through many publications in conferences and journals. Toward the end of the project we asked ourselves if there was anything else left to say that our publications did not say. The answer was that indeed much was left unsaid. The publications for the most part presented technological solutions to particular problems encountered at the time of publication. What was missing was any kind of integration—a larger conclusion, a bigger picture based on more than three years of experience. We decided that a book with the focus on the larger picture was the answer.

Rather than concentrating on point solutions to specific technical problems, the book would give a perspective of a three-year experience. Each chapter tries to look back three years and move forward to share a three-year perspective with the reader. This was the best way we could imagine to communicate what we learned in the project. This kind of presentation in each chapter gives the reader the opportunity to see the whole picture: our assumptions, our starting point, and where we ended up. As a reader, you can judge how our experiences may or may not apply in your context.

The project investigated different aspects of software architecture. In Chapter 1, "ARES Conceptual Framework for Software Architecture," Alexander Ran tries to abstract and summarize from these different aspects the project's collective understanding of an architecture-oriented approach to software engineering. In some ways, this chapter is the main result of the ARES project to be communicated to the community. Experienced software engineers and architects may read this chapter immediately and identify with many points it makes. Less experienced engineers probably will find this chapter unconvincing or hard to read initially. They will be better off reading the chapter quickly at the beginning and then returning to read it more carefully after they have read the rest of the book.

The rest of the book contains three "technology" chapters and three "experience" chapters. The technology chapters (2 through 4) abstract the technological aspects of our experience in a particular area. For example, Chapter 4 ("Software Architecture Recovery") tries to organize the processes that we used in applying architecture recovery to the ABB case study. It is not a research presentation as much as an attempt to document the approaches that worked in the case study. But rather than presenting the details of the case study, it presents methodological approaches that may be useful in other case studies of interest to the reader.

Thus, in reading one of the experience chapters (5 through 7), you can form your own conclusions about the experiment and the experience. A technology chapter presents our conclusions about the applicability of technology to real-world situations. The technology and experience chapters may be read in any order if the reader prefers to jump to a favorite subject.

Acknowledgments

Many people contributed to the ARES project in different ways. We would like to thank the following people from the different partners who participated in the project during different times in the project: Ruud Dewig, Alexander Gurschler, Karin Hajek, Vesna Hassler, Manfred Hauswirth, Hans Jonkers, René Klösch, Sturle Mastberg, Henk Obbink, Marcello Reina, Claudio Riva, Liesbeth Steffens, and Rob van Ommering.

The following reviewers provided valuable comments on an earlier copy of the manuscript that helped improve the book: Len Bass, Frank Buschmann, Paul C. Clements, Henry McNair, Robert Nord, Jim Purtilo, and Stephan Stoecker. David Weiss provided comments on the initial ideas for the book.

We would like to thank Deborah Lafferty, our editor at Addison-Wesley, for her enthusiasm, energy, ideas, and overall support in all aspects of the book preparation. We would also like to thank our copy editor, Stephanie Hiebert, who managed the process under very tight time constraints. It has been a pleasure to work with and learn from her.

We acknowledge gratefully the work of Doris Fisar, who edited and formatted various versions of the manuscript, all quite cheerfully.

Introduction

This book is a result of a three-year cooperative research project conducted by a consortium of six partners: Imperial College of Science and Technology (London), Technical University of Vienna, Polytechnic University of Madrid, Asea Brown Boveri (ABB) Corporate Research, Philips Corporate Research, and Nokia Research Center. The purpose of the research was to understand which techniques, methods, or tools could be used to improve the process and product of software architecture for families of software-intensive products.

ARES was a problem-oriented research project. Rather than developing a set of solutions and then looking for the problems they can solve, we invested considerable effort in analyzing and understanding existing problems of industrial software development using the software architecture perspective. Only afterward did we look for the appropriate solutions, evaluate their feasibility, and, finally, apply the solutions to real, full-size problems. This approach ensured the relevance, applicability, and scalability of ARES results.

The first phase of ARES was devoted entirely to the analysis and understanding of the real industrial problems that fall in the domain of software architecture. The main result of this phase was the selection of case studies, model problems, and evaluation criteria for technological solutions to problems of software architecture in industry. Rather than inventing new solutions, our main purpose all along was to understand which existing solutions work in the reality of industrial software development. Thus we devoted considerable time to evaluating the existing technology capable of addressing the problems we had identified during the problem analysis phase.

The second phase of the project was devoted to field testing and further development of known solutions, making them applicable to real, full-size problems. The industrial case studies selected during the first phase played the central role in making sure that ARES results were readily applicable in specific domains of interest to the industrial partners, as well as scalable to address real problems.

We were well aware that by far the hardest problem of improving the product development capabilities is technology transfer. Rather than using the common "research then transfer" approach, we planned to use the "industry as laboratory" approach. All research was conducted and results were validated in the context of existing industrial products that exhibit definite architectural problems. Achievements and results then were measured by improvements in the sharing of components (platform) and structure (family architecture) between an existing set of related software products whose development and maintenance was split because of the limitations of the current methods of software development.

As a general rule, we avoided any new development when results of earlier research could be used to advantage. Wherever possible we followed the evolutionary path with respect to current practices of the industrial partners. To ensure that our work is relevant for developing families of software-intensive products, we applied all methods, techniques, and tools to several industrial case studies using existing products.

ARES has generated and accumulated significant experience of tested and usable methods for architecture-based industrial-software development. This book is an attempt to share that experience with researchers, engineers, and managers involved in the development of software-intensive products.

ARES Motivation

In the late 1980s and early 1990s the complexity of embedded software crossed a critical threshold that necessitated a change in software development practices. Requirements for flexibility, openness, adaptability, and growing sophistication in functionality had made software the central part of most embedded systems. Software development costs began to drive the development costs and development times of new products. At that time software managers and engineers of several companies involved in the development of software-intensive products reported problems that can be placed into at least one of the following categories:

- **Difficulties in developing variants of software for the same product as a family.** Often variants of a product intended for different, geographically remote markets need to be developed simultaneously by different projects and teams. This situation is especially common when the product has to interact with local infrastructures that are different for each intended market. Though different variants in the projects that were examined shared large portions of their functionality, in most cases only a small portion of design and implementation was shared, if any. The variants ended up having different structures, or parts were not easily separable, or the interfaces of the parts providing similar functionality were incompatible, or the perceived effort of unifying the implementation was too large. In most cases, parallel development of dissimilar variants could not be brought together.[1]

- **Explosion of versions caused by rapid market- and technology-driven evolution and diversification of products, even in a narrow application domain.** Successively developed variants of the same product, intuitively, have better potential for sharing of implementation than simultaneously

---

[1]Attempts to develop first a common baseline, a platform, and then use it for different product variants did not work well either, in particular in new application domains where market requirements were not fully understood prior to trials of product deployment.

developed product variants. In practice, however, to provide different sets of features, implementation was changed in multiple places and units of change did not correspond to clearly identifiable elements of design. The variance was managed by use of a conditional inclusion of source code text or other similar techniques. After a few releases of different variants, however, the cost of maintaining nonlocal dependencies of conditionally included text could not be justified and implementation again had to be split into multiple, independently maintained and further diversified variants.

- **Low degree of reuse, despite functional similarity and the use of OOD and OOP.** Many expectations for achieving better results in building software for product families were associated with using object-oriented design (OOD) and object-oriented programming (OOP). In a few projects that we reviewed, we found no evidence that OOD significantly alleviates the problems of explosive diversification of software designs and implementations for product variants.

- **Inability to predict or control performance of a large distributed real-time system.** Although performance of a real-time system might be as important as its functionality, software developers were more comfortable discussing what the software was doing than when and for how long it was doing it. There seemed to be a definite lack of knowledge of what actually happens when the system is running: which threads interrupt which threads, where potential resource contention points are, which activities must or may be performed in parallel and which ones need to be sequenced. In the few cases in which the performance model of the regular operation was understood to some degree, the sequences and performance of startup and shutdown were still a mystery to system developers. Almost the same could be said about overload or failure recovery situations. In several cases in which system performance was problematic (in operational state or startup, or in overload), performance models were built. In all cases these models revealed the semiaccidental nature of choices made by developers regarding the execution structure.

- **High degree of unforeseen coupling between subsystems, resulting in poor localization of change, high communication overhead, and loss of modularity.** Systems with an elaborate structure of software components often did not pass simple assessment of coupling. Excessive coupling suggested that though some structuring of the software was performed, there was a lack of reasoning beyond this basic level. Either software developers did not realize the need, or they did not have the tools to address the concerns of modularity or to reason about it.

- **Lack of conformance between high-level design documents and software implementation.** Design documents were generally unreliable. Sometimes documented designs were not implemented as described, or essential information was missing from existing documents, or they were outdated by changes that were introduced in software implementation without being reflected back into the designs. As a result, the system could be understood only on the implementation level, and all subsequent changes led to further divergence between implementation and design.

Several distinct sources of complexity were apparent:

- **Size.** The size of software has grown significantly because more and more features are implemented in software.
- **Concurrency and distribution.** Multiprocessor-based solutions are increasingly prevalent.
- **Diversification.** Software must be more and more diversified because of globalization of companies and the need to approach different market segments.

All these sources of complexity pointed to the need to think about software in terms different from its source code elements, on a level of abstraction that can be called architectural. And, indeed, a case-by-case study of reported problems revealed that most of them were due to insufficient attention to architectural decisions made during the design and development of those systems, inability to represent and communicate these decisions, or difficulties in maintaining conformance between existing descriptions of architectural decisions and software implementation. We identified three related facets to these problems:

1. **Technological.** Methods, techniques, and tools for describing, analyzing, comparing, extracting, and evolving software architecture were missing.
2. **Organizational.** The development process did not allocate resources and did not include steps for making, communicating, or evaluating architectural decisions. Organizational aspects were due in part to the technological problems and in part to the project orientation of development processes, since architectures become more prominent in the scope of a family or a domain than in the scope of a single project.
3. **Social.** There was no shared culture of software development. By "culture" we mean the collection of common ways ensuring that the decisions made in different phases, at different places, by different people are conforming and compatible. In the context of evolving systems and large, geographically distributed development teams, this factor is of crucial importance.

These conclusions provided the initial motivation for the ARES project. After several meetings between software engineers from Nokia and Philips, we decided that cooperative research would be beneficial for both companies. Discussions with technical experts from other industrial corporations made it clear that the described situation was quite common and research could benefit many companies developing software-intensive products. Thus we decided to initiate a Europe-wide project and proceeded to build a consortium that could combine its experience to propose a practical approach to the architectural design of embedded software for families of software-intensive products.

ARES Team

Within several months we succeeded in building a strong consortium of partners having common interest and complementary capabilities to carry out the research. Here is a short characterization of the partner groups that made up the ARES research team.

Imperial College of Science and Technology, London

The Department of Computing at Imperial College is widely recognized as one of the leading centers of research and advanced training in computer science and software engineering in Europe. The Distributed Software Engineering (DSE) section focuses on methods, tools, and environments for the development of composite, heterogeneous, and distributed software-intensive systems. The DSE section has a strong interest in the development and management of component-based systems with particular emphasis on the architectural aspects of software systems. The DSE staff pioneered architecture-centered software development with the Darwin architectural description language and the Regis support environment for implementing distributed component-based architectures. Thus the Imperial College team took the lead for architecture description research in ARES.

Technical University of Vienna

The Distributed Systems Group (DSG) in the Information Systems Institute of the Technical University of Vienna is involved in teaching and research in all aspects of distributed computing, with particular emphasis on component-based software engineering of distributed systems and services.

DSG had proven expertise in reverse engineering of software and had strong interest in moving toward architecture recovery, architecture redesign, codification of domain-specific architectural knowledge, and process modeling for architecture-based software development. Thus DSG was an ideal partner to lead the ARES architecture recovery research.

Polytechnic University of Madrid

The Telematic Engineering Department (DIT) of the Polytechnic University of Madrid (Universidad Politécnica de Madrid, or UPM) has teaching and research responsibilities in the fields of communication software engineering, communication network and services, artificial intelligence, switching systems, databases, operating systems, computer architecture, programming, and software engineering.

DIT-UPM maintains close relationships and industrial contacts with most parts of the Spanish and multinational industries in the telecommunication field. DIT-UPM's particular interest in the ARES project was in specification, design, deployment, and validation of advanced services for open distributed architectures and real-time systems. Strong experience in real-time systems, metrics, and technology transfer made DIT-UPM a natural choice for leading ARES research on architecture assessment, addressing quality requirements through the analysis of architectures, and organizing architectural knowledge.

Asea Brown Boveri Corporate Research

ABB Corporate Research had long had experience in object-oriented development and formal specification languages. Object-oriented analysis techniques are used within ABB for high-level analysis and specification of ABB products. Through the International Telecommunication Union (ITU, formerly CCITT), ABB contributed to the definition and standardization of the object-oriented specification language SDL-92, used within the telecommunication area. Safety and quality aspects are important for many ABB products, including its train control system (TCS). Coincidentally with the beginning of ARES, ABB Corporate Research started an effort to reengineer the TCS software in order to use an architecture-centered approach to software for a family of train control systems. This was an ideal pilot for ARES technology.

Philips Corporate Research

The IST (Information and Software Technology) sector of Philips Corporate Research is a knowledge center on software design methodologies at Philips. It is involved in the research, knowledge transfer, and consulting on software products and software design methods. An important topic is the improvement of software development methodologies used within Philips.

The software development improvement activities are mainly in the fields of medical systems, communication systems, and consumer electronics. Research and knowledge transfer are focused on specification and modeling (including architecture) of software systems, and on data management in and about software systems. Knowledge transfer is performed mainly through projects with product groups.

Nokia Research Center

Nokia Research Center is the corporate research and development organization of the Nokia Group. Its mission is to monitor future technologies in close cooperation with the business groups of Nokia. The Software Technology Laboratory (SWT) had experience in development and transfer of modern software engineering technologies into Nokia business units. The laboratory participates in the development of complex telecommunication systems and provides consulting in software engineering processes. The Software Architecture Group (SAG) was established within SWT with a target of improving Nokia corporate competence in software architecture. Prior to the initiation of ARES, Nokia SAG had conducted a number of studies and identified problem areas in designing architectures for embedded software for product families. Good understanding of problems involved in the architectural design of industrial software put Nokia SAG in an excellent position to lead the ARES project.

ARES Process Model for Architecture-Centered Software Development

To develop the plan for the project, we had to put in place an initial model of architecture-centered software development. Such a model was intended to help us identify the missing capabilities and make a realistic plan for developing these capabilities in the context of cooperative research. We thought that in such a Europe-wide project it might be too hard to research organizational and social facets of architecture-centered software development; therefore we limited ourselves to considering only the technical issues.

We started with a very generic model of architecture-centered software development, consisting of three activities:

1. Making architectural decisions
2. Documenting architectural decisions
3. Managing the consistency of architectural descriptions and other software-related information, including design documents, source code, test cases, execution traces, and so on.

We also made several important underlying assumptions:

- Architectural decisions are made to address quality requirements such as reliability, availability, or security.
- Architectures can be described with a degree of formality to make the architectural description amenable to analysis.
- Each software system (or family of software systems) has an architecture.
- The architecture of software can be recovered from its source code, configuration files, and other "nonarchitectural" descriptions.

In the course of ARES research we had to revise both the model and the implicit assumptions. It is important to present these here, however, to make both the directions and the results of ARES research understandable to readers of this book. We refined and elaborated the initial model into a framework of processes and assets associated with architecture-centered software development. The research would look for techniques, methods, and tools capable of supporting the processes of this framework and would field-test them with existing industrial systems.

Figure 0.1 illustrates our framework of processes associated with architecture-centered software development. Let's walk through this diagram. Architecture descriptions are the most important (central) asset of architecture-centered software development. Even though this assumption seems quite intuitive, it is rarely true in practice. An important question ARES attempted to answer in this relation was, What architectural descriptions could be regarded as important assets of software development? It turned out there is no short answer to this question.

Architecture development requires input of domain knowledge, experience of product development, and understanding of quality requirements, as well as knowledge of generic

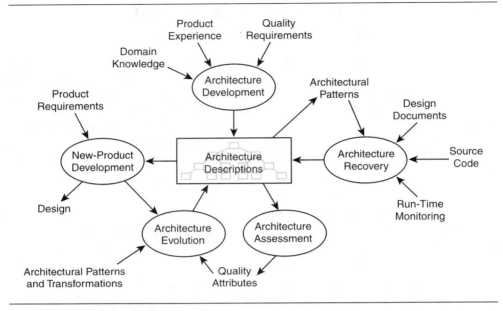

FIGURE 0.1   Framework of Processes and Assets Associated with Architecture-Centered Software Development

and domain-specific architectural patterns. In which form do these need to be available, and how do architecture development processes use this input? A partial answer to this question is implicit in Figure 0.1. The diagram is based on the assumption that by applying different architectural patterns, one can achieve different qualities in the derived architecture. This idea opens the possibility of assessing an architecture on the basis of employed architectural patterns.

One can also evolve architectures toward desired qualities by substituting appropriate architectural patterns. This suggests that architectural patterns should be characterized by qualities they support. Architectural descriptions, then, should be made in terms of architectural patterns employed in the system.

The architecture recovery process attempts to match known architectural patterns with data from run-time monitoring, design documentation, and source code, thus recovering a system's architecture in terms of recognized patterns. To enable this process, descriptions of architectural patterns need to include information of how they might be reflected by designs, source code, or run-time events.

Finally, product development combines existing architectures and product-specific requirements to produce designs, not architectures. When predefined architectures do not satisfy product requirements, an architecture evolution process needs to be employed rather than a product development process.

There is no predefined order of processes in this framework. Processes interact through feedback loops, leading to an iterative process that may be triggered by new input on any of the input lines. The processes are relatively independent and are only loosely coupled, thus increasing stability and robustness of the framework.

On the basis of the framework for architectural design described here, we defined as the main objective for the ARES project to enable software developers to explicitly describe, assess, and manage architectures of embedded software families. To reach this goal we planned to select, extend, or develop a framework of methods, processes, and prototype tools for incorporating architectural reasoning during the life cycle of an embedded software family.

In terms of technology, the research was conducted along the following lines:

- Description of software architecture
- Architecture recovery
- Architectural assessment and analysis of software

Proper deployment of architecture-centered development can affect many aspects of software development and the properties of the final products. To focus both the research and the evaluation of the results, we chose as the main goal of the ARES research to improve the capabilities of developing software for product families. In the next section we present in more detail the specific problems of building software for product families.

ARES Objectives

The following discussion describes in more detail the relation of architecture-centered development to product families, and specific objectives and results that support processes of the envisioned framework for architecture-centered software development.

Description of Software Architecture

Our initial assessment of current practice before beginning the ARES project stated the following: In current practice, descriptions of software architecture are informal, are incomplete, lack detail, do not allow reasoning about the qualities of the system, and may not be meaningfully compared or tested for their consistency with the implementation. As a result, software developers lack the means to document and communicate their architectural decisions. Because architectural decisions are implicit and unexpressed, implemented software architectures may not be fully understood, effectively communicated, or reused. In the context of large teams, the lack of an effective mechanism to communicate the architecture of software causes rapid degradation of structure and makes changes to software increasingly difficult and unsafe.

Our objective then was to develop and validate a method for precise description of software architecture that can serve as a basis for the following:

- Understanding and effective communication
- Comparison, analysis, and quality assessment
- Reuse and evolution

In particular, the developed method for software architecture description should demonstrate the following:

- Improved understandability of existing software when described using the architectural description language
- New possibilities to analyze the software using the architectural description
- New possibilities for reuse as a result of better separation of concerns (components and connectors) or more powerful parameterization of designs
- Explicit definition of legitimate dimensions for evolution within the selected architecture

Architectural Assessment and Analysis of Software Design

It is customary to divide the set of requirements of a system into two categories:

1. Requirements that are directly related to the function of the constructed system; the services the system provides are usually called **functional requirements.** Functional requirements are usually satisfied by specific components that perform the required function.

2. Requirements that may not be allocated to specific components, but rather depend on the overall organization and interconnection of the components and the main decomposition principles or pervasive policies of software design; these are often called nonfunctional requirements. Such requirements may address system safety, usability, timeliness, fault tolerance, performance, and so on. We believe that the term **quality requirements** better expresses the nature of this category of requirements. Quality requirements may not be addressed on the component level. Satisfaction of the quality requirements is one of the most important functions of software architecture.

Our initial assessment of current practice before beginning the ARES project stated the following: In current practice, there is no definite method to precisely specify software quality requirements and to examine architectural decisions with respect to the quality requirements. Most of the architectural decisions are made by default, on the basis of the intuitive understanding and earlier experience of the designers.

Our objective then was to provide a framework for making architectural decisions that allows us to do the following:

- Precisely specify software quality requirements
- Assess architectural descriptions for their satisfaction of specified quality requirements

- Select the design alternative that satisfies best the requirements and constraints of the problem

Software Architecture Recovery and Reengineering

The use of methods for precise architecture description and the possibility of assessing architectural descriptions for their qualities offers significant advantages in the development of new software. However, significant investment has been made in existing software and continues in its maintenance and further development.

How can the new software architecture methods be applied to existing software? Architecture recovery methods, techniques, and tools provided by ARES were planned to enable software developers to construct architectural descriptions of existing software. This capability will also address the problem of maintaining consistency between the description of software architecture and its implementation in an executable programming language.

Analysis of architectural descriptions of related products will also help reveal domain-specific architectural patterns that may serve to merge separately developed software into a family, based on the common architecture, or to unify a number of programs over a shared platform that provides the commonly used generic services and capabilities.

Focus on Product Families

Many companies are forced to continuously diversify their products in order to address the needs and requirements of different market segments. For example, to allow competitive pricing of lower-end products we build products that have similar functionality but different hardware capacity. Alternatively, products may be differentiated by the set of supported functional features. Products that must interoperate with their environment—for example, communication products that are designed for different transmission and signaling standards—are often subject to regional diversity. Consumer products are often designed to meet expectations of different age groups, different levels of users' technical sophistication, and possible cultural differences. As a result, products have different sets of functional features, provide different user interfaces, are implemented on different hardware, and have to interact closely with different kinds of environments. But a TV set is a TV set. It is intuitively acceptable that a large part of software that controls a TV set should not depend on the differences in transmission standards, hardware capabilities, or the specifics of the user interface.

Usually different product versions are developed by different projects and often by different teams. Even when each project starts with an identical baseline implementation, at the end of the project it is hard to determine which parts of the implementation are version-specific and which are version-independent. As a result, each product version needs to be maintained separately.

Interaction between product diversification and evolution leads to a significant increase in the effort necessary to introduce a new feature or change an aspect of product functionality in any way. Each change that is applicable to several versions of the product needs to be implemented, documented, and tested multiple times.

Dealing with diversification and evolution is a big problem, and many software development managers are well aware of it. Therefore we selected it as the main focus of ARES and as an assessment criterion for project results. We were convinced that our capability in creating software architectures translates directly into our capability to build and manage software for product families, and ARES results corroborated this idea.

The ARES project took the following as its targets:

- To understand and generalize existing experience of building software for product families
- To identify the main problems faced by developers of complex software for product families
- Where appropriate, to propose solutions for these problems

The four directions of ARES research are

1. Specification of software architecture
2. Architecture recovery
3. Architectural assessment in the software design process
4. Development and evolution of family architecture

Development and evolution of family architecture creates an interdependent framework. Support for development of software product families is the unifying goal of the project. Specification of software architecture provides a common language for the rest of the project. The specification method must explicitly address the family aspects by offering new possibilities for reuse because of better separation of concerns, more powerful parameterization of designs, and explicit definition of legitimate dimensions for evolution within the selected architecture. Architecture recovery uncovers family-specific architectural patterns that may be used to merge related but separately developed applications into a family. The architecture recovery methods must provide a means for dealing with existing software. Architectural assessment is based on the architectural descriptions and addresses modularity, configurability, and localization of change, which are important for family architectures.

1

ARES Conceptual Framework for Software Architecture

Alexander Ran

In the previous chapter we introduced the framework of processes associated with architecture-centered software development, as we understood it in the early stage of the ARES project. In this chapter we present a conceptual framework for software architecture that we developed during the project. A conceptual framework for software architecture is a model of what software architecture is. It is a set of organizing principles that help software architects invent or discover the abstract descriptions of complex software that represent its architecture.

A conceptual framework for software architecture should offer the software development team a model that can be used to design the architecture of new software or to understand, describe, and evaluate the architecture of existing software. At the time of this writing, there is a definite lack of comprehensive practical models of this kind. In this chapter we present some useful ways to think about complex software in order to control important qualities related to its development, performance, and evolution.

1.1 Genealogy of ARES Conceptual Framework for Software Architecture

In recent years, many important contributions have been made to the study of software architecture. The seminal paper by Perry and Wolf (1992) laid the foundation for the study of the subject. The book by Shaw and Garlan (1996) gives a broad perspective on research contributions aiming at solving difficult problems faced by software architects. The book by Bass, Clements, and Kazman (1998) offers in-depth coverage of software architecture in practice, demonstrating how system-level problems are addressed by experienced software architects working on real projects. Finally, Boehm's work (Boehm et al. 1999) puts architecture in the perspective of the organizations involved in procurement, development, deployment, and use of software, thereby making the architecture correspond to business goals and leading to a win-win situation for all stakeholders.

Here we are concerned primarily with the technical aspects of software architecture unified in a consistent conceptual framework. Probably the first work that addressed this goal specifically was "The 4+1 View Model of Architecture" by Philippe Kruchten (1995) of Rational. This work was in informal circulation from the early 1990s and eventually was published by IEEE Software in 1995.

The 4+1 View model offered a simple and understandable way to think about software architecture of complex systems, by organizing descriptions of software related to different concerns in five categories, called **views.** The four main views are

1. The **logical view,** which is the object model of the design (when an object-oriented design method is used)

2. The **process view,** which captures the concurrency and synchronization aspects of the design

3. The **physical view,** which describes the mappings of the software onto the hardware and reflects its distribution aspect

4. The **development view,** which describes the static organization of the software in its development environment

Descriptions of software in these four views are illustrated and validated with an additional view that contains selected use cases and scenarios. Each view shows a specific aspect of the modeled system. Until now this has been perhaps the most influential approach in terms of popularity in industry. Naturally, the ARES conceptual framework follows the 4+1 View model in many ways.

Soni, Nord, and Hofmeister (1995) took the subject one step further. After studying a considerable number of software-intensive systems built by Siemens, they identified four different architectural views used by designers to describe the software:

1. **Conceptual architecture.** Major design elements and their relationships

2. **Module interconnection architecture.** Functional decomposition, interfaces, and layers

3. **Execution architecture.** The dynamic structure of the system

4. **Code architecture.** Organization of source code, libraries, and binaries

This work confirmed the need for multiple descriptions of software done from different perspectives and demonstrated that the specific perspectives may be different from the set included in the "4+1" views. In addition, Soni, Nord, and Hofmeister called their views architectures, which may be interpreted as a statement that these are, at least partly, independent models rather than different views on the same thing. The paper, however, does not suggest this interpretation. It analyzes relationships among these views, identifies the concerns addressed by each view, and discusses characteristics of development and delivery environments that influence the designs of the different views. Another important contribution of this work is in identifying the need to partition the architecture of software into infrastructure (technical architecture) and application (business architecture).

This work fundamentally influenced our understanding, and we have used these important ideas in the ARES conceptual framework for software architecture. We also made some additional contributions:

- Clarifying the relationship between architecture and requirements
- Rethinking the role and content of conceptual architecture
- Introducing the notion of component domains as the bases for organizing requirements and separate architectural structures
- Separating the notion of multiple architectural structures from multiple architectural views
- Introducing the notion of software texture as an important part of software architecture
- Establishing a hierarchy of architectural scopes as an organizing principle for product family architecture

More than 30 software engineers and researchers from six different organizations and at least eight countries worked on the ARES project. It should be no surprise, then, that there is no single ARES view on every question or concept related to software architecture. However, we believe that this presentation is based on an understanding that correlates positively with the understanding of the ARES team as a whole.

This chapter presents an interpretation of the main concepts of software architecture, concentrating on the technical aspects and only briefly touching on some of the issues related to process and organization. A separate book would have to be written to present in depth the ARES conceptual framework for software architecture. This chapter is only a short summary, a brief overview of the subject, necessary to create the basis for communication about the architecture of software for product families.

In later chapters, ARES researchers present their experience of architecture-centered software development. Because the ARES conceptual framework was formulated as one of the conclusions of the ARES project, some of the research reported in the following chapters is based on concepts that have not yet reached their final form. This chapter should be helpful also in these circumstances and provide the reader a perspective for interpreting records of thinking in transition. The material of this chapter should also be useful to anybody involved in building families of software-intensive products and willing to take an architecture-centered perspective.

1.2   Software Architecture: A Tool for Dealing with Complexity

Before exploring the main concepts of software architecture, we wish to state our understanding regarding the primary need for software architecture—the main reason for its existence—including when it is reasonable and necessary to address the architecture of software and when we need to consider only software design, if anything at all.

The general interest in architecture emerged when software built by companies crossed a certain threshold of complexity. This happened across industries sometime between the mid-1970s and mid-1980s. The general situation could be characterized as a loss of intellectual control over the software being developed in industry.

This loss of intellectual control could be recognized from multiple symptoms. A common symptom was monotonic growth of software almost unrelated to added functionality, usually as a result of fear to touch the existing code. Engineers were not sure anymore what any particular part of software was doing—that is, where and how it was used. Any request for change in functionality could be addressed only by adding more code. A very typical symptom of lost intellectual control was integration failure. Multiple poorly understood relationships between different components made integration a never-ending process. Correcting one observed problem inevitably led to the introduction of several new ones. Another common symptom was performance barriers that could not be significantly affected by the use of faster hardware. More precisely, nobody seemed to know which hardware component needed to be faster to improve system performance. One of the most painful symptoms was uncontrollable diversification of software created for different customers or markets. Even though products differed only in small parts of their functionality, there was often a wholly separate version and configuration for each market or customer.

Not everybody, however, lost the intellectual control over software development. Projects and products that retained intellectual control over their software employed a different level of understanding the software—an understanding that could be called architectural. Therefore, study of what software architecture is promised to help software developers regain intellectual control over the development of complex software.

We understand software architecture as a conceptual tool for dealing with the complexity of software. There are several essential sources of software complexity:

- **Open-endedness, imprecise specification.** It seems impossible in practice to precisely specify the function of software before the software is built.

- **Indirectness, intangibility.** We don't directly construct the performing system itself. We create source code that will go through a variable sequence of nontrivial transformations to produce the executing system.

- **Concurrency of execution.** Generally we understand space and spatial relationships better than we understand time and temporal relationships. In addition, programming technology is very much geared toward the step-by-step definition of processes. Many systems built in industry, however, have multiple processors and multiple concurrent threads of execution.

- **Concurrency of construction.** Another aspect of concurrency is concurrent engineering: We cannot build software sequentially piece by piece; rather, large teams have to build different interdependent pieces concurrently.

- **Diversification.** In industry, we rarely build one-of-a-kind systems. Usually we build product families or product lines in which each product has different features that need to be provided by a single implementation with a minimal amount of configuration, customization, and rework.

- **Size.** When numbers of design elements such as functions and classes are measured in hundreds of thousands, a different representation of software is required.

Proper architecture of software should reduce the complexity that results from at least one of these factors.

1.3   Conceptual Framework for Software Architecture

A **conceptual framework for software architecture (CFSA)** is the foundation on which software architects base their design decisions. For an organization to be able to influence and/or assess design decisions made by software architects, the CFSA needs to be explicitly defined and actively managed.

At a minimum, the CFSA defines a model for software architecture. It may also include product-related models, strategies, policies, and tools for making, assessing, and implementing design decisions consistent with the framework. Thus the CFSA provides necessary input and context for software architects working in the specific organization that owns the CFSA. From the management (or customer) point of view, the CFSA is a tool that can be used to influence the architecture and thus the quality and fitness of the product under development.

Rather than trying to define CFSA, we start here by describing the ARES CFSA and leave finding a suitable definition for later.

1.3.1   Fundamental Concepts of the ARES CFSA

The following concepts underlie the ARES CFSA.

Scope

In most circumstances an architecture is intended for more than one instance of a system. Characterization of the class of systems for which the architecture is applicable defines its **architectural scope.** There is usually a hierarchy of scopes that play an important role in an application domain, a corporation, a company, a product division, or some such entity. Software architecture should be created for a specific architectural scope, consistently extending the architecture of its enclosing scope, providing context for and constraining the architectures created in its subscopes. Specifying the scope for architecture is an important part of architecture itself.

Concerns

Software architecture can play an essential (and independent) role in software development only if it addresses specific **architectural concerns** related to system life cycle that are not addressed by other software development functions and activities. These concerns are not necessarily evident from system requirement documents or any other system descriptions. Identifying and documenting architectural concerns and their owners, also called stakeholders, is an important part of software architecture.

Requirements

Architectural concerns should be refined into **architecturally significant requirements** that are specific in terms of desired system properties and the way in which achieving these properties influences or constrains the architecture.

Component Domains

Software exists in multiple forms simultaneously. Some of the most common forms are source or object code components, executable components, and executing components. There are relationships, but no direct correspondence, among these different kinds of components. Each kind of component forms its own **component domain.** In each component domain, software architecture (as an approach to complexity) addresses different concerns through independent or loosely dependent design decisions within the component domain. Identifying the component domains relevant in view of architecturally significant requirements is an essential part of software architecture.

Structure

In each component domain, independent architectural structures may exist. An **architectural structure** is created by the partition of software into components in a component domain and their composition into an integrated whole. Architectural structures should be traceable to concrete system elements, rather than being mere conceptual abstractions. Different architectural structures may be interdependent, but they are not different views of the same entity. Architectural structures are an important part of software architecture.

Views

Architectural views are models of architectural structures or other elements of software architecture. Views are used throughout the architecture life cycle for specific purposes of understanding and analyzing the different aspects of system development and performance. The major characteristic of a view is its *purpose* and *utility.* Views are not complete descriptions. In fact, views need to omit otherwise important architectural information in order to be useful for their specific purpose. The major issue with views is consistency with the system rather than completeness. Architectural views are a necessary part of architecture on the way to designing architectural structures and different aspects of system design.

Texture

Recurring microstructure of the software components is at least as important as the system structure. We call recurring microstructure of components **texture** and consider it an important part of software architecture.

Concepts

From the perspective that considers software architecture to be an approach to dealing with complexity, probably the most important decision is the selection of **architectural concepts** used to think about the system. The existence of architectural concepts is often taken for granted. As we explain later, however, architectural concepts are not found in the application domain or in the implementation domain, but need to be invented in order to simplify the design, construction, and representation of complex software. All other parts of software architecture more or less directly depend on the invention (selection) of architectural concepts. We consider inventing architectural concepts to be the most crucial part of software architecture.

1.3.2   The ARES Metamodel of Software Architecture

In each component domain we model the architecture of software as having four parts or facets:

1. Architecturally significant requirements
2. Concept definitions, which we also call conceptual architecture
3. Structures, or partition and integration (components and composition)
4. Texture, or recurring microstructure

Figure 1.1 illustrates this model. We use these four facets to organize activities (and products) of creating, documenting, and understanding the architecture of software. This means that when faced with any of these tasks, we need to fill in each of the categories by answering the corresponding questions:

1. What are the architecturally significant requirements for this system in different phases of its construction, use, and evolution?
2. What are the key concepts for understanding and designing this system?
3. What is the structure of this system? Or, what are its components and how are they composed into an integrated whole?
4. What is the texture of this system? Or, what are the mechanisms and patterns that make the whole consistent and manageable (as opposed to a patchwork of accidental pieces)?

Separation of concerns is one of the most fundamental principles for the successful design and construction of complex systems. We tried to apply this principle uniformly to the design of the ARES CFSA. We separate concerns of development, configuration, delivery, execution, change, and other important processes and phases in the software life cycle.

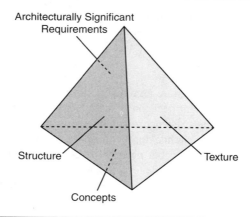

FIGURE 1.1   ARES Model of Software Architecture

There are two patterns of making partitions that we use extensively: layering and clustering. **Layering** is related to open-endedness and diversification. It establishes intermediate boundaries and platforms of stability and creates a path for incrementally reaching the goal of development. **Clustering** helps deal with size and concurrency of development.

In the following sections we will explore this model in more detail.

1.4   What Is Software Architecture?

The first phase of many new projects developing software-intensive products is the design phase of the system software architecture. Often one of the first steps in this process is building a common understanding among the project members about what software architecture is. Active research of software architecture during the 1980s and 1990s has produced a wealth of definitions that attempt to capture the essence of software architecture by abstraction. Together these concepts yield the following definition:

> Software architecture is defined as components, connectors, constraints, and rationale.

Intellectually, this definition is quite satisfactory. However, in the context of developing and describing software architecture for a product we need a definition that provides answers to very concrete questions:

- How is architecture related to requirements?
- When is architecture sufficiently understood to proceed with the system development?
- Where lies the boundary between architecture and design?
- Does each product, release, or version have a separate architecture, or should there be just one architecture for all products in a product family, or even in an application domain?

The definition we will give later directly addresses these and similar questions. This definition does not contradict or replace the understanding of representing architecture as components, connectors, constraints, and rationale. It simply puts the emphasis on providing concrete guidance in the process of developing and describing the architecture of software.

First and foremost, architecture is a set of concepts through which we impose order on complexity. The concepts we use to think about software determine what is omitted from consideration and what is emphasized, what is grouped and what is separated. Other, more common expressions of architecture are in most circumstances elaborations done using invented architectural concepts to answer specific questions.

We build software to perform the function specified by functional and quality requirements. **Functional requirements** specify what software has to do. **Quality requirements** state how well it should be done. Quality requirements qualify the function in terms of desired performance, availability, reliability, usability, configurability, or integrability of the system. (These are often called "ilities.")

In addition to the explicit functional and quality requirements, well-designed software addresses other concerns that constitute implicit requirements for change, reusability, or other kinds of evolution, interoperability with other systems, and so on.

Even though there may be many different requirements specifying different functionality, qualities, or needed evolution flexibility, only a few representative requirements influence the architecture and thus are architecturally significant. The need to focus on architecturally significant requirements leads to the following definition for software architecture:

> Software architecture is a set of concepts and design decisions that enable effective satisfaction of architecturally significant explicit functional and quality requirements and implicit requirements presented by the problem and the solution domains.

This definition emphasizes several aspects. First, the reason for software architecture is *satisfaction of requirements.* Not all requirements are architecturally significant. There are different classes of requirements that must be understood in order to create an architecture. Implicit requirements come from both problem and solution domains. Architecture can only enable the satisfaction of requirements; it cannot guarantee their satisfaction. Finally, this definition does not emphasize structure-related decisions over other kinds of decisions. The reason is that the relative weight of structure-related decisions in real systems could be limited.

To limit the responsibilities of the architecture team, we need to answer the question, Where does the boundary between architecture and design lie? When setting the scope for the tasks of the software architecture group, we need to exclude from architectural concerns detailed design decisions made at the component level. Though such decisions may directly influence the capability of the system to satisfy important requirements, they do not influence the design of other components; thus the cost of revising these decisions is limited. Such issues belong to component design. Therefore

> Software architecture is a set of concepts and design decisions that must be made prior to concurrent engineering to enable effective satisfaction of architecturally significant explicit functional and quality requirements and implicit requirements presented by the problem and the solution domains.

All successful companies nowadays plan product families rather than single products. Therefore, in practice, software architecture always needs to address product family concerns. Products that perform similar functions and share parts form a product family. Multiple releases of a single product that include the enhancement of either functional or quality features and have to be supported during overlapping periods of time in essence also constitute a product family. The main problem in developing software product families is how to achieve sharing of effort and parts when developing variant products while providing variation in their features and capabilities. Software architecture for a product family must specifically address evolution and diversification of products even if these are not explicitly stated in the requirements.

Some design decisions that affect both the satisfaction of system requirements and concurrent design have to do with software structure. This is the reason that software architecture is often identified with the structure of software. However, not all the design decisions that are essential for satisfying system requirements and enabling concurrent engineering are concerned with the structure. Examples include decisions determining the texture of software that include the selection of major component models, design patterns and pervasive design policies as, for example, flow control, load monitoring, execution tracing and logging. In addition, the selection of implementation languages and platforms, trade-off decisions, and process-related decisions fall in the category of architectural concerns. Therefore, our working definition states the following:

> **Software architecture** is a set of concepts and design decisions about the structure and texture of software that must be made prior to concurrent engineering to enable effective satisfaction of architecturally significant explicit functional and quality requirements and implicit requirements of the product family, the problem, and the solution domains.

1.5   Architecturally Significant Requirements

A common misinterpretation of the connection between solution and problem domains is the belief that architecture is determined by requirements. Consequently, some projects needlessly wait to specify requirements completely before starting architectural design—a point that is hard to reach in reality without having a good understanding of architecture.

In other cases, detailed product requirements exist because of standards, for example, and architectural design is expected to address product requirements—which is impossible without going into the detail of product implementation. In reality, only a small fraction of product requirements have any influence on architecture. Identifying these requirements is the first step in any architectural work.

1.5.1   Identifying Architecturally Significant Requirements

An important question that needs to be answered by a CFSA is how architecturally significant requirements can be identified. Although the answer to this question is definitely domain-dependent, some general rules do apply. Here are some suggestions for identifying requirements that qualify as architecturally significant requirements:

- Requirements that cannot be satisfied by one (or a small set of) system components without dependence on the rest of the system. These usually include all systemwide properties and quality requirements.

- Requirements that address properties of different categories of components—for example, how components are named, or referred to, by other components.

- Requirements that address processes of manipulating multiple components—for example, system building, configuring, or upgrading.

- Properties of a product or product family that make it unique, competitive, and worth building. These are the most important architecturally significant requirements.

It is essential to build the product right. It is even more important to build the right product. Boehm describes a process for identifying the right product as defined by success-critical stakeholders (i.e., those stakeholders whose agreement and eventual satisfaction is necessary for the success of the product) (Boehm et al. 1999):

1. Identify the success-critical stakeholders.
2. Identify the stakeholders' win conditions (i.e., the circumstances under which the stakeholder will be satisfied).
3. Identify win-condition conflict issues.
4. Negotiate top-level win–win agreements.
5. Invent options for mutual gain.
6. Explore option trade-offs.
7. Manage expectations.
8. Incorporate win–win agreements into specifications and plans.
9. Repeat steps 1 through 8 until the product is fully developed.
10. Confront and resolve new win–lose and lose–lose risk items.

This process offers a good framework for defining architecturally significant requirements for the right product.

1.5.2   Structuring Architecturally Significant Requirements

It is generally accepted that the architecture of software directly affects systemwide properties such as availability, reliability, and security. Well-structured software also supports requirements for change, reusability, interoperability with other systems, and so on. If all different requirements were supported by the same architectural structure, it would be impossible to satisfy them independently. And indeed this is often the case. For example, requirements concerning performance and reliability interact because software execution structure affects both kinds of properties.

Often system requirements may be grouped so that requirements in different groups may be addressed by different and at least partly independent software structures established by partitions of software in different component domains. Such partitions exist simultaneously and often are independent of each other. Here are a few examples:

- We address run-time requirements by partitioning software into execution threads of varying priority (or utility), specifying thread scheduling policies, regulating the use of shared resources, and so on.

- We address change and reuse requirements by partitioning software into modules—substitutable, unit-testable components having well-defined boundaries, predictable interaction with the environment, and minimal, well-specified dependencies on other modules.

- We address portability requirements by defining software layers and establishing the conformance of layers and their interfaces to existing standards.

- We address requirements for independent restart or independent failure modes by partitioning the software into a set of separately loadable and executable processes.

Architecturally significant requirements must be grouped so that requirements in different groups may be satisfied independently. Requirements *within* each group may interact and even conflict. A good rule of thumb for finding independent requirements is to group them by the time of the software life cycle they address. Very often requirements that address software development and change can be satisfied almost independently from requirements that address run-time behavior or software upgrade, for example. We will discuss this in more detail in connection with different software component domains (see Section 1.7).

The number of architecturally significant requirements in each group should be small, from three to five. Whenever possible, architecturally significant requirements in each group should be prioritized.

1.6   Architectural Concepts

Most people think of the architecture of software as some kind of structure represented as a diagram that conveys the overall design of the software. That idea is, of course, fairly intuitive and accurate. However, this intuition leads people to believe that the first and the main question that needs to be answered by software architects is, What is the overall structure of this software and how does this structure support the requirements of the final product? This is indeed a very important question, but it is not the first to ask.

Often different functional features are allocated to different components. This feature allocation is motivated by the need to create variant products that support only subsets of features. Feature-based partitioning is also effective for work division, since each feature may have an associated cluster of knowledge in both the application and the implementation domains. A complex system that warrants the effort of architectural description often implements hundreds of different features. It is unrealistic to expect an architecture prescription to list hundreds of different components, as well as their relationships and interactions. Because features are different and often complementary, omitting the components and their functions from the model would simply result in an incomplete and possibly incorrect model. Therefore, a useful conceptual architecture must exist on a different level of abstraction from an implementation blueprint.

Any structure can be described as a set of elements related in certain ways to one another. A typical approach to architectural design is therefore to select a set of elements and explore their relationships from multiple viewpoints and describe them using graphical notation that nowadays tends to borrow from object-oriented modeling techniques. The emphasis thus falls primarily on exploring relationships. Because software elements interact in multiple ways, various dynamic models, such as state charts, message sequence charts, or action and activity charts, play an important role in describing relationships. Software architects are often expected to produce extensive descriptions of static and dynamic relationships between sets of selected elements that represent the functioning system. Such descriptions are often required by project management prior to more detailed design. These expectations create several types of problems.

Understood in this way, the architect's task is impossible because of the large number of possible interactions and special cases, the flux in the understanding of detail, and simply the lack of information in the early development stages. Of course, it is feasible to produce an architecture description of the kind we have mentioned that gives an incomplete view of the functioning system. Unfortunately, in addition to being incomplete, such descriptions differ from design documents only in level of *detail* rather than in level of *abstraction*. They do not provide an adequate framework for more detailed design and implementation.

These problems are a consequence of the approach. Because of the emphasis on the structure, the elements of architectural partitions have no conceptual depth. They are just names, and nothing can be deduced about their behavior and function. The only way to describe them or define them is to exhaustively describe how they carry out their responsibilities in every situation.

The real task of a software architect during the early iterations of architectural design is different. The software architect's goal is to invent a set of conceptual elements and describe general rules that can be used to determine their behavior in different situations. Thus conceptual architecture should be a kind of theory about a small set of concepts. The structure of the system, along with the interactions that occur between different elements, can be created later using the conceptual architecture to guide the thinking and establish the rules that determine the specific structure consistent with the conceptual architecture.

Clearly, this is an idealization. We do not know how to build theories about software, and we do not create software designs by proving theorems. This, however, should not change the goal and therefore the process of designing a software architecture. The first and possibly the main task of architects during early development is to invent the key concepts and describe their general properties, rather than to engage in an exhaustive allocation of functional use cases over a set of elements whose only properties are names.

A practical way to describe a conceptual architecture is with a metaphor that connects all major concepts of the architecture. Such a metaphor is not a blueprint for the specific system. It is an archetype that captures the essence of key conceptual elements that can be used to construct different systems consistent with the given conceptual architecture.

For most software systems, it is possible to identify three classes of important concepts: application domain concepts, implementation domain concepts, and architectural concepts. **Application domain concepts** result from application domain analysis and jointly form the domain model. **Implementation domain concepts** result from implementation domain analysis and jointly define the virtual machine model or platform. **Architectural concepts** are not found from analysis of requirements or implementation platform. Key concepts for the architecture of software need to be invented to simplify the task of bridging the gap between the product requirements and the implementation platform.

Thus one of the primary tasks of software architects is to establish and communicate to the rest of the team the important concepts necessary for effective software design and implementation. A proven way to approach this goal is to create partial models that relate different architectural concepts to their roles in addressing architectural problems and concerns. Together, these models make up the conceptual architecture of software. The conceptual architecture of software is a model of important concepts used in the design of software, including their properties and relationships.

Conceptual architecture is created before the system is designed to any significant degree of detail, and it usually exists more as a vague intuition than a precise structure. To communicate these intuitions to the development team, to define architectural partitions, and to develop detailed designs, architects must rely more on evocative metaphors and analogies than on formal descriptions. This is the primary reason that verbal interaction is considered so important for successful communication of conceptual architecture.

Once conceptual architecture is understood, or possibly along with the development of conceptual architecture, structural model(s) of software must be built to provide guidance that is more specific for implementing the product.

1.7　Component Domains

However much we speak about software components, there is still much confusion regarding what a component is. One may say that components result from the partition of a composite entity. One may also say that a composite entity is a result of the composition of several components. Either way there should be an entity that can be partitioned. Software is not a single entity in the sense that it has multiple, partially independent planes of existence, each having its own type of component: a component domain.

Software exists in at least the following planes:

- **Design or write plane,** in which it is being designed and written
- **Build plane,** in which a template for executable images is constructed
- **Setup or configuration plane,** in which a template for the executable image is instantiated with configuration data or transformed in other ways to fit a specific delivery platform
- **Restart plane,** in which a group of related processes is started, stopped, and otherwise collectively managed
- **Execution plane,** in which the software is executing its function

These are not different views of one thing. Rather, these are in many respects different things. Thus, viewed through its components, software exists as a set of modules, a set of concurrent threads, a set of processes, a set of executables, a set of source code files, and so on. In different existence planes, software is partitioned into components of the corresponding component domain. There may be a different number of software components in different component domains of a software system, and in each component domain different relationships may exist between the components. Partitions that separate concerns create architectures that are more stable and have wider applicability and better potential for reuse. The reason is that changes in requirements are likely to affect the partition in a single plane while leaving the other planes unchanged.

As it happens, important partitions of software in different component domains may be very different from each other. For example, the partition into modules has little or no relationship to the partition into execution threads. Partitioning into modules enables incremental construction, testing, evolution, and reuse of specific functionality. Partitioning into execution threads simplifies system design while addressing performance and possibly reliability and availability requirements. Layers of a protocol stack are an example of partitioning data communication functionality into modules. The same module structure, such as a protocol stack, may be assigned to or split over an arbitrary structure of interacting execution threads. Thus the two structures need not be related.

As another example, consider the partition of software into processes. This partition is used to address requirements for independent loading and protection. Though processes sometimes bind execution threads, often execution threads (in the sense of strictly sequenced actions) span multiple processes. Such could be the case when parts of a protocol stack need to be independently (re)loadable and/or upgradable. One way to address these requirements is by partitioning the stack into different processes. Even with the existence of these multiple processes, a packet passes through the protocol stack in a single execution thread. In addition, the very existence of a remote procedure call mechanism is due to the fact that a sequence of actions making a single logical execution thread may be partitioned into multiple processes.

1.8   Architectural Structures

A structure of software in a component domain is created by a partition of software into components and their composition into an integrated whole. For every system it is necessary to determine which structures of software affect architecturally significant requirements and to group the requirements in such a way that each group is supported primarily by independent structures that exist in different component domains.

One effective way to identify independent (or partly independent) requirements is by different stages of software life cycle with which they are concerned. A typical (though somewhat simplified) set of stages when different structures of software play major roles includes write time, build time, configuration time, upgrade time, start time, run time, and shutdown time. The most important software structure at write time is the structure of modules. Thus write time–related requirements, such as feature addition and evolution, porting, and diversification, are addressed primarily by appropriate module structures that play a major role at write time.

Similarly, start time–related requirements (such as order, presence, independent operation, and failure modes) are addressed primarily by appropriate executable structures—the startup or shutdown unit or component. In addition, of course, run time–related requirements, such as performance or availability, are addressed by the structures of objects and execution threads—the domain of run-time software components. Table 1.1 lists some of the most common partitions, along with their requirement and component domains, and the software life-cycle stages concerned.

Many projects make the mistake of trying to impose a single partition in multiple component domains, such as equating threads with objects, which are equated with modules, which in turn are equated with files. Such an approach never succeeds fully, and adjustments eventually must be made, but the damage of the initial intent is often hard to repair. This

TABLE 1.1   Architectural Structures of Software

Structure and Life-Cycle Stage	Requirements Domain	Component Domain
Execution structure is essential at run time.	Performance, availability, reliability	Execution threads, communication channels, schedulers, shared resources
Loading structure is essential at (re)start or shutdown time.	Independent restart or upgrade, protection	Processes or executables, data stores
Configuration structure is essential at configuration time.	Configurability, multiplatform delivery	Nonstandard; usually data files and special configuration interfaces
Module structure is essential at write time.	Change management (for evolution, porting, diversification), incremental or concurrent development, reuse	Modules, provided and required interfaces

invariably leads to problems in development and occasionally in final products. We have collected several real-life reports of such developments.

In one case, implementation of a complex functional feature was split between two groups. Two functional clusters were defined, along with the necessary interfaces. Unnecessarily, the modules also ended up in different processes and had to interact at run time using slower interprocess communication mechanisms.

Another example involved a system that was partitioned into a set of distributed processes. The partition was motivated by considerations of required parallelism, availability, and fault tolerance. This partition was subsequently used to allocate additional functionality, which affected resource requirements and timing characteristics, violating the original design. As a cure, non-real-time functionality was allocated to new components. However, because the software architecture was identified with its process structure, these components became independent processes. Consequently, the components had complex interfaces and performance was compromised.

Our current understanding suggests that designing a software architecture must start with specific architectural concerns, specify the partition in different component domains, along with a scheme for integration and coordination of the parts, and explain how this specific partition and the corresponding integration of the software address the specified architectural concerns. Examples of architectural concerns may include timeliness, capacity, availability, effective division of work, conformance to standards, use of existing parts, or controlled propagation of change. To address these concerns, different partitions may exist in different component domains.

From the point of view of software reuse, architecture that separates concerns pertinent to different requirement and component domains also results in more reusable components. Therefore it is important to recognize multiple software existence planes (as described earlier in this chapter), with the associated component domains and independent partitions of software, and their relations to different requirement domains.

1.9   Architectural Views

Multiple architectural structures should not be confused with architectural views. Architectural structures are concrete and different from each other. Architectural views are abstractions, and different views may be different abstractions of the same entity. Take, for example, layers and subsystems—two commonly used architectural views of software. **Subsystems** are essentially groupings of modules and are best described by specifying the modules they contain. Subsystems are commonly *vertical* sections; that is, they usually aggregate modules that implement related functions. (We refer to these later as clusters of functionality.) **Layers** are *horizontal* sections that may have different scope within the system. Layers may be confined to a single subsystem or even a part of the subsystem, or they may extend right across different subsystems.

Layers may be established to address portability requirements by requiring conformance to a set of interfaces specified by existing standards. A related view that employs layering is used to manage incremental implementation and functionality delivery. The increment view shows software development increments that can be used for early system integration. This (usually) layered view of system functionality may cut across multiple subsystems.

These three cases—(1) subsystems, (2) functional or portability layering, and (3) layers of incremental development—represent views of module partition. It is important to understand this to avoid conflicts in description and update through views.

Architectural views play the same role in dealing with architectural information as data views play in database management systems. We can better understand the value and limitations of architectural views using the lessons learned about data views in the database community. There are two major issues with data views: maintenance and update. View maintenance includes processes for ensuring consistency of the view with the data (and transitively consistency of multiple views). View maintenance may be difficult, but it is feasible and practical as long as view derivation from the data is not too complex. On the other hand, update of data through views is attractive but in general does not work.

These conclusions influenced to a significant degree our understanding and use of architectural views in the ARES project. We understand views as presenting information derived from concrete architectural structures. Views are defined by the derivation procedures, rather than by the information they present. Views can be sketched to understand the architectural structures before they are designed. Once architectural structures exist, views can be changed only after the change is effected in the corresponding architectural structures. For example, we often need to describe interfaces provided (or required) by a certain layer or subsystem. Remember that these interfaces are derived as interfaces of the modules included in the layer or the subsystem.

The term "architectural views" is commonly used to mean a broader category of architectural descriptions following the well-known work of Philippe Kruchten on the 4+1 View model of software architecture. In the 4+1 model, views denote different areas of concern and categories of descriptions rather than views in the sense of abstraction of information regarding concrete architectural structures of software.

There are several good reasons to clearly separate concrete software structures that exist in different component domains from abstract views necessary for managing specific concerns, such as work division, incremental integration, or portability. Whereas the conceptual architecture and architectural views of software may need to be built prior to more detailed design, concrete architectural structures are best described along with detailed design and often after implementation is completed. In addition, the degree of detail and precision in describing conceptual models, architectural views, and architectural structures is different. Finally, it is significantly easier to communicate to software developers the importance of concrete architectural structures than it is to convey abstract conceptual models or architectural views. Understanding the relationships among conceptual architecture, architectural views, and concrete architectural structures makes the architecture more accessible to the development team and thus increases the expected lifetime of the architecture.

1.10   Layers of Functionality

The purpose of software is to implement (or model) a collection of functions in the problem or application domain using available functions in the solution or implementation domain. "Application domain" here means the direct context for which the software is built, possibly excluding the computer system on which the software will operate. Examples of application domains include financial applications, inventory management, networking, process control, and factory automation. The existence of an application domain usually implies the existence of rules, notions, vocabulary, and other types of expert knowledge that may be set apart from general knowledge and other application domains.

An implementation domain for software-based solutions has at least two independent dimensions: run-time (dynamic) and construction-time (static). (These are related to different existence planes of software, as discussed earlier. Most of the discussion that follows applies to other planes as well.)

The most basic run-time implementation domain consists of the hardware machine, which may include a processor, various types of memory, and special-purpose computing, control, or input/output devices. When the functionality that the hardware machine provides is sufficiently close to the functionality that is required in the application domain, it is possible to design the software that bridges the gap directly. However, usually functions provided by hardware machines are too low-level for most application domains. That is, it is too complex to design software that provides the function required in the application domain using directly only the function provided by the hardware machine. In such situations we design a virtual machine that supports the implementation of the functionality required in the application domain more easily than the original machine, and it is easier to implement the virtual machine on top of the hardware machine than it is to implement the required application. Therefore, software is typically structured as a hierarchy and/or aggregation of virtual machines providing functions successively closer to the application domain.

Though it may be possible to design architecture whose components rely directly on hardware functions to provide functionality specific to the application domain, such vertical partitions hinder reuse in several ways. For example, some lower-layer functions may be used by different components of higher layers, and because pure vertical partitions hide all intermediate layers within component implementation, identical functionality is (re)developed multiple times.

To support reuse, a conceptual framework for software architecture requires layering of functionality. However, layers of functionality should not be confused with components. The former are boundaries that help find stable components. Architecture that precludes software modules from spanning multiple functionality layers supports better reuse of components. Such layering, however, should exist only at write time. Claims that layered designs have worse performance are usually due to misunderstanding of write-time and run-time component domains of software architecture and the independent structures that may exist in these component domains.

A typical example of functionality layers may include a foundation components layer, an abstract model of hardware, an infrastructure layer, an application domain framework, and an application components layer. Figure 1.2 illustrates hierarchical functional layering

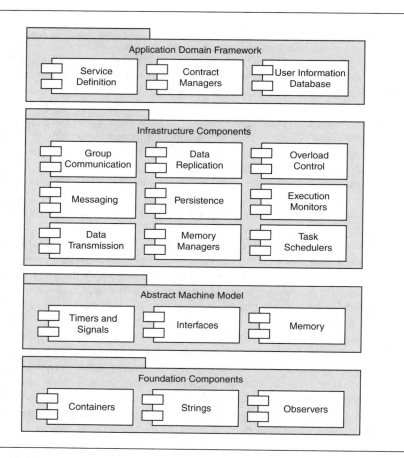

FIGURE 1.2   Functional Layering

for a service application, naming typical components found in the corresponding functionality layers.

Criteria for identifying different functionality layers include the following:

- They use different sets of main concepts.
- Their design and implementation require different knowledge and skills.
- They have different rates of change.
- They have different domains of use.

The lines that divide different functionality layers are not sharp. They are a matter of subjective judgment and an important architectural decision. However, what is most important is that such a decision is explicitly made using appropriate considerations.

1.11 Clusters of Functionality

Layers create *horizontal* boundaries that should be respected by components. Often there are natural *vertical* boundaries that can be identified independently in each layer of functionality. Such vertical boundaries establish functional clusters. Components then can be designed to fall fully within functional cells made by the intersection of layers and clusters.

Figure 1.3 shows clusters of functionality that can be defined in the infrastructure partition we used earlier to demonstrate layers of functionality. The main purpose of functionality clusters is work division. Therefore these partitions exist primarily in the write-time component

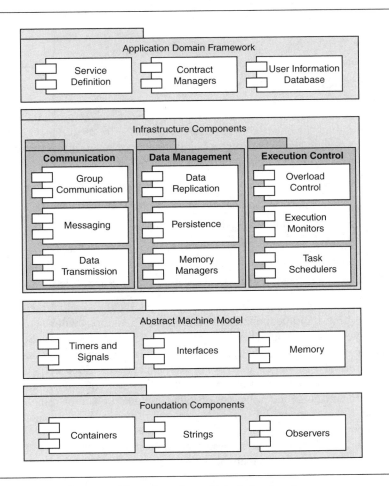

FIGURE 1.3   Clusters of Functionality within Infrastructure

domain. It is important to ensure that boundaries between functionality clusters are not carried over (unnecessarily) into the run-time component domain. However, there may be a reason for having functionality cluster views for build-time and configuration-time component domains, since these may depend on, or at least be affected by, the development structures.

Identifying clusters of functionality is an important architectural decision. Once clusters of functionality have been identified, they may be used to assign responsibility and work to different teams and team members. Criteria for identifying different functionality clusters include the following:

- Their design and implementation require different knowledge and skills.
- They can be developed and tested independently.

The dividing lines between different functionality clusters are usually clear because they follow simple intuition and common sense.

1.12 Abstract Machine Model

Software architecture of embedded software, as a rule, has to include an abstract machine model that represents the underlying hardware. The reason for creating an abstract machine model as a part of architecture is simple: Many (or at least several) functions of the system depend on the underlying machine in multiple ways:

- For naming, addressing, or referring to different parts of the machine
- For managing and communicating information about the machine
- For reasoning about the capabilities of the machine
- For measuring and monitoring performance of the machine
- For managing resources of the machine
- For detecting faults of the machine—that is, locating and isolating faulty parts

If the architecture does not include a single model and a single representation of the underlying machine, multiple models and multiple representations will be created and maintained by different components. This duplication is unnecessarily wasteful. Such models and representations probably would be inconsistent, requiring complex translation when communicating information about the underlying machine between different parts of the system, or would even make sharing this information impossible. Consequently, system performance would suffer, and the goals and principles of sound architecture within a single system would thus be violated. This is a special case of the general principle that core concepts shared by multiple components must be present in the architecture.

Of course, we all were taught to design portable software that does not depend on the hardware on which it executes. Is there not some contradiction here? We don't think so. Software should not depend on irrelevant details of hardware design, or on any other irrelevant details for that matter. The purpose of the abstract machine model is exactly this: to identify, separate, and represent relevant properties and capabilities of the machine. Which details of the machine are relevant depends on the scope of the architecture, the problem domain, and possibly the specific product requirements.

When we speak about the "machine," we do not necessarily mean raw hardware. We mean more the virtual machine, the platform on which the software will execute. This machine very often includes at least parts of the operating system and possibly other software components. For common application types designed for standard execution platforms, the operating system is the abstract machine. The abstract machine model for these applications is a model of the operating system. Such a model may be concerned with users, ownership, file systems, file descriptors, processes, threads, and so on. We are not taught to create or accustomed to creating this model as part of an architecture because it is already there (at least one would hope so) in the documentation of the operating system.

One of the important goals of operating systems is, of course, to provide software applications with a stable interface (read "an abstract model") to access the capability of the machine. However, even when the machine is a "standard computer" and the variability of the parts and their capabilities is limited, this goal is achieved only partially by the operating system. Many software applications require access to capabilities of the machine not directly or adequately supported by the operating system.

In some cases, even software architecture designed for a standard execution platform needs an explicit abstract machine model. An application very sensitive to memory access time may need to have a more detailed memory model than is presented by a typical operating system. It may need to know the actual sizes and kinds of available physical memory, their access times, transfer times, and so on.

In the case of embedded software, the variability of the underlying machine makes it unrealistic to expect that the operating system could adequately represent the elements of the machine, as well as their properties and capabilities. Therefore, an essential part of any architectural model for embedded software is the abstract machine model for every architectural scope (domain, family, evolving system, and so on) for which the architecture is specified.

1.13 Texture of Software

The texture of software is created by recurring (uniform) microstructure of its components. Certain aspects of software functionality are hard to localize using common programming languages and techniques. Such functionality cannot be implemented once and then used in different components; rather it must be implemented multiple times. This fact raises the importance of choices and consistency in the implementation of such functionality so that it becomes a major part of the software architecture. Decisions that affect the texture of software have a significant impact on the system, and they are as hard to revise as decisions regarding the structure. Consistency of the texture is very often a problem because the decisions appear to be local to component, cluster, or layer design. It is not easy to identify the common concerns present in the implementation of different components without concentrating on the texture of the software.

Well-designed software has consistent texture. Software components need to observe policies for security, flow control, overload control, and fault detection and handling; they must rely on infrastructure for communication, coordination, state maintenance, execution tracing, and so on. To achieve consistency in component design, the architecture should provide the necessary information. This information can be provided in the form of aspects, policies, and patterns—each of which we examine in more detail in the discussion that follows. The texture of software is created by a combination of observed standards; uniformly applied styles, patterns, and policies; and the use of specific infrastructure, component models, and even programming languages. Examples of software texture that must be designed and regulated by rules and standards include uniform component model realization, error reporting, exception identification and handling, and execution tracing mechanisms.

1.13.1 Aspects

In addition to their application-related function, software components have to attend to other concerns, for example:

- Configuring functionality and implementation
- Providing interfaces for management
- Monitoring and reporting on execution
- Reporting errors
- Identifying and handling exceptions
- Supporting testing
- Managing persistent state
- Binding required service access points to service providing components
- Maintaining state consistency with other components

Each system may have a different list of extrafunctional concerns that must be addressed by all or a majority of components. These are architectural aspects of component design. This use of the notion of **aspects** is consistent with the Building Blocks method (van der Linden and Müller 1995b). Identification of the common aspects of component design is one of the most important decisions that should be specified by software architecture. It is essential that all aspects be addressed in a consistent, similar (if possible, identical) way in the design of all components. Thus software architecture must define recommended ways of addressing the aspects—a process accomplished by the use of patterns, decision trees, and policies. Usually there is more than one way to address an aspect. Often in the same family of products some aspects need to be dealt with in multiple ways. Decision trees (see Chapter 6) offer a powerful mechanism for representing families of patterns and selecting between members. Finally, the selection of appropriate patterns, and other uniformly applied decisions, should be documented as a list of policies.

1.13.2 Patterns

In recent years, software design patterns have become one of the trendiest topics among software designers. Much has been written about patterns generally, and many specific patterns have been presented, so we assume readers are familiar with the topic and we present here only some points that are commonly overlooked.

For us, a **pattern** is an experience-proven solution to a problem recurring in a defined context that resolves an apparent conflict inherent either in the problem requirements or in the context. Very often the solution part of patterns is overemphasized. In reality, identification of recurring problems is the most essential part. Once the problems are understood, solutions are easy to find. Therefore, as the main focus of patterns in our conceptual framework for software architecture, we emphasize the definition of the context and analysis of problems recurring in this context.

Technically, the same kinds of solutions apply to many different problems. Whether patterns that employ the same or similar solutions to different problems are different patterns is a question that comes up again and again. We believe they are. Their major role is to help designers identify problems in their design and to make them aware that a solution is needed. The specific solution may be less important and often can be refined at a later stage.

Patterns are domain-specific. Our emphasis on the problem and the context may have made this point clear already: Essential problems are different in different domains. Though there are some abstract similarities, what really matters is the ability of software designers to recognize problems as they meet them. Therefore, architecture descriptions must include domain-specific instances of the general problems and patterns.

Patterns exist for every kind of concern and on every level of abstraction. Patterns are not restricted to overcoming limitations of programming languages or improving the reuse and configurability of software by incorporating additional levels of indirection. Patterns can be found for effective resource allocation, configuration management, performance monitoring, or software stability evaluation. It is impossible to lay down all these patterns at the beginning of a single project. Therefore it is more important to establish the organization and processes for incremental identification, clustering, and refinement of patterns. The use of design decision trees (see Chapter 6) may be helpful in this process.

1.13.3 Policies

Policies in our CFSA are design choices that must be applied uniformly to the design and implementation of every component in order to be effective. This makes it clear why determining policies is an essential part of architecture.

A simple example of policy can be the selection of a communication flow control mechanism used in distributed software. When sending a request for a remote service, the client component needs to allocate time within which the remote component is expected to respond. The reason is that remote components and their communication channels may have independent modes of failure. But what happens if no response arrives within the allocated time interval? There are, of course, patterns that address this situation.

As is well known, this situation may be due to different problems: possible transient or persistent failure of remote components, transient or persistent failure in communication channels to remote components, or transient overload of the remote component. In each case the response needs to be different. In most systems, however, dealing with all possible cases is not worthwhile. Rather, the most common situation should be selected and a response to the symptom should be established as a policy. For example, assuming that time-outs in responses of remote components occur only as a result of transient overload conditions, the flow control should require a time window in which no further requests are made if a response is late. To be effective, this behavior should be used uniformly by all components. Therefore, it must be defined in the software architecture.

Typical concerns that can be addressed by policies include the following:

- Detecting and handling errors in communication
- Detecting and handling exceptions
- Tracing and monitoring execution
- Allocating internal resources
- Providing procedures for component startup and shutdown
- Controlling communication flow
- Implementing certain security measures
- Monitoring and controlling execution load

As a rule, the list of concerns addressed by policies should be grouped according to design aspects common to all components. It is unrealistic to expect all policies to be determined before component design. It is important, however, to set up the structures and processes that will enable the architects to recognize issues that need to be addressed by policies during component design.

1.14 Hierarchy of Architectural Scopes

An important task of the software architect is to define the proper scope for the architectural models. As architecture defines the scope of component use, proper definition of the scope of an architectural model defines the (re)usability scope of components. The context in which a software component is used may be very general or very specific.

A very specific context is defined by the software architecture of a specific system, including implementation choices of data communication formats, control transfer policies, or other relevant details. A very general context would talk about only very abstract partition and allocation of responsibilities between the component and its context—for example, by describing the partition as client/server, event loop, or repository-based.

These kinds of descriptions are commonly called architectural styles. From the generality of architectural styles to the specificity of single-system implementation is a continuum of choices. Some points on this continuum are especially useful:

- Variant software architecture
- Dynamic-variant software architecture
- Evolving-system software architecture
- Product family software architecture
- Domain-specific software architecture
- Reference software architecture

One should understand that there are no fixed architectural scopes in the architecture of a specific product. Architectural scopes partition the architecture for the sake of effectiveness, and this is the only criterion for their validity. Identifying the architectural scopes relevant in a specific case is an important part of the architect's work. Only in rare circumstances do more than three architectural scopes need to be considered. Here we provide definitional descriptions of some of the typical architectural scopes just mentioned.

Reference software architecture is the collection of concepts and patterns of structure and texture that allow the systems conforming to the same reference architecture to interoperate and to be managed by the same tools and procedures. Probably the most famous example of reference architecture is the OSI-layered model of communicating systems. Because the emphasis is on interoperation, reference architectures focus primarily in the runtime component domain.

Domain-specific software architecture (DSSA) defines essential domain concepts and functional partitions (structure and application programming interfaces) that enable the development of shared platforms, components, and component frameworks for construction of software in the specified domain. DSSA is typically concerned with domain-specific infrastructure. This may include the selection of operating system, middleware, and data persistence services. DSSA may also specify other components and component frameworks that provide more domain-specific functionality that is useful for most systems in the domain. For example, DSSA for communication network elements may include a node configuration framework, and user authentication and access authorization components.

Because domain-specific architecture emphasizes shared platforms, it focuses mainly on the build-time and the load-time component domains. However, because DSSA separates essential functionality, it is visible in the write-time component domain as well. DSSA should be defined at the level of abstraction on which the variation between different systems in the domain is not visible.

Product family software architecture (PFSA) defines the concepts, structure, and texture necessary to achieve variation in features of variant products while achieving maximum sharing of parts in the implementation. It is similar in intent to DSSA, except that whereas DSSA focuses on commonality and uniformity, family architecture focuses on achieving variability. An appropriate scope for the family can be determined by the bounded complexity of the family architecture. A situation of too many differences between variant products or too many dependencies will be reflected in the complexity of the family architecture. This is the reason that PFSA defines a smaller architectural scope than DSSA.

Note that product families exist primarily on the implementation level and therefore may include variant products intended for different uses. Those variant products may differ from each other in their essential features. These differences often imply that PFSA does not make decisions regarding specific product component structure, but only establishes patterns or mechanisms for creating structures common in the product family. PFSA usually focuses primarily on the write-time component domain. However, it may address run-time concerns common to the whole family by specifying the texture of variant products necessary to support variation across the product family in reliability requirements or other (not function-specific) aspects.

Evolving-system software architecture (ESSA) defines the stable structure and flexibility parameters of the specific system. ESSA defines support for variability in the capacity of the essential features and selection of the secondary (or optional) features provided by the product. ESSA specifies the component structure of the system in write-time and run-time component domains. ESSA is specifically focused on provisions for extension and evolution, as well as variation in optional features and feature capacity as may appear in a single product evolution or in a line of products that coexist at the same time.

Dynamic-variant software architecture defines the structure and texture of software that enables dynamic configuration of the system. Dynamic-variant architecture was always important for embedded software that had to support multiple hardware configurations. This architectural scope is becoming increasingly important for desktop software, as many systems need to provide support for add-on and plug-in components.

The architecture of a specific variant describes a single architectural choice in terms of component structure in every relevant component domain. It is the highest level of abstraction at which system performance characteristics can be analyzed, though provisions for performance can be made within wider architectural scopes.

We recommend the partition of architectural descriptions along a hierarchy of architectural scopes for several reasons. It is rare that a family of products is conceived before even a single variant product is built. If architectural description of the initial variant product makes distinctions between decisions that belong to different architectural scopes when subsequent products are developed, planning of the product family could be done at the architectural level rather than at the implementation level. Grouping of architectural decisions (and descriptions) into architectural scopes would also make evident which architectural scopes and corresponding concerns are addressed by the given architecture. This approach would assist the assessment of risks and effort beyond a single project.

The recommendation of grouping architectural descriptions into architectural scopes should not be interpreted as a suggestion to address concerns of wider architectural scope in every project dealing with the development of a specific system. On the contrary, we suggest that such projects address concerns of only their specific architectural scope while reusing the work already done to address concerns of the wider scopes. Thus if the aim is to create an evolving system, the specific variant architecture needs to be described in relation to dynamic-variant architecture, which in turn is defined in relation to evolving-system architecture.

However, if the work on the wider architectural scopes has not been done or is not known to project personnel, project management should plan appropriate actions and take the corresponding risks into account.

1.15 Final Remarks

Separation of concerns is one of the most basic principles of software design. A good conceptual framework for software architecture should support the separation of concerns addressed by software components. This was the main motivation behind the design of the ARES CFSA. The main ideas of our framework are the following:

- Architecturally significant requirements should be identified and managed separately from product requirements. They should be grouped in a way that allows independent satisfaction of requirements in different groups.

- Conceptual architecture is a model of key concepts rather than a blueprint for software construction.

- Software is not a single entity. It exists simultaneously in multiple planes, each having its own component domain. Partitions in different component domains should be established independently, each addressing a different group of architecturally significant requirements.

- Multiple intermediate functionality layers need to be established between the application domain function specified by requirements and the functionality provided by hardware. In the write plane, software components should not span multiple functionality layers.

- Within each functionality layer, multiple functionality clusters can be defined to form natural boundaries within which components are identified, developed, and maintained.

- Consistency of software texture is achieved by defining in the architecture the common aspects that need to be addressed in the design of all components. For each aspect, the architecture needs to specify systemwide policies and patterns of component microstructure that address typical concerns and problems associated with this aspect of component design.

- Software architects should identify and define the set of architectural scopes relevant for the specific system. Architectural decisions and descriptions should be allocated to a well-defined architectural scope. Each software component should belong to a specific architectural scope that determines the scope of its intended reusability and the scope of allowed dependencies.

2

Software Architecture Description

Jeff Kramer, Jeff Magee, Keng Ng, Naranker Dulay

Software architects use descriptions to document and communicate views of their architectures. Notations and languages that can be used to define architectures succinctly and precisely are thus of particular importance. In this chapter we give an overview of several approaches that claim to be usable for architecture description. As we will see, no approach covers all architectural views or provides a notation for all architectural planes. And in all cases, concern for product families is ignored or treated poorly.

The basis of our approach is the observation that one of the most important ways in which we cope with large and complex systems is through abstraction. Architectural views are specific kinds of abstractions. For instance, the development view sees systems as compositions of interacting components. To this end, the variously termed coordination, configuration, and, more recently, architectural description languages (ADLs) facilitate description, comprehension, and reasoning at that level. They provide a clean separation between the behavior and the interactions of individual components.

The interest in software architecture descriptions is based on the belief that describing the development view, which incorporates a separate structural view, provides a sound and useful level of abstraction for describing and understanding large systems. The recognition of high-level textures as client/server, or layered, systems provides further aid to the comprehension of overall systems design. It has been recognized, most notably by Garlan and Shaw (1993) and Perry and Wolf (1992), that when systems are constructed from many components, the organization, or architecture, of the overall system presents a new set of design problems. One of the central architectural concerns identified by Garlan and Perry (1994) is the high-level description of systems based on graphs of interacting components.

Depending on the architectural view and plane (specific views and planes were described in Chapter 1), a component may have different meanings and thus different descriptions. Within the process view a component has state, exhibits some well-defined behavior, and has a unique identity. The **identity** of a component distinguishes it from all other components; its **behavior** is its outwardly visible and testable activity; and its **state** consists of the cumulative results of its behavior. In many architecture views **components** are the primary points of computation in a system and **connectors** define the interactions between these components. We can specify architectural descriptions for these views explicitly and precisely using a special-purpose language, known as an **architectural description language (ADL).** An ADL provides notations for representing architectural structures and textures in a given view.

There are clearly many important views for many planes in software design, including views for system behavior and quality aspects such as resource, timing, and performance issues. We see these views as orthogonal and complementary to the structural aspects of a system. It is our belief that a single architecture description of a system provides the ideal skeleton to which different views can be attached. It provides a framework so that the same basic architecture description can be used to derive and construct the system and to analyze it with respect to different properties (see Figure 2.1).

In this chapter we will describe the specific problems currently encountered in the development of industrial-software product families and propose two ADLs to address them: Darwin and Koala. Darwin is the earlier ADL and was extended to express the diversity and evolutionary aspects that are crucial within product family development. Koala is a more specialized ADL that was developed by the ARES project for embedded software. Koala places greater emphasis on the deployment architecture and has been fine-tuned for performance and efficiency in resource usage for consumer electronics applications. We will show how these ADLs can be used to provide structure and texture to a system.

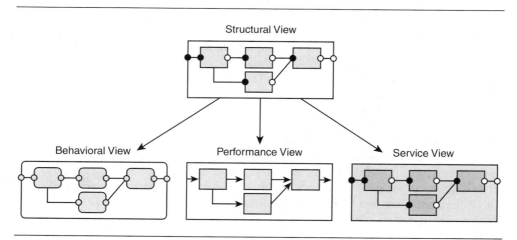

FIGURE 2.1 Multiple System Views

2.1   Current Research in ADLs

Architectural description languages are notations specially developed for expressing and representing architectural structures and textures. An ADL specification is typically a high-level description of the system structure and texture that addresses the design plane and focuses on the development view. It is often referred to as a structural model. To date, much of the work on ADLs has concentrated on providing precise descriptions of connectors, which provide the glue for combining components into systems (Garlan and Perry 1995) and accommodating diverse connector types (Allan and Garlan 1994, Shaw et al. 1995). The current generation of ADLs has placed less emphasis on the description of complex and changing system structures. As exemplified by UniCon (Shaw et al. 1995), ADLs of this generation describe the overall system structure by declaring a static set of component instances and connectors. Recent efforts in industrial research environments such as Siemens (Schwanke, Strack, and Werthmann-Auzinger 1996) and Andersen Consulting (Kozaczynski and Ning 1996) have adopted a similar approach.

ADLs have previously been known in the literature as structural configuration languages, module interconnection languages, graphical interconnection languages, and network specification languages. The main objective of most of these older ADLs was to increase program-structuring ability by providing more general structuring mechanisms on the basis of explicit component interconnection.

In the subsections that follow, we briefly review a selection of existing ADLs and architectural description tools and highlight their salient features.

2.1.1   PCL (Proteus Configuration Language)

PCL is a modeling language that provides facilities for the integrated modeling of hardware, software, and documentation structures (Sommerville and Dean 1994). It is designed to model the variability within system families. PCL assumes that each family comprises a stable part, which is common to all versions, and a variable part, which is version-dependent. Conditional expressions are used to describe situations in which parts of the structure will be included for any particular version. Object-oriented modeling techniques such as inheritance can also be used to add details to specific components with common ancestors.

As can be expected from its name, PCL plays a role in the configuration plane. However, PCL was designed as a documentation language and, as such, does not include mechanisms for specifying configuration rules against which a specified configuration can be checked.

2.1.2   DARTS

DARTS is the graphical language for describing the architecture of LOTOS specifications (Turner 1993). It is used as a tool to visualize the architecture of large LOTOS specifications and to allow designers to think in terms of relations among components, and it avoids irrelevant details from the architecture standpoint. It is integrated in a LOTOS environment with tools to edit, convert from or to LOTOS specifications, and animate architectural descriptions.

DARTS has a bias toward the process view.

2.1.3 ROOM (Real-Time Object-Oriented Modeling)

ROOM is an object-oriented methodology targeted at the development of real-time systems (Selic, Ward, and Gullekson 1994). The structuring mechanism used consists of actors, ports, and bindings. An actor is an encapsulated component, which models an abstract role in a system and communicates with its environment by passing messages through its interface ports. Messages are passed along bindings, which connect two or more ports. An actor can be hierarchical, and because actor classes are also organized into class hierarchies, entire system hierarchies can be refined and reused through standard inheritance mechanisms.

ROOM has a focus in the process view. System behavior and dynamics in ROOM are modeled using a variation of Harel's StateCharts (Harel 1987), which allows for efficient tool implementation.

2.1.4 EDLC (Evolutionary Domain Life Cycle)

EDLC is an iterative software life-cycle model that encourages the reuse of software requirements and architectures (Gomaa et al. 1994). Among its objectives is the support for development of families of systems within an application domain, instead of the development of single systems. EDLC advocates a component-based compositional approach to system building and extends traditional object-oriented methods to model variations and dependencies between system components. Descriptions of the dependencies of features on objects are used to generate target systems from a generic architecture. A prototype domain-modeling environment exists to support the EDLC method.

The EDLC focus is the design plane and the development view.

2.1.5 UniCon

UniCon allows the overall system architecture to be described in terms of a static set of component instances and connectors (Shaw et al. 1995). A connector mediates the interaction of two or more components; the type of connection it provides, as well as the roles to be played by the components it connects, must be specified. A set of built-in component types (e.g., filter, module, sequential file) and connector types (e.g., pipe, file, remote procedure call) are provided as standard by the language. This structure gives support for specific textures within the architecture. UniCon deals with the development view and the design plane.

The system structure is fixed at specification time. Consequently UniCon does not provide support for dynamic and evolving structures.

2.1.6   LEAP (Lockheed Environment for Automatic Engineering)

LEAP is a graphical development environment that supports the capture of design knowledge and the synthesis of domain-specific system descriptions (Graves 1992). The target application area is distributed reactive systems. Component descriptions in the form of templates are used to structure the design and synthesis knowledge, allowing new systems to be constructed through template instantiation and composition. The template approach leads to a specific texture of all systems written in LEAP. Domain-specific requirements and rules can be used to customize software components for individual applications. LEAP deals only with the design plane.

2.1.7   Aesop

Aesop is a meta-CASE system dealing with textures (Garlan, Allen, and Ockerbloom 1994). It is used to develop style-specific architectural environments, where a style is an idiom or pattern (e.g., pipe/filter or client/server system) or a reference model (e.g., OSI seven-layer model for communication). Aesop generates a style-specific environment (called a fable) by combining style descriptions with a shared toolkit of common facilities.

Fables support the development of component-based systems, which can be represented as labeled graphs of components and connectors, both of which can be described hierarchically. A generic fable allows the creation of box-and-line diagrams with no semantic interpretations. A pipe/filter fable, on the other hand, has additional built-in knowledge of this style of systems (e.g., pipes are directional and cannot be decomposed). The graphical editor of a fable ensures that the stylistic constraints of the corresponding style are enforced.

Aesop deals with the design plane.

2.2   ADL Requirements for ARES

Although there are many benefits of having an explicit ADL for architecture description, existing ADLs do not go far enough in solving the more specific problems encountered in the design and implementation of embedded software families. Our experience with the ARES case studies identified the following important issues not tackled by the current generation of ADLs.

2.2.1   Level of Abstraction

For descriptions of the logical, process, and development views, an ADL should be able to present high-level abstractions. We should be able to deal with several planes and several views for a product family. Notations for object-oriented design methods such as OMT (Object Modeling Technique), Booch, and more recently UML (Unified Modeling Language) have proven to be useful in identifying and describing various aspects of the system architecture. However, these languages are aimed mainly at design and provide a very low level of abstraction.

The semantics of components is overly rich and often unwieldy. Moreover, the semantics hinders the possibility of reinterpreting the description elements in such a way that multiple views for other planes are allowed. Instead, for a selected set of views separate descriptions are needed, and it is often not clear how such separate descriptions can be connected. When used for architecture description, object-oriented design methods force the architect to consider many aspects that are either unnecessary or too detailed; they provide specific textures, whereas the architect should provide the texture that is best suited for his or her product family.

2.2.2 System Construction in Addition to System Documentation

It would clearly be beneficial if the description of the logical view could be used within the other views directly. In this way system structure modifications could be applied to the description and automatically propagated to the eventual implementation. For an architectural description to be used for the configuration and build planes, the ADL needs to have an operational semantics for the elaboration of specifications such that they may be used at initialization time to direct the generation of the desired system. Having a stable architecture throughout the development process is also useful for maintaining the developer's orientation through the different views and planes. The architecture can then be viewed as a skeleton around which the different software artifacts related to the system can be hung. In terms of tool support, the architecture provides the ideal framework for aiding system navigation.

2.2.3 Handling of Variations within a Product Family

The most significant architectural requirements for product families are related to the handling of variations. Variation is not restricted to the elements of the configuration plane; the elements in other planes also vary. As noted earlier, most existing ADLs focus on the description of a fixed system structure with little or no provision for the description of variations within the architecture. Although this approach is adequate for describing a single instance of a system, it lacks the flexibility needed for handling the (often minor) differences in architecture between family instances. Related systems within an application domain often share a similar, general architecture, but with slight variations due to the difference in feature set and other requirements. It is clearly desirable to represent the variability within such a product family at an architectural level rather than at the program code level. The capture and representation of features in an ADL are thus important issues.

An ADL must provide support for describing the part of the architecture that is common to all instances of the family, as well as a means of capturing information relating to the nonstandard part of the product family. From such a generic architectural description of the product family, it should then be possible to generate specific, feature-driven system configurations. In other words, it should be possible to produce a single family architecture from which features and variations can be selectively included in particular systems. The advantage of this approach is that it obviates the need to develop and maintain multiple versions of the product family independently, while at the same time reducing the subsequent errors caused by conflicting feature sets.

2.2.4 Definition of Dynamic Structures

Most ADLs have concentrated on specifying the organization of components and connectors, which are static. Although such description is adequate for many systems, it is often desirable to be able to evolve the structure of a system at run time to adapt to changes in requirements and to make better use of system resources. In fact, present-day operating systems support the dynamic adaptation of software via DLLs (dynamic link libraries) and component brokers. Even though these facilities are presently not widely used within embedded systems, they will become important in the future.

When an ADL specification is used to drive system construction, the structure of the resulting system in terms of its component instances and their interconnection is fixed at build time. Support for dynamic structure in an ADL will allow the software architecture to evolve during system execution.

2.2.5 Multiple System Views and Attributes

As we argued earlier, it should be possible to embed or associate views with the basic architectural description. Although it may not always be sensible to represent this information with the ADL itself, there clearly needs to be a way of relating it to the architectural components. Where appropriate, there should be ways of cross-referencing and translating among views. The ADL would provide an ideal organizational framework for managing this diverse pool of information. With the appropriate tool support, the elicitation, storage, and presentation of such information can all be automated to minimize the tedium of such mechanical tasks.

2.2.6 Description of Hierarchical and Layered Architectures

Hierarchical and layered architectures provide a means of coping with the problem of manageability—that is, the degree to which the ADL can represent large and complex systems. They allow a system to be viewed and analyzed at different levels of abstraction and detail. Support for hierarchy allows a complex system to be partitioned into smaller, more manageable pieces, and larger system components to be built out of smaller building blocks through composition. Indeed, the use of such techniques is widespread in the case studies that are used in the ARES project, ranging from consumer electronics to train protection systems. What has been lacking is proper language and tool support to ensure their systematic and principled use. Note that the hierarchical decomposition allows localization of configurations and mixing of the design and configuration planes: A compound component is built out of a (local) configuration of other components. Moreover, components at a high level in the hierarchy may have a meaning in the build and execution planes, whereas lower-level components have a meaning only in the design plane.

In addition to components, the interfaces of the components themselves can be complex in large and complex systems. Hence language support is needed to deal with the complexity of interfaces, in addition to dealing with components.

2.2.7   Tool Support for Architectural Visualization and Manipulation

The structural part of software architecture is quite amenable to representation in a graphical form. Therefore, in addition to the more traditional textual representation, there should be one or more ways of visualizing the different aspects of the architecture in a graphical form. Apart from syntactic structural development views, there should be support for other semantic views of a system, such as the process view, incorporating behavior in terms of state transitions or data flow, or component interactions in terms of message sequence charts. These kinds of information can be treated as additional system attributes, which can be attached to (as a tag) the basic structural framework.

Tool support is essential in order to exploit the many benefits of graphical representations. In addition to aiding system comprehension through visualization, automation can help with mechanical tasks such as system navigation, method guidance, diagram layout, code generation, syntax checking, and consistency management. It makes mundane and tedious tasks more manageable and less error-prone.

2.3   Darwin

Darwin was chosen as the vehicle for experimentation within the ARES project primarily because it already satisfied most of the requirements for the development of software product families. Furthermore, because it had been produced by one of the ARES partners, both the language and its associated tools were more amenable to modification and extension in order to support all our requirements for an ADL.

Darwin is an ADL that evolved from our earlier work on configuration programming for distributed systems (Kramer 1990, Kramer and Magee 1985). Like its predecessor, Conic (Magee, Kramer, and Sloman 1989), Darwin describes a program as a hierarchical configuration of components. Primitive components (those at the leaves of the program hierarchy) interact by accessing services. Each intercomponent interaction is represented by a binding between a required service and a provided service. Components and connectors do not have a predetermined semantics. This means that Darwin descriptions can be used for descriptions of various planes and views. Darwin has both a graphical and a textual representation. The Darwin specification of system architecture can also be used as a framework for structuring behavioral specifications during design and analysis and is used directly to drive system building during construction.

2.3.1 Components and Services

Darwin views components in terms of both the services they provide (to other components) and the services they require (from other components). For example, the component in Figure 2.2 is a filter component, which provides a single service (`prev`) and requires two services (`next` and `output`). The diagrammatic convention used here is that filled-in circles represent services provided by a component, and empty circles represent services required by a component. The type of the service is specified in angle brackets. In the example, the interaction mechanism used to implement the service is a port, which accepts messages of type `int`. Darwin does not interpret service-type information, but makes it available to the underlying execution platform. Depending on the view, different types may be used that can be interpreted automatically. For instance, in the Regis system (Magee, Dulay, and Kramer 1994a) dealing with the deployment view, type information is used to select the correct communication code directly. In addition to providing several predefined interaction mechanisms, Regis permits users to define their own. When used with a conventional distributed platform such as CORBA (Object Management Group 1991), service types name an IDL (interface definition language) specification, which is then used to generate the correct client and server stubs.

In general, a component may provide many services and require many services. The names of required and provided services are local to the component type specification. In a distributed environment, a component does not need to know the global names of external services or where they are to be found. Components may thus be specified, implemented, and tested independently of the rest of the system of which they will form a part. We call this property **context independence.**

Context independence permits the reuse of components during construction (through multiple instantiation) and simplifies replacement during maintenance.

2.3.2 Instantiation and Binding

The primary purpose of the Darwin language is to allow system architects to construct **composite component types** from both instances of basic computational components and other composite components. The resulting system is a hierarchically structured composite

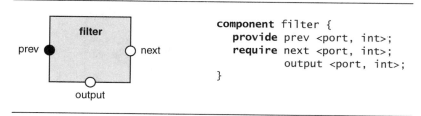

FIGURE 2.2 Component Type `filter`

component that, when elaborated at execution time, results in a collection of instances of computational components that are concurrent and potentially distributed. Composite components and systems are thus formed in Darwin by declaration of the instances of components and binding of the services required by one component to the services provided in another, as shown in Figure 2.3 for a simple client/server system.

A binding is legal only if the service type of the requirement matches the service type of the provision. As noted earlier, Darwin only manages service types; it does not interpret them, so the matching predicate must be supplied by the system being used to specify the service type. The matching predicate is dependent on the plane and the view involved. In the current Darwin tool set, the default is to do a simple name equivalence test. Many requirements may be bound to a single service provision (in a many-to-one binding); however, a service requirement may be bound to only a single service provision. The problem of using Darwin to describe architectures using one-to-many bindings is discussed later in the chapter.

2.3.3   Guarded and Replicated Configurations

The example shown in Figure 2.4 defines a variable-length `pipeline` of `filter` instances in which the input of each instance is bound to its predecessor's output. The length of the `pipeline` is determined by a parameter of the composite component, which is substituted at elaboration time of the Darwin configuration program.

The `pipeline` component type is implemented by an array of `filter` instances whose dimensions are defined by the array declaration. The `forall` replicator construct declares the actual instances and their bindings. Each instance must be declared explicitly because the instances may have different parameter values. The `when` guard construct can be used to conditionally include instances and/or bindings in an elaborated system.

```
component Server {
    provide p;
}

component Client {
    require r;
}

component System {
    inst
        A:Client;
        B:Server;
    bind
            A.r - B.p;
}
```

FIGURE 2.3 Client/Server Configuration

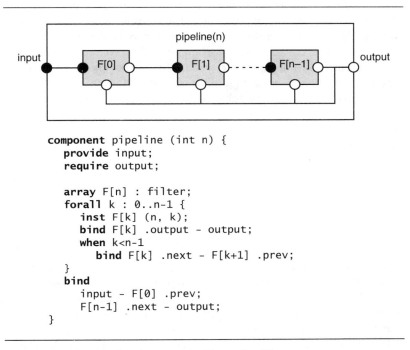

```
component pipeline (int n) {
    provide input;
    require output;

    array F[n] : filter;
    forall k : 0..n-1 {
        inst F[k] (n, k);
        bind F[k] .output - output;
        when k<n-1
            bind F[k] .next - F[k+1] .prev;
    }
    bind
        input - F[0] .prev;
        F[n-1] .next - output;
}
```

FIGURE 2.4 Composite-Component Type pipeline

Requirements that cannot be satisfied inside a component can be made visible at a higher level by being bound to an interface requirement, as has been done in the example for the filter F[n-1] requirement next, which is bound to output. Similarly, services provided internally that are required outside can be bound to an interface service provision—for example, input - F[0].prev. Because an interface requirement represents an external provision, it is consistent that many internal requirements may be bound to an interface requirement—for example, F[k].output - output.

Darwin also supports recursively defined components and allows component types as parameters so that template component types can be defined (Magee, Dulay, and Kramer 1994b). In addition, it provides support for dynamic structures, which will allow the software architecture to evolve during system execution in order to adapt to changes in requirements and to make better use of system resources.

2.3.4   Composite Interfaces

In the same way that Darwin allows composite components to be constructed from simpler ones, it allows individual services to be grouped into composite interfaces. This capability of treating a set of related services as a single interface is particularly useful in larger systems in which, unless an abstraction mechanism for interfaces is provided, the large number of services that become exposed at the top levels of the component hierarchy makes a system highly unmanageable. From a design perspective, it also makes sense to be able to view related services as one. For example, a file server component may provide, among others, services such as `openFile`, `readFile`, `writeFile`, and `closeFile`. For a client component, it is more convenient to be presented with just a single `fileIO` interface with the four individual services as subinterfaces. In Darwin, the description will look like this:

```
interface fileIO {
        openFile;
        readFile;
        writeFile;
        closeFile;
}
```

Declared in this way, a client of the file server component will see only one `fileIO` service. From within the file server itself, all four subservices will be visible and bindable to its internal subcomponents. Figure 2.5 shows a graphical representation of this composite interface.

Although previous ADLs, such as Conic, support arrays of services and have constructs for binding service arrays in complex topologies, they lack a construct to bundle together and bind a number of nonhomogeneous services. Darwin's support for composite interfaces and consequently the ability to view multiple services as one and perform bindings between these grouped services goes a long way to solving this problem.

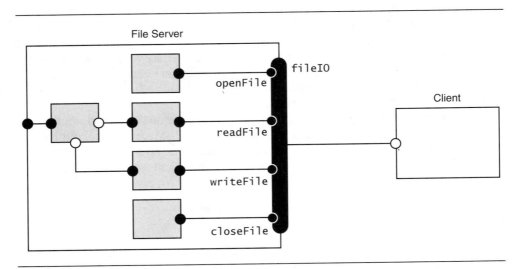

FIGURE 2.5   Composite Interface

2.3.5   Generic Types

One of the most powerful features of higher-level programming languages is support for **generic types** (e.g., template classes in C++). In Darwin, such types allow abstract template architectures to be described. Placeholders can be defined that can then be substituted with real component types when the system is eventually built.

The following example is taken from the TV set example (see Section 2.5.5). The tv_set component takes two generic component type parameters that act as placeholders for the terrestrial and satellite tuners, respectively:

```
component tv_set (
   ‹terrestrial_tuner›, ‹satellite_tuner›,
   int tv_type, int tv_std, bool pip_selected)
{
   inst tt : ‹terrestrial_tuner› (tv_type);
   when (tv_type == HIGH_END_TV) {
      inst st : ‹satellite_tuner› (tv_type);
      when (pip_selected) {
         inst p : pip (tv_std);
         inst tt2 : ‹terrestrial_tuner› (tv_type, tv_std);
         inst st2 : ‹satellite_tuner› (tv_type, tv_std);
      }
   }
}
```

We can now instantiate different instances of tv_set, as in the following:

```
component t_tuner1 { ... }
component t_tuner2 { ... }
component s_tuner1 { ... }
component s_tuner2 { ... }

inst example1 : tv_set (t_tuner1, s_tuner1, HIGH_END_TV, NICAM,
true);
   inst example2 : tv_set (t_tuner2, s_tuner2, LOW_END_TV, PAL,
false);
```

2.3.6   Partial Component Types

When working with complex parameterized architectures, the ability to partially build new component types can greatly simplify descriptions and more accurately enumerate the different members of a product family. A **partial component type** is one that has some of its parameters defined, thus allowing parts of a system to be fixed while other features or variations are left undefined until the later stages in the development process. This capability is particularly useful for consumer electronics software, in which the production of code for memory chips of limited size is a major concern.

```
component tv_set1 = tv_set (t_tuner1, s_tuner1);
component tv_set2 = tv_set (t_tuner2, s_tuner2);
```

The components `tv_set1` and `tv_set2` are partially evaluated features of the full `tv_set` component. They still require parameters for `tv_type`, `tv_std`, and `pip_selected`. We can instantiate specific components as in the following example:

```
inst example1 : tv_set1 (HIGH_END_TV, NICAM, true);
inst example2 : tv_set2 (LOW_END_TV, PAL, false);
```

We can also create further partially evaluated types from them, as in the following:

```
component high_end_tv_set1 = tv_set1 (HIGH_END_TV);
component NICAM_tv_set1 = tv_set1 ( , NICAM );
```

2.3.7 Namespaces

If the number of distinct features and component types is large, the global namespace that Darwin employs for constants and component types can give rise to clashes and errors. A simple remedy is to allow constants and component types to be encapsulated within component types. Any component that requires knowledge of any of the features can then just include this new component within its description, thereby allowing it to access the values of all the features within this feature set. This solution also has the advantage that features that influence components only at the lower levels of the system hierarchy are not seen at the upper levels. A namespace hierarchy can easily be managed in this way.

In the following examples we nest the definitions of television component types with a tv component. We also group together television constant definitions for better namespace management.

```
component tv {
   component tv_constants {
      const int HIGH_END_TV = 0;
      const int LOW_END_TV = 1;

      const int PAL = 0;
      const int NICAM = 1;
   }

   component pip (int tv_std) { ... }
```

```
component terrestrial_tuner (int tv_type, int tv_std) { ... }

component satellite_tuner (int tv_type, int tv_std) { ... }

component tv_set (int tv_type, int tv_std, bool pip_selected)

}
```

We can now provide access to constants and types, as in the following examples:

```
tv :: tv_constants :: HIGH_END_TV
tv :: pip
tv :: terrestrial_tuner
tv :: satellite_tuner
tv :: tv_set
```

2.4   Tool Support for Darwin

Our approach to software architecture and its embodiment in Darwin is the basis for a collection of automated tools that together support the design, analysis, and implementation of distributed programs.

The Software Architect's Assistant (SAA) (Ng, Kramer, and Magee 1996) is a visual environment for system design and development. It provides the user with automated, intelligent assistance throughout the software design process. As a graphical CASE tool, SAA has the knowledge of Darwin language syntax built in, thus ensuring that only the input of legal Darwin constructs is allowed. SAA's facilities include the display of multiple integrated graphical and textual architectural views, a flexible mechanism for recording design information, and the automatic generation of program code and formatted reports from design diagrams. Software reuse is supported through the use of component libraries. In addition, SAA enables the designer to produce specific system structures from the definitions of generic software architectures. Figure 2.6 shows a typical screen shot of SAA, displaying multiple views.

The Labelled Transition System Analyser (LTSA) (Magee, Dulay, and Kramer 1997, Magee, Kramer, and Giannakopoulou 1998, 1999) is a verification tool for concurrent systems. It mechanically checks that the specification of a concurrent system satisfies the properties required of its behavior. In addition, LTSA supports specification animation to facilitate interactive exploration of system behavior. A system in LTSA is modeled as a set of interacting finite state machines. The properties required of the system are also modeled as state machines. LTSA performs compositional reachability analysis to search exhaustively for violations of the desired properties. More formally, each component of a specification is described as a labeled transition system (LTS), which contains all the states a component

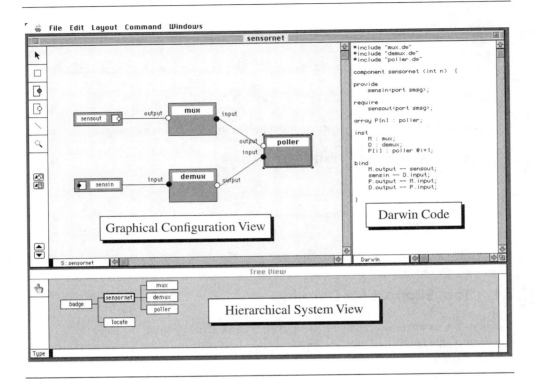

FIGURE 2.6   The Software Architect's Assistant

may reach and all the transitions it may perform. However, explicit description of an LTS in terms of its states, set of action labels, and a transition relation is cumbersome for other than small systems. Consequently, LTSA supports a process algebra notation called FSP (for "finite state processes") for concise description of component behavior. The tool allows the LTS corresponding to an FSP specification to be viewed graphically.

Darwin provides LTSA with the architectural framework for partitioning and composing LTS descriptions. The compositional hierarchy used for compositional reachability analysis can be derived directly from a Darwin description. Indeed, SAA supports the automatic generation of this information, which can be fed directly into the LTSA (see Figure 2.7). Hence, used together, the two tools form an integrated environment for program design and analysis.

Regis (Magee, Dulay, and Kramer 1994b) is a programming environment aimed at supporting the development and execution of distributed programs. It embodies a constructive approach to the development of programs based on separating program structure from communication and computation. Darwin is used as the configuration language for structuring Regis components. In other words, Regis programs are constructed from a Darwin configuration description consisting of a hierarchically structured specification of interconnected

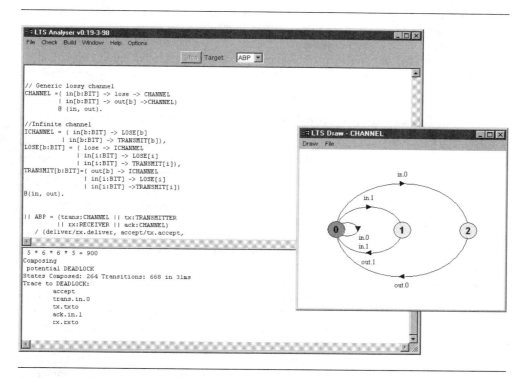

FIGURE 2.7   The Labelled Transition System Analyser

component instances. When elaborated at execution time, this specification results in a network of intercommunicating active components, which can be distributed across a local area network. The computational components in Regis are, in fact, C++ objects. They interact via communication objects, which are also programmed in C++.

2.5   The Use of Darwin in ARES

In this section we focus on the application of the Darwin ADL to the description of architectures for software families. We identify real problems currently encountered in the development of a television software family as test cases and, in each case, demonstrate how Darwin could solve or alleviate the difficulties in the system development process.

One of the key problems in the development of a system family is in relating the features that differentiate the members of a family to an overall architecture for that family. The current state of the art addresses such variance at the code or programming-language level; that is, it is addressed only in the deployment view. It is our belief that the problem of variance description is better tackled at the more abstract logical and development views. Individual family members, then, are obtained through the mapping of features to component instances of the general architecture, or by customization of a component through parameterization.

The notion of a component is thus a key concept in the specification of system families.

2.5.1 Problems of Architectural Description and Understanding

The use of modules or components for encapsulation and information hiding is well understood and is being practiced in software development at Philips. However, this is done only within the deployment view, in which the languages (C/C++) and tools being used have inadequate support for compound components and other advanced features of architectural styles. The deployment view guides the selection of the development view. Because of the complexity of the system, the resultant software architecture ends up having a flat structure consisting of many dozens of components. Although at the logical view these components are organized in a hierarchical fashion, the chosen approach for the development view does not support an easily used mechanism to enforce strict encapsulation and access control for the components in question.

Here is a typical scenario of the current practice in software development: A developer requires a particular feature or functionality. He finds—for example, through the UNIX grep utility—a function, f, whose name suggests that it does what is required. However, function f is in the interface of a component, c, that is encapsulated by another component, d, and thus is not supposed to be accessible from outside d. The developer is not aware of this and includes the header file of c, instead of that of d. This situation is illustrated in Figure 2.8.

A more concrete example can be found in the television case study (see Chapter 5). Because they lacked a clear understanding of components, the developers were not always sure whether they were dealing with a compound component or with a subcomponent of the compound. This confusion can best be illustrated by Figure 2.9, which presents two views of the tuner component.

The left-hand view considers the tuner component as a compound component that is subdivided into a hardware component, a driver component, and a component providing tuner

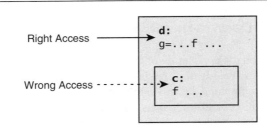

FIGURE 2.8 Encapsulation of Functionality

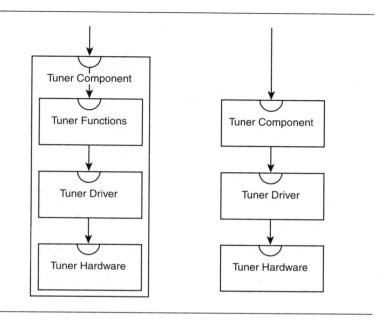

FIGURE 2.9   Compound Tuner Component

functions. The right-hand view considers the tuner component not as a compound compo-nent, but rather as a component cluster containing related components. The views are used interchangeably and are assumed to be equivalent, leading to confusion and violation of basic concepts.

To a large extent, the problems mentioned here have been caused by the fact that the specification and implementation languages used for the television software do not offer the necessary constructs for describing compound components. In addition, no tool support was available to enforce strict adherence to properties such as encapsulation and information hiding.

To maximize the advantages of component-based software development, it is crucial that the component structure be carried forward and maintained, through all planes and views. If this is done, there is a clear understanding between the programmers and the designers as to what constitutes a "real" compound component, what is a cluster, and so on. Furthermore, we avoid the problem of divergence between the original design (which has a component structure) and the eventual implementation, which will often no longer exhibit such a structure. The use of an ADL will clearly go a long way to solving this problem.

The use of an ADL will further add the necessary discipline to the design and imple-mentation processes. It will force the designers to make explicit difficult choices about which components could and should be encapsulated, which interfaces should be exported, and other architectural decisions. Of equal importance, it will force the designers to adhere to such decisions once they have been made.

2.5.2   Support for Architectural Description in Darwin

Darwin, as an ADL, was specifically designed for the description of hierarchical, component-based software architecture. As such, the compound component is a basic and essential concept within the language. In Darwin, such a component is referred to as a composite component and provides encapsulation of its subcomponents. Composite components in Darwin unify the concepts of compound components and clusters (described earlier in the chapter) into a coherent and flexible system structuring abstraction. They are the means for specifying large systems in a hierarchical and modular way.

Using composite components to hierarchically group subcomponents in systems is conceptually clear and powerful. However, composite components also need to explicitly expose the underlying interaction structure of a program. The need to show and promote such structures is crucial because it allows components to be defined in a context-independent way. A context-independent component does not need to know the specific components with which it will interact, but it has a specific interaction interface. In Darwin, such an interface of a component is described in terms of the services the component provides to its environment, as well as the services it requires of its environment.

Using the example in Figure 2.9, the Darwin description for the tuner component would look like Figure 2.10. Note that because Darwin provides proper encapsulation, only the services provided at the interface of the composite tuner component are visible to other com-

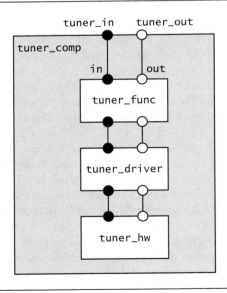

```
component tuner_comp {
    provide tuner_in;
    require tuner_out;

    inst tunf: tuner_func;
         tund: tuner_driver;
         tunh: tuner_hw;

    bind tunf.out-tuner_out;
         tuner_in-tunf.in;
         .....
         .....
}
```

FIGURE 2.10   Darwin Description of the Tuner Component

ponents. The three subcomponents are not accessible from outside their parent. Any functions provided by any of these components that need to be accessed by external components will have to be exported via the interface of their parent, as done with the `provide` feature in the figure.

An important architectural consideration is the requirement in many systems of safety of interactions—that is, the ability to restrict or prevent unintended interactions. In Darwin, the interaction structure of a program is described at the architectural level, as bindings within composite components. This clear separation between structure and computation is distinct from the current approach in which both computation and component interaction are embedded within program code, making the structure much harder to comprehend. Making interaction structure and interaction safety the concerns of composite components leads to systems that consist of hierarchically structured networks of loosely coupled, configuration-independent components.

We can gain power and safety by ensuring that components are explicitly typed and that component types have clearly defined and typed interface(s). If circumstances allow, such component types can then be used to instantiate as many instances of the component as are needed and in any number of applications. This capability promotes the use of libraries of reusable and interchangeable components.

In comparison to the current industrial practice, our uniform treatment of composite and primitive components leads to a black-box approach to components. Ideally it should not be possible to distinguish between components that are primitive and components that are composite, and if the interfaces are the same, composite components and primitive components can be used interchangeably. Because composite components can be instantiated in other composite components, they support hierarchical program structuring better than modular programming languages, which do not allow modules of modules or multiple copies of a single module.

Clustering components without strong encapsulation, as was done in the television software, represents a weaker form of structuring but could be supported if composite components were allowed to be specified as "white boxes." Any subcomponent within a white-box component would then be explicitly accessible from outside the white box. Of course, such direct access has consequences in terms of context independence and the ability to interchange components. For such reasons, clustering is not considered a particularly worthwhile structuring abstraction and hence is not explicitly supported by Darwin. The use of clustering for coordinating and managing components across the component hierarchy—for example, for resource allocation, migration, failure recovery, and security—is more ideally handled by the use of concepts that are known in the application domain.

It should be pointed out that in the Darwin approach to system development, the software architectural view is maintained throughout the system life cycle. It provides the overall framework within which the description of computation is embedded (in the primitive components), thereby helping to ensure conformance among the original, logical view, the development view, and the deployment view, regardless of the programming language used. With the appropriate tool support as demonstrated by the Software Architect's Assistant, such conformance can be automatically checked and maintained.

2.5.3 Description of Variance in Product Families

Variation within a product family exists in many forms. Traditionally it has been coded directly in the program source code as option settings and compiler flags. This low-level approach to describing variation is error-prone and provides little aid for reasoning. When the range of variation within a product family is large, as is often the case in industrial applications, the need for more structured and systematic techniques and tools for specifying and reasoning about variation is all the greater.

Within the Philips television product family are three main sources of variation:

1. Differences in user interface, partially originating in cultural differences
2. Differences in transmission standards
3. Differences between low-end and high-end television sets

Diversity in user interface is dynamic and short-term. Preferably the exact features of the user interface are determined just before production time, even though the main components will have to be determined at design time. This kind of variation exhibits itself in the different combinations of the primitive user interface functions—for example, the way in which input signals such as button presses are translated into a series of actions. Future changes to the physical input devices and the interpretation of user actions means that user interface variations cannot be completely predetermined.

Variation in transmission standards is static and long-term; that is, the collection of transmission standards usually remains unchanged for many years. However, new standards, such as those for digital transmission, are still arising—hence the need to cater to a growing set of standards. It is often a requirement that it be possible for each type of television to comply with any one of the many standards. Sometimes one television needs to be able to support more than one standard. The variations determined by the standards are mainly low-level functions—for example, how to get information out of the transmitted signal. Certain kinds of information can be selected for only certain formats. For instance, the teletext functionality is available only for the standards used within Europe. Such limitation means that a large part of high-level functionality is meaningless when such a standard does not exist. Ideally this functionality will not be present for these variants.

The third kind of variation reflects the difference in the feature sets of high-end and low-end televisions. This kind of variation is presently determined before product development starts, and it is usually related to the size of available hardware for the particular television. For example, limitation in memory size usually means that some features in lower-end televisions must be excluded or that the functionality provided must be reduced or less flexible. In software terms, this limitation shows itself in the different, often lower, values for certain system constants dealing with sizes of tables and so on.

2.5.4 Support for Variance Description in Darwin

In using an ADL such as Darwin, the main objective is to elevate the description of variance from the program code level (using compiler flags and option bits) to the architectural or component level. The aim is to have a structured approach to the description of a product family, and to the subsequent generation of specific family instances from such a generic architecture.

As already described, Darwin supports the concept of software components, which allows the encapsulation of system features or functionality. By mapping system functionality to components, we can implement the presence or absence of features by including or excluding the associated Darwin component(s). In the simplest scenario, producing a specific variant of a product then becomes a matter of plugging together the components that support the desired functionality. Although this is the basic idea for variance description using an ADL, it would be unreasonable to expect software designers to handcraft the architecture for each individual instance of a product family.

In Darwin, a component type can be used to describe the generic architecture of an entire product family. From such a description, specific instances of the family can be generated on the basis of the set of features required for that family instance. Language constructs exist to support the specification of conditional creation of components and their bindings, thus allowing different system structures to be produced from a single description of a component type.

Three mechanisms are available in Darwin for modeling the definition and selection of features: global constants, parameter passing, and function calls. In this way Darwin provides support for the configuration plane.

Features as Constant Definitions

The first technique is to use globally defined constants. These constants are similar to compiler flags and thus have the same drawbacks. For example, in the simple example that follows, the teletext component t is created only if the value of the `teletext` constant is `true`.

```
const bool teletext = true;
component microTV {
   when (teletext) {
      inst t: teletext_component;
   }
   ......
}
```

Using global constants to define features and build variants allows static compile-time variants to be described but requires all dependent components to be recompiled for each distinct type of television. In practice, for complex systems the whole architecture would have to be rebuilt.

Features as Component Parameters

The second technique is to parameterize components with the features they use. The use of component parameters in this way is similar to the use of compiler flags at the component level.

```
component microTV (bool teletext) {
   when (teletext) {
      inst t: teletext_component;
   }
   . . . . . .
}
```

Defining features as component parameters rather than as global constants is a more flexible technique because it allows more than one variant to coexist within a system. Furthermore, components with variants need to be compiled only once and can be reused as many times as needed. Feature parameterization works well when the number of features is small, but it quickly becomes unwieldy for complex systems with a large number of features and options. We can alleviate this problem by grouping features into feature sets to partition the namespace of the features into more manageable subsets. The disadvantage of this approach is that it requires the set of features to be completely known when the component is specified, which is not always the case.

Features as Function Calls
The third technique is to select features by calling functions that look up feature values:

```
component microTV () {
   when (teletext ()) {
      inst t: teletext_component;
   }
   . . . . . .
}
```

Feature functions are the most flexible technique for building and elaborating variant components because they allow features to be defined and selected orthogonally to the Darwin ADL. This mechanism is particularly useful when the feature set is defined in a more expressive way (e.g., as in a SQL database) and/or where more complex algorithms are needed for selection. The mechanism of diversity parameters in Koala (see Section 2.6), is based on this mechanism.

2.5.5   Description of a Simple Television in Darwin

In this section we illustrate how Darwin can be used to describe the generic architecture of a family of televisions, with particular focus on the different ways in which variation can be handled.

A television can be described informally as follows:

> A television set can have both terrestrial and satellite tuners. High-end televisions have them both. Low-end televisions have only a terrestrial tuner. In addition, transmission standards vary: PAL, NICAM, and so on. In each television only one

such standard is available. Both kinds of variation can be determined before construction time. However, we want to have a design covering all variants. A third source of variation is the user interface. Certain (high-end) televisions have PIP (picture-in-picture). In order to accommodate this feature, a second tuner (of each kind) has to be available. For PIP there are a lot of options: fixed in place on the screen, movable on the screen, resizable, selectable from PIP to full screen, interchangeable between full screen and PIP. The precise collection of these features will be determined just before production time.

In the following code example we present one solution to modeling this television. The solution is not the only one possible but it highlights some of the possibilities. We model the diverse number of PIP predicates by a dynamic function call (`pip_option`) while using parameterization to designate television types (high-end or low-end) and standards (PAL, NICAM, and so on) and whether PIP is required (`pip_selected`).

```
// Note that in practice the constant definitions and
// each component type would be separately defined
// and included where necessary.
const int HIGH_END_TV = 0;
const int LOW_END_TV = 1;

const int PAL = 0;
const int NICAM = 1;

component pip (int tv_std) {
    when pip_option (tv_std, "fixed_place_on_screen") {...}
    ...
}


component terrestrial_tuner (int tv_type, int tv_std) {...}

component satellite_tuner (int tv_type, int tv_std) {...}

component tv_set (int tv_type, int tv_std, bool pip_selected) {
    inst tt : terrestrial_tuner (tv_type);
    when (tv_type == HIGH_END_TV) {
        inst st : satellite_tuner (tv_type);
    when (pip_selected) {
            inst p : pip (tv_std);
            inst tt2 : terrestrial_tuner (tv_type, tv_std);
        }
    }
}
```

Although we have so far concentrated on the support for variance through component inclusion or exclusion, we can also handle individual, low-level features at the programming level, which corresponds to the primitive components in Darwin.

2.6   Koala

Koala is an ADL born out of our experience in applying Darwin to the television case study. Unlike Darwin, Koala is not intended to be an open and general description language for software architecture. Instead, Koala is an ADL specially designed for and targeted at embedded software for consumer electronics. Based on Darwin, Koala shares all of Darwin's major concepts and ideals, but it has been fine-tuned for performance and efficiency in resource usage. This refinement is necessary because, for cost considerations, the computing hardware in high-end consumer electronics products today is comparable in power only to personal computers of some ten years ago. Hence there is much stronger emphasis in Koala on the deployment architecture and the ability to derive efficient implementation from its description in an ADL. It thereby provides a specific texture to systems written with it. Tool support is available to use the hierarchical decomposition efficiently within the design and configuration planes.

The subsections that follow describe the Koala ADL, highlighting the major new concepts introduced in this language and the rationale behind their introduction.

2.6.1   Components and Interfaces

As in Darwin, a Koala component is an encapsulated piece of software. It is a unit of development as well as a unit of architectural design. Components are graphically represented as rectangles, and interfaces as small squares containing triangles (see Figure 2.11). The semantics enforced by Koala provides a texture in which the interfaces are collections of function calls. We do not adhere to the Darwin dichotomy of black and white circles. Instead, the squares with triangles are introduced to impose a specific semantics of interfaces: The direction of the triangle indicates the direction of the corresponding function call. The similarity with integrated circuits is intentional: Engineers in the television domain readily understand such illustrations.

As in Darwin, components can be combined into hierarchical structures. In addition, in Koala we make a distinction between component types and component instances. A **component type** is a reusable component in isolation; it is typically defined within the design plane. A **component instance** is an occurrence of such a component in a particular configuration, which is an activity dealt with in the configuration plane. Koala, like Darwin, supports the mixture of these planes, through hierarchical decomposition. Most components

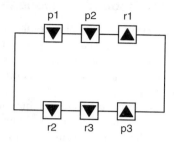

FIGURE 2.11   A Koala Component

found in consumer electronics tend to be single instances; that is, they occur only once in a configuration. However, support for multiple instantiation is also provided.

As in Darwin, the component model is hierarchical, allowing complex components to be built out of simpler ones. During development, the system can be partitioned and assigned to engineers on the basis of their areas of expertise. Work on different components can thus take place concurrently.

Similarly, Koala makes a distinction between interface types and instances. To be more precise, an **interface type** is a syntactic and semantic description of an interface, and an **interface instance** is an interface occurring in a component. In the deployment view, an interface type is described in an interface definition language (IDL):

```
Interface VolumeControl {
    void setVolume (Volume v);
}
```

The Koala IDL resembles COM (Component Object Model) and Java interface descriptions in which function prototypes are listed in the C syntax. Koala interfaces can contain only functions. Types are automatically made available wherever they occur in interfaces. Constants are treated as functions.

As we foresee evolution of our systems, we have to cope with upgrades of interfaces. We follow the COM convention that an interface type, once defined, may never be changed. Still, new generations of components may require the definition of new interface types that are small extensions of existing types. Although we can bind a requires interface of type I_1 to a provides interface of type I_2 (consisting of all the functions in I_1, plus a few extra) by inserting a glue module (see Section 2.6.3), the syntactic and code overhead for doing so is quite large. Therefore we allow the tip of an interface to be bound to the base of another interface if the first interface is of a subtype of the second. This is the case if the set of functions in I_1 is a subset of the set in I_2.

2.6.2 Configurations and Compound Components

In Koala we construct configurations by instantiating components and connecting their interfaces. A requires interface must always be bound to precisely one provides interface, but a provides interface may be bound to several (or zero) requires interfaces.

A configuration is described in a component description language (CDL). The description contains two sections, one declaring the component instances and one connecting their interfaces. Needless to say, the description closely resembles hardware parts and net lists that are commonly used by hardware engineers. Note that component instances have names unique to the configuration in which they are instantiated. Figure 2.12 shows a Koala representation of the tuner configuration depicted in Figure 2.9.

When dealing with hierarchy, connections between interfaces can be routed in various ways. The general rule is that the tip of each interface triangle must be connected to precisely one base, and that each base may be connected to zero or more tips. This rule allows for shortcuts between interfaces on the border of the component, a feature that can be used to obey strict layering conventions without any implementation overhead. Figure 2.13 depicts a Koala compound component that encapsulates the tuner software.

2.6.3 Gluing Interfaces

A direct connection between interfaces is not always sufficient. It assumes that components match each other in their interfaces, and this is often not the case in the evolution of consumer electronics software over many years. Moreover, consider ActiveX components that

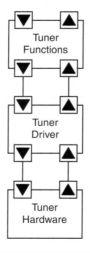

FIGURE 2.12 A Configuration Example

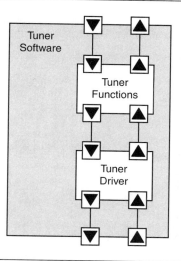

FIGURE 2.13   A Compound Component in Koala

are (claimed to be) highly reusable but that must be glued with Visual Basic. We can define glue components, but the managerial overhead of doing so is too large. Therefore we introduce the concept of glue modules (see Figure 2.14). In this picture a glue module is introduced to enhance the tuner functionality. A simple tuner can be set at predefined frequencies only, and it determines whether those frequencies carry signals. A searching tuner searches for the next frequency that carries a signal.

A module has a unique name within the component type in which it appears. If a tip of an interface is connected to a module, then its functions are implemented in that module. If a base of an interface is connected to a module, then the module may use those functions (possibly). The naming conventions are extended to cope with this new situation.

For each module the Koala tool generates a header file. The component designer adds one or more C files to implement the respective functions. This mechanism is also used to implement basic or primitive components, which contain no instances of other components: By connecting `provides` and `requires` interfaces to one or more modules, the designer can control the generation of header files. Note that the introduction of glue modules provides Koala systems with a specific texture in which each piece of code is part of a module and each connection is through a series of connected interfaces.

2.6.4   Diversity Interfaces and Switches

Our experience shows that components can be made reusable only if they are heavily parameterized (compare the long property lists of Visual Basic components). Traditionally,

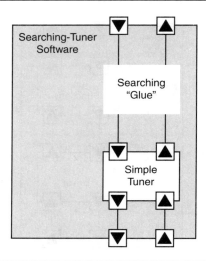

FIGURE 2.14   Gluing Components

heavy parameterization has resulted in components using lots of RAM and ROM. In resource-constrained systems, we can parameterize our components heavily only if we have a way of removing undesired flexibility when inserting the component in a configuration. The parameterization is necessary for the family of products, and not for individual products. Thus we came to the decision to use the "Features as Function Calls" mechanism for diversity (see Section 2.5.4). Because a component communicates with its environment always via interfaces, we have dedicated special `requires` interfaces, called **diversity interfaces,** for the diversity functions. Note that this decision implies that the implementation of diversity functions lies outside of the component (as opposed to Visual Basic, in which properties are implemented within the component). Note that our mechanism in fact unifies the notions of parameterization and binding, by reducing the component parameter assignment to a binding operation. Diversity interfaces can be used to control the internal diversity of components. However, they can also be used to deal with structural diversity.

Suppose component A uses component B_1 in one product and B_2 in another. We can simply define two configurations to handle the implementation, but component A may be part of a complex compound component, and we do not want to duplicate the rest of it. Our basic solution is to insert a module between the `requires` interface of A and the `provides` interfaces of B_1 and B_2. Because this is a recurring pattern, we will now introduce a special concept for handling it.

A **switch** is an element that can be used to route connections between interfaces. Its "top" must be connected to the tip of one interface, and each of its "bottoms" can be connected to the base of a different interface. The switch setting is controlled through a diversity interface. Note that the use of diversity interfaces and switches provides texture to Koala designs.

Figure 2.15 depicts a component that incorporates a switch. This component implements a tuner that searches for frequencies that carry signals. On the basis of a diversity parameter (required by the leftmost interface), searching is done in hardware or in software.

2.6.5   Optional Interfaces

In Koala, interfaces can be added to existing components, provided that they are declared optional (represented as a dashed box). Our treatment of optional interfaces resembles the COM Query Interface mechanism.

In Figure 2.16 optional interfaces are introduced in a component that may act either as a simple tuner or as an searching tuner. The searching functionality is carried by an optional interface that may not always be available. The presence of the interface depends on the diversity parameter. In addition, the searching tuner has an optional interface, whose availability depends on the presence or absence of a tuner that can search in hardware.

2.6.6   Events

Instead of defining an event-handling mechanism within the Koala model, we simply advise component designers to signal events through outgoing (`requires`) interfaces (just as in Visual Basic). Another component that uses signaling services of the component can provide an event-handling interface that can be connected to the event-signaling interface. In a multithreaded system, functions in event interfaces are called on the thread of the

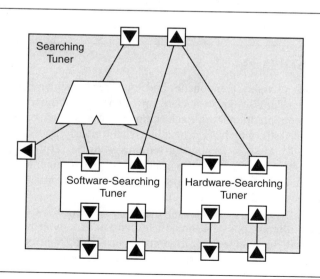

FIGURE 2.15   A Koala Switch

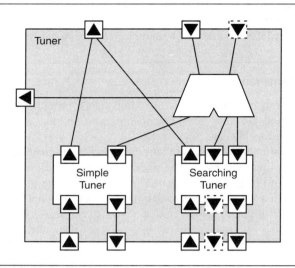

FIGURE 2.16 Optional Interfaces

component raising the event, so the general rule is that the handling must be quick and non-blocking.

The Koala examples we have given use events in this way. In addition to interfaces pointing to the bottoms, we have interfaces pointing to the tops. The latter interfaces are the event-carrying interfaces.

2.6.7 Threads and Tasks

Our systems consist of many components but few threads (remember the resource constraints). We therefore advise not to declare threads in basic components, but instead to declare them at the configuration level. Each component may implement its time-consuming activities in terms of tasks, which are scheduled synchronously by a task manager running in a global thread. To do so, a component requires a thread ID through a virtual thread interface, and it creates its tasks on such virtual threads. At configuration time, the (many) virtual threads are mapped to the (few) physical threads, thus enabling the principle of **task inversion** (sometimes called thread sharing).

A component may have tasks that operate on different timescales and thus have to be implemented in different physical threads. It then requires two (or more) virtual thread interfaces, which will be mapped to different physical threads at configuration time. In this case the component must make sure that internally the different activities are properly synchronized.

2.6.8   Configuration Plane and Binding

Because of resource constraints, Koala components are implemented in C. Moreover, the execution plane is simple. No adaptations of components are foreseen at execution time. In the deployment view a component is a set of C and header files in a single directory, which may freely include and use each other but may not reference any file outside of the directory.

The trend in binding techniques is to shift the moment of binding from compile time to link time to initialization time to run time. The Koala model supports various forms of late binding.

2.7   Final Remarks

This chapter has provided a general overview of the role of software architecture description in software development. In particular, we have focused on architectural description using architectural description languages. ADLs are notations specially designed for expressing and representing architectural structure and texture. The aim is to have an explicit description of system structure, as distinct from system behavior and interaction details.

An ADL is used to specify software architecture in terms of components and connectors. A system description thus consists of an interconnection of components by connectors. For complex systems, composition is a powerful mechanism for system design and construction. Composite components can be built from smaller components, yielding a component hierarchy in which the individual components can be independently developed and analyzed. By applying the same compositional technique to program specification and code, we can use the system architecture as a means for both program analysis and construction.

Software architecture description has an even bigger role to play in the development of software families. The typical high level of similarity among members or instances of a software family makes the use of a generic family architecture a very attractive approach to software development. The Darwin ADL was designed as a general structuring language to support such capability. Darwin is a concise declarative language that describes software structure in terms of components and their bindings. Darwin components have well-defined interfaces that make them context-independent and thus amenable for reuse in different systems. In addition, in order to overcome the problem of scalability, a composite component can be recursively composed out of simpler components. Consequently, a Darwin system consists of a hierarchy of interconnected components.

Although not specifically designed to tackle the problems of software families, Darwin has enough flexibility and expressiveness to model such systems through the use of parameterized components and conditional guards. Such features are particularly useful for the description of variations within the product family. Furthermore, Darwin's support for advanced features such as generic components and partial types adds flexibility by allowing architectural decisions to be delayed and by promoting the reuse of structural templates.

In the ARES case studies to which Darwin has been applied, it has proven itself a useful tool for the description and comprehension of family systems. However, real-world constraints in the consumer electronics industry dictate that more consideration should be given to performance and resource constraints of consumer electronics software. The fusion of industrial requirements and research ideas resulted in the Koala ADL, which was designed from the outset with those issues in mind. Koala adopted many of the principles and concepts embodied in Darwin but has been customized for a smooth transition to deployment, enabling better performance and resource usage. At the same time, it was designed to ensure that, as a design notation and approach, it could readily be introduced into the industrial-software development process without causing too much change and disruption to the existing practice. Since its introduction, Koala has been successfully deployed in the development of the next generation of software for consumer television sets.

In addition to the importance of having an explicit notation for architecture description, it has become clear that automated tool support is an essential part of software development. This is particularly true in the case of the development of software families, which comes with a new dimension of problems, including the capture and representation of feature variations, the mapping of features to components, and the derivation of specific family instances from a generic software architecture. Although many of these are design issues, the availability of automated tool support will go a long way toward making such tasks manageable, practical, and testable. Tools such as the Software Architect's Assistant and the Labelled Transition System Analyser have demonstrated this improved capability.

Although much progress has been made in the application of architectural techniques to the design and implementation of commercial family software, we are continuing our close collaborative work between academic and industrial partners to test the validity of our approach and tools. With the help of more case studies and experience gained from real-world application, we envisage further improvements on both fronts.

Software Architecture Assessment

3

Juan C. Dueñas, Alejandro Alonso,
William L. de Oliveira, María S. García,
Juan A. de la Puente, Gonzalo León

Architecture assessment is the activity of checking an architecture to ascertain whether it satisfies the required architecturally significant requirements; therefore assessment concentrates mainly on the evaluation of structure, texture, and concepts with respect to architecturally significant quality requirements, also called quality attributes. This chapter describes the assessment techniques used during the ARES project and how they were enhanced during the project, either by their novel application or by improvements to the basic techniques. Their applicability for each of the ARES cases is explained, and the results are integrated in a common decision-making framework.

The assessment of software architectures is still an open issue for the research community: There is no clear understanding of how or when to perform it. From the industrial viewpoint, some things are clearer: Means of early validation of abstract models are needed (Dikel et al. 1997). Along with this requirement for early assessment, other specific requirements for each business domain have been satisfied by the use of techniques such as simulation of statistical models and response-time analysis.

Software architecture has a strong impact on the final quality of the system because it can enable or inhibit the system's quality attributes (Bass, Clements, and Kazman 1998), thus limiting the degree of quality that a system can achieve. However, software architecture is not sufficient for the satisfaction of the quality requirements: Poor design and coding practices, inadequate testing, and many other activities in the development cycle can defeat the benefits provided by a sound architecture.

Currently, the main difficulties in assessment activities are

- The lack of a deep understanding of quality attributes
- The high level of abstraction in the available architecture

- The lack of formalism in architectural descriptions
- The absence of experience in assessment

Furthermore, architectural assessment cannot be understood in isolation. It is a part of the general architectural process; thus architectural assessment is closely related to other architectural issues presented in this book (see Figure 0.1 in the Introduction), such as the following:

- **Architecture description.** The kind of available architecture description determines the kind of applicable assessment technique. Some assessment techniques can operate on informal models (Kazman et al. 1994). Others require formal, unambiguous models.

- **Architecture recovery.** Architectures are made explicit mainly for successful systems with a long life span; for many such systems, the original design documentation is lost or inaccurate. Architecture recovery activities are important not only because they are necessary for obtaining the architecture required to perform the assessment, but because other sources of information useful for the evaluation must also be recovered. This fact allows us to extend the definition of architectural assessment as the process of evaluation of an architecture against certain characteristics, including the set of activities required for relating the architecture to other assessment information obtained in other phases of the development.

In the next section we present previously proposed approaches to architectural assessment and real-life problems that make them hard to apply in practice. We follow with industrial applications of existing techniques and how they were adapted during the ARES project. Then we describe a general decision-making framework for architecture assessment. We end the chapter with open issues and the main conclusions of our research.

3.1 Approaches to Architectural Assessment

The first question about architectural assessment is when it must be done. Following the well-known principles of reducing the effect of errors in the development costs, the answer is easy: as early as possible (Abowd et al. 1997). The design activity follows from the software architecture; once it has been proven that a given architecture is not the proper one, an alternative must be adopted. However, architectural assessment is more difficult as it is applied to more abstract architectural models, so a balance must be found between abstraction and applicability of the techniques described here.

Another important topic is the software process. The usual academic discourse about the development and use of software architecture includes assessment activities within the traditional waterfall process model, in which each phase of the software development process follows in an orderly way after the completion of the previous phase. In practice, however, software architecture is often cost-effective only for already successful systems that must evolve. Often this means that the artifacts in the design plane architecture of these systems need to be recovered from existing artifacts in the build, configuration, restart, and execution planes. In addition, the available deployment view may have to be lifted to recover the process, development, and logical views. In that case architecture assessment may be combined with an architecture recovery process. If the software architecture is used in a forward engineering process—that is, in the development of a new system—only speculative methods for evaluation are at hand.

The most direct answer to the question of how to assess software architecture depends on the answer to another question: What are the features to assess? As stated in Chapter 1, system requirements can be divided into roughly two categories:

1. **Functional requirements,** which can be directly related to the function that the given system must provide

2. **Quality requirements,** which cannot be allocated to specific components in the system, but depend on their overall organization and interconnection, as well as on the main decomposition principles or pervasive policies of software design

There are several techniques for assessment; each is suitable for eliciting different kinds of information and capable of checking different requirements. Our interest at this point concerns the quality requirements. The most general partition splits them into qualitative aspects of the software architecture and quantitative, measurable aspects. Correspondingly, there are two major classes of assessment techniques: *questioning techniques* and *measuring techniques.* It is often desirable to use quantitative methods or measures on software architecture because of the possibilities for automation. However, this solution, although cost-effective, is still far from offering complete results. In the ARES project, for example, we used the following techniques:

- **Metrics,** quantitative interpretations about observable measurements on the architecture. Their advantage is that they give unambiguous, specific values; the drawback is that we must make assumptions about their use, so they return values that may be too specific. Often these values are obtained from views in the build or execution plane.

- **Experiments,** including statistical simulations and tests of prototypes. The advantages are that the prototype behavior relates to actual use of the system, and the assumptions are clearer than those for metrics and can be derived directly from scenarios. The problems are the cost to obtain a prototype and, because the prototype is tested in the execution plane, the possible mismatches between the prototype and the design plane of the software architecture.

Many other techniques, specific for each domain, are available. For example, one branch of exploration in the ARES project focused on time properties of real-time systems, in which the main requirement is the predictability of the response time. The rate monotonic analysis technique was used as the basis for response-time analysis. **Rate monotonic analysis** is a set of techniques for analyzing the time behavior of hard real-time systems on the basis of fixed-priority scheduling (Klein et al. 1993). The focus of the work was to make this technique more usable in industry, by developing support for families of products, integrating in the model additional scheduling policies, and supporting the semiautomatic generation of global system models.

Within the ARES project the main effort was devoted to the exploration of metrics as an assessment technique for software architecture. We reused previously-defined metrics for design models and adapted them for use with architecture. We also used the simulation of software architecture models for assessment. Finally, we used time analysis to evaluate architectures of product families. Table 3.1 presents a brief list of the available assessment techniques, with some of their main characteristics. The table also includes the following techniques not used in the ARES project:

- **Scenario-based techniques,** such as software architecture analysis method (SAAM), that describe a specific interaction between a stakeholder and the system
- **Questionnaire-based techniques,** in the form of lists of open questions applicable to all kinds of architectures, regarding both the process and the software architecture product
- **Checklist-based techniques,** such as a set of specific questions for a given application domain

Next we present the metrics and the response-time analysis techniques studied during the ARES project.

TABLE 3.1 Properties of Assessment Techniques

	Technique	Generality	Detail Level	Phase	Target
Questioning Techniques	Questionnaire	General	Coarse	Early	Artifact, process
	Checklist	Domain-specific	Varied	Middle	Artifact, process
	Scenarios	System-specific	Medium	Middle	Artifact
Measuring Techniques	Metrics	General or domain-specific	Fine	Middle	Artifact
	Prototype, simulation, experiment	Domain-specific	Varied	Early	Artifact

Source: Bass, Clements, and Kazman 1998.

3.1.1   Design Evaluation

Assessment of design by means of metrics is a technique that has been applied for more than 20 years. However, it has been used mainly to assess products in the later phases of development: the source code first, then detailed designs. These phases are more closely connected to the deployment view of the system and views of the build, configuration, restart, and execution planes.

The literature contains the following kinds of metrics for these artifacts:

- **Size.** Module size (Bieman and Ott 1994, *ITU Specification* 1993, Lindqvist et al. 1995), design size (Miguel et al. 1996), code size (Fenton and Pfleeger 1997, *ITU Specification* 1993), and code volume (*IEEE Std 982.1* 1988)
- **Complexity.** Module complexity (Fenton and Pfleeger 1997, *IEEE Std 982.1* 1988, Miguel et al. 1996), design complexity (Briand, Morasca, and Basili 1994, Burns 1994, *IEEE Std 982.1* 1988), and program complexity (Burns 1994, Fenton and Pfleeger 1997, *IEEE Std 982.1* 1988)
- **Modularity** (Fenton and Pfleeger 1997)
- **Cohesion.** Design cohesion (Fenton and Pfleeger 1997), code cohesion (Miguel et al. 1996), and functional cohesion (Bieman and Ott 1994)
- **Coupling** (Briand, Morasca, and Basili 1994, Fenton and Pfleeger 1997, Miguel et al. 1996)

All these metrics can be considered internal: Their purpose is to evaluate a software product separately from its environment. They make it possible to evaluate quality by means of static analysis before actual use of the model.

The measurements of internal metrics often use figures based on the amount or frequency of the appearance of low-level software elements in the product representation (such as the graphical representation or table of control flow, data flow, or state transition structure), and they can be obtained without the program's being executed. Until recently, however, no metrics were available in the literature for software architecture. To assess architectures we adapted some common design and source code metrics to the elements that appear in software architecture models (in the development view). We give examples of such adaptations in Section 3.2.

3.1.2   Response-Time Analysis

Some systems have time requirements such that the correctness of the system depends not only on the logical correctness of its results, but also on the amount of time it takes those results to be produced. Such systems are called **real-time systems.** Sometimes real-time systems are developed without the time requirements being considered until the implementation phase, and their time properties are checked only by execution of the final code. If the time requirements are not met, the cost of fixing the problem at this stage is comparatively high. The whole application may even have to be redesigned.

Note that the problem here is not performance, but the response time of the system. The important questions are, What is the worst-case scenario for the amount of time the system actions take? and Does this amount of time meet the corresponding time requirement? A system may have good performance in general but fail to meet the time requirements for some activities. This failure renders the system incorrect and, possibly, unsafe.

We can solve this problem in part by assessing the time properties early in the development cycle, on the basis of the process view of the architecture. This is the central problem of response-time analysis: *How can we have some knowledge of the system response time early in the development cycle?*

Nowadays we have some tools and methods to analyze the response time of a system based on a high-level description of software. In most cases these descriptions can be derived from the process view of the architecture. From the point of view of time assessment, there are three types of system models (Fenton and Pfleeger 1997).

1. **Specification models** are used to capture the system requirements in terms of its external behavior from the user standpoint. There is no concern about computational resources, and time requirements are related mainly to the response time to external events. Analysis of this model is used mainly to ensure the consistency and completeness of the time requirements. Little can be said about the time behavior of the system because the computational resources are considered to be infinite.

2. **Design models** are used to represent the decisions taken throughout the system design cycle. These models are concerned with the deployment view of the architecture because they consider the allocation of resources such as processors, memory, communication links, and so on. There are several types of submodels:

   - The partition of the system into subsystems
   - The allocation of activities and data to processors and the interfaces between subsystems
   - The software architecture inside each processor
   - The code organization

   The available techniques can be used to estimate the response time of the system on the basis of the system structure and estimates of the time requirements of the modules and activities in the system.

3. **Implementation models,** the lowest abstraction level, describe the product implementation in terms of the programming code.

In this chapter we present techniques for calculating in an analytical way (i.e., not by simulation) the response time of systems on the basis of design models. There are several published methods for assessing the response time of real-time systems, some of which are based on fixed-priority scheduling. The basic method has been extended for dealing with periodic and aperiodic tasks, and jitter (*ITU Specification* 1993, Klein et al. 1993).

Although at the beginning of ARES some response-time analysis techniques for hard real-time systems were available, their use in industry was limited because of their novelty, as well as some unresolved issues, such as the following:

- Experience with these techniques is limited.
- Industrial applications are not always priority-based and preemptive.
- Guidelines for the industrial application of these techniques are lacking.
- Tools and methods for supporting the response-time analysis of product families are lacking.

The most mature and usable approaches for analyzing the system response time are based on the real-time analysis model in Klein et al. 1993. This type of analysis requires that we develop a model of the system by identifying system events, the sequences of activities executed to handle them, and the resource usage by each of these activities. With this information and the scheduling policies of the resources in hand, we can use various analysis techniques to assess whether the time requirements can be met. These techniques range from simple utilization-bound analysis to response-time computation under a variety of assumptions. With these techniques *it is possible to have feedback on the fulfillment of the time requirements early in the development cycle and to take corrective action if necessary.*

In developing the response-time assessment techniques for ARES, we tried to solve some of the open issues mentioned earlier. These techniques are based on calculation of the system response time and comparison of this value with the time requirements. We summarize these assessment techniques in Section 3.2.1. In the rest of this section we present the basic ideas required for response-time analysis.

3.1.3 Basic Concepts for Time Assessment

The list that follows describes the basic concepts for building the models to be used for time assessment based on the rate monotonic analysis described in Klein et al. 1993.

- **Event sequences.** An *event* is an instantaneous change of state, and an **event sequence** is a succession of events of the same kind occurring at definite times. An event sequence is characterized by an *arrival pattern.* There are several kinds of arrival patterns—for example, periodic, irregular, bounded, bursty, unbounded.

- **Response to an event.** Every time an event occurs, the system performs some *actions,* which together make up the **response** to the event. For this purpose, actions can be ordered in different ways: sequential, parallel, or select. Actions require some *resources* in order to be executed. Every time an action begins or ends, a scheduling decision has to be made in order to allocate resources to actions. The amount of resources required and the duration of each action are important scheduling parameters. Actions have some *attributes* that characterize their timing behavior: priority, usage, atomicity, jitter tolerance. Another important issue is the *allocation,* or *scheduling, policy* being used for each resource.

- **Time requirements.** Responses can have **time requirements,** which usually consist of a *time window* relative to the event arrival time, within which the actions required in response to the event must be performed. The end of the window is called the *deadline* of the response. Timing requirements can be

- **Hard.** The timing requirement must be met at all times.

- **Soft.** Only the average response time must be within the specified window.

- **Firm.** There is both a soft requirement (for a single response instance) and a hard requirement (for the overall response time).

3.2   Advances in the Industrial Application of Assessment

In their application to the relevant case studies—a telecommunication switch (Nokia), a family of TV sets (Philips), and a train safety control system (ABB)—architectural assessment techniques were both researched and improved as part of the ARES project. In this section we will deal with only the parts of the architecture required to apply a certain assessment approach. A well-known framework for the classification of architectural information that helps organize the inputs for assessment is the 4+1 View model (see Chapter 1).

The telecommunication case study reveals a common problem: The logical view and the development view cannot be clearly separated. Kruchten (1995) mentions that the larger the system is, the larger are the differences between the views. In fact, the problem is not that the same model is used for both views, but that conflicting requirements from each view result in a model with duplicated elements or with badly defined interfaces between elements.

The aims of architectural assessment are to predict or check the fulfillment of system requirements: maintainability, scalability, response time, and resource usage. All of these factors contribute to the evolution of successful systems—by reducing costs in the modification, by being able to support more users with few modifications, or by using the given resources more efficiently. In the subsections that follow we present the three main analysis techniques applied in order to fulfill these requirements for the ARES case studies.

3.2.1   Structural Analysis

Structural analysis is the application of metrics to a model of the system structure. Metrics can be applied to architectures under only certain circumstances:

- **When formal, machine-readable models of the architecture are available.** If these models exist, metrics can be applied even when no later by-products exist (such as in the implementation code).

- **When the degree of model description is uniform.** Metric results can be inaccurate or even plainly wrong if the level of detail is not consistent throughout the architecture. This fact reveals a source of subjectivity, for it is the designer who evaluates the degree of detail of each subsystem to be submitted to the assessment process.

- **When the means for validation are available.** Applying metrics does not provide useful results by itself, but the consistent and continuous application of metrics does. In the case of product lines, comparing the individual products with their metric values provides valuable information for validation. Initially, only the validation made by human experts can help correlate the metric results with the system quality values, taking the existence of domain analysis results or the identification of architectural styles as inputs for this process.

Once these conditions are met, the structural analysis process—the application of metrics—can provide results that are useful in themselves, without being related to the quality attributes of the system. Examples include the following:

- **Average values for size, cohesion, and coupling** of the components in the architecture, either for the subsystems of a given model, or for different versions of a given subsystem. In the latter case, the temporal evolution of the architectural metric results can give a hint about the future evolution of the system.

- **Divergences of average values** that help reveal potentially dangerous practices or bad structures. The comparison can be made between subsystems of a given model or between different versions of the same subsystem.

- **Sensitivity analysis or variability of system results** with different variants of subsystems.

Having presented the conditions under which metrics may be applied to architectures, and the applicable metrics, we next discuss the adaptation and use of metrics for architectures—first the metrics that operate on subsystems of a certain model, and then some of the metrics available to quantify characteristics derived from the full models.

Component and Connector Metrics

In the architectural description language of the telecommunication case study, an in-house variant of SDL (Specification and Description Language) (Lindqvist et al. 1995), components and connectors can be recognized that clearly describe the construction of the system. Thus simply by counting the number of elements, we can obtain a first measure of the size of components or connectors:

1. **Number of exported elements,** the number of elements, defined in the context of the component considered, that are visible to others externally. This metric is usually provided for data elements (parameters, abstract data types, input–output elements and messages), or for computational elements (procedures, processes, functions).

2. **Number of imported elements,** the number of elements, defined in the context of other components, that are visible only to the component in consideration. The elements considered are the same as for the number of exported elements.

3. **Interface size,** the sum of the number of exported elements and the number of imported elements.

4. **Number of defined elements,** the number of components defined internally to the component in consideration. For the Nokia case study, this metric counted the number of modules, procedures, processes, items of shared data, and so on.

5. **Number of defined connectors,** the number of connectors defined internally to the component in consideration. In this case, the items counted were accesses to data items, procedure calls, remote procedure calls, signals, and input–output operations.

6. **Implementation size,** the sum of defined elements and connectors for a given component.

With the definition of these simple metrics, we can obtain values for the following:

- The size of the component, calculated as the sum of interface and implementation sizes
- The data and information flow complexity of the component
- Pure information flow complexity (*IEEE Std 982.1* 1988), calculated as follows: $(\text{fan-in} \times \text{fan-out})^2$
- Weighted information flow complexity (*IEEE Std 982.1* 1988), calculated as follows: $\text{size} \times (\text{fan-in} \times \text{fan-out})^2$
- External complexity of the component (Miguel et al. 1996), calculated as follows: $e_1(\text{inflow} \times \text{outflow}) + e_2(\text{fan-in} \times \text{fan-out})$

where the new terms required can be directly obtained from the metrics defined earlier:

- inflow = number of imported data elements
- fan-in = inflow + number of data elements that the component defines as input
- outflow = number of exported data elements
- fan-out = outflow + number of data elements that the component defines as output
- e_1 and e_2 are weighting factors

In the architectural language for the telecommunication switch case study, the structural element that presents the abstraction level necessary for architectural description is called program block. Thus the internal metrics will be applied to this element. Table 3.2 presents the results of the application of the simple metrics to different program blocks in the case study, which for confidentiality we have renamed A, B, C, D, and E.

Even with this small set of measures, it is easy to see that program block E is considerably larger than C, basically because of the higher number of functions that it must perform, reflected also in the interface size. The figures suggest that maintenance efforts will be focused on program block E. At the same time, program block A offers many services to the others, as evidenced by its larger interface size; therefore the effort to perform the integration

TABLE 3.2   Simple Structural Metrics for the Case Study Program Blocks

	A	B	C	D	E
Number of exported elements					
Number of exported procedures	12	0	0	0	91
Number of exported signals	52	0	0	0	0
Number of imported elements					
Number of imported procedures	33	3	3	1	5
Number of imported signals	54	0	0	0	0
Interface size					
Interface size of program block	151	3	3	1	96
Number of defined elements					
Number of defined processes	1	4	3	3	3
Number of defined modules	0	0	0	0	0
Number of defined databases	0	0	0	0	0
Number of defined types	17	93	50	29	53
Number of defined constants	17	68	6	16	43
Number of defined alarms	0	0	0	0	0
Number of defined procedures	12	0	0	0	91
Number of defined functions	111	126	118	113	129
Number of defined connectors					
Number of defined signals	0	4	4	1	0
Implementation size					
Implementation size of program block	158	295	181	162	319
Program block size					
Program block size	309	298	184	163	415

testing with this program block will be higher. Requirements related to both maintenance effort and integration test effort *may* be among the architecturally significant requirements of this family. The assessment indicates that the system architecture may violate these requirements in the two program blocks A and E.

Architectural Configuration Metrics

Representation of the development view often consists of connected graphs of components and connectors. This information is needed to determine whether appropriate components are connected, whether their interfaces match, whether the connectors enable proper communication, and whether their combined semantics results in the desired behavior. In concert with the development view, the deployment view enables assessment of concurrent and distributed aspects of an architecture—for example, potential for deadlocks and starvation, performance, reliability, security, and so on.

The development view also allows us to analyze how much the architecture adheres to design heuristics. For example, we can determine whether an architecture is too deep, which may affect performance because of message traffic across many levels and/or process boundaries, or too broad, which may result in too many dependencies among components.

Although we devoted some effort during the ARES project to studying these more complex metrics, their usefulness is still far from being proven. The following are some of the simpler metrics available that have been adapted for architectural use:

1. **Morphology metrics** (Fenton and Pfleeger 1997). Many morphological characteristics are based on graph representations in terms of nodes and edges and can be directly measured, including the following:

   - **Size,** measured as number of nodes, number of edges, or a combination of these characteristics

   - **Depth,** measured as the length of the longest path from the root node to a leaf node

   - **Width,** measured as the maximum number of nodes at any one level

   - **Edge-to-node ratio,** which can be considered a connectivity density measure because it increases as we add more connections among nodes

2. **Graph-theoretic complexity metrics** (*IEEE Std 982.1* 1988):

   - **Static complexity,** a function (C) based on the countable properties of the components (nodes) and intercomponent connections (edges) in the network: $C = \text{edges} - \text{nodes} + 1$.

   - **Dynamic complexity,** a measure of software architecture in the execution plane as represented by a network of components during execution, rather than at rest, as is the case for the static measures. It is calculated using the formula for static complexity at various points in time.

3. **Coupling,** defined by Gaffney and Cruickshank (1992) as follows:

$$\text{Coupling} = (\Sigma_{i = 1\ to\ n} Z_i)/n$$

where

   - $Z_i = (\Sigma_{j = 1\ to\ m_i} M_{ij})/m_i$—that is, the average number of input and output items shared with component i

     - M_{ij} = number of input items + number of output items shared between components i and j

       - m_i = number of components that share input or output with component i

   - n = number of components in the software architecture

Tool Support

The tool support for the application of such metrics is usually not very complex. Several strategies were tested during the ARES project, ranging from the use of scripting languages on textual tables representing the development view of the architecture, to the integration of these metric extractors in architectural recovery and management environments.

The structural analysis results make up part of the architectural information. The kind of tool support for the application, management, and storage of the metrics and their results must correspond to the same technology as in the rest of the development environment. That is, metrics tools need to be maintained to keep up with the evolution of metrics technology. The best current option is to use a management information database, using hypertext technologies, that helps update and relate the architectural items to the metrics and their results. The metric results, in addition, must be made public to the development teams.

Conclusions of Application

Applying structural analysis to the architecture allows us to derive the following conclusions:

- There is no correlation between metric values and quality values that is general enough to supersede the effects of the development environment, process, and tools.

- There is an intuitive correlation between metric values and quality values that can help in the decision-making process but does not yet lead to automatic decision-making artifacts.

- To know the correlation between metric values and quality values more accurately, it is necessary to establish a sustained architectural quality effort in the organization that, after several applications of the metrics, may be able to generalize the results.

3.2.2   Behavioral Analysis

We have already mentioned that there is a close relationship between the requirements that can be checked and the range of available techniques for assessment. Part of our work in the ARES project focused on the study of metrics-based techniques for structural properties such as maintainability. These techniques can be used for checking other sets of requirements, although their usefulness is limited, as is the case for requirements that reflect behavioral issues of the system being built.

One of the analytical techniques that can be used is *rate monotonic analysis,* provided that the architecture contains information about activities, resource usage, and time. Another interesting group is *dynamic analysis techniques,* which includes the study of behavioral requirements by simulating the system behavior using an operational model (Smith and Williams 1993). This kind of model is a representation of the system, able to simulate the evolution of a particular characteristic, such as the internal state, over time; that is, an operational model is able to be executed by an abstract processor, often called a simulator. Developers resort to dynamic analysis techniques when analytical techniques are not able to cope with the problem because of size, complexity, or lack of information. In the ideal situation, the behavior of the system under development could be modeled formally with a set of equations, and these equations could be solved. In practice, obtaining these equations is almost impossible, so dynamic analysis is the only real choice.

Whereas for structural analysis the only required input is the model (an artifact of the design plane), dynamic analysis (simulation) requires two kinds of inputs: the models of the observable behavior (the executable models or prototypes) and the use cases that exercise this model. The latter may include both design plane and execution plane artifacts. Moreover, it requires connections between the logical and the process architectures. The quality of the results depends on the degree to which the use cases reflect the real usage of the system.

The framework for using simulation to assess software architecture models has the following characteristics:

1. **Target requirements.** Simulation is useful mainly for requirements that deal with system behavior, such as performance, scalability, end-to-end response time, and resource usage. The common factor among all of these requirements is that they refer to the system usage within an operating environment. Thus the simulation needs not only the system model but also information about its operating environment, represented by the interface between the system and the rest of the world, and this information is often harder to handle than the system model.

2. **Information needs.** The results of simulation must be easily related to the artifacts of the design plane, such as components and connectors in the development view. Problems may result because there are no direct relations between the architecture and the components used in the simulation models. When the artifacts are in the behavioral view, connecting the simulation model with the results may be easy.

3. **Development effort.** The main problems of simulation are effort and cost: the cost of turning the architecture into a simulation model, or, if a later product such as code is available, the cost of using that product as the bridge between the architecture and the simulation model.

4. **Accuracy of models.** Another problem with simulation is the accuracy of the model, which limits the accuracy of the results. Interestingly, many architectural models, because of abstraction level and incompleteness, are not directly suitable for simulation and thereby may be a potential source of inaccuracy.

5. **Use cases.** As already mentioned, the model of the operating environment is a key factor for the success of the simulation because the validity of the results is driven by the appropriateness of the usage scenarios, or use cases. To develop such a model we can use the scenarios that appear in the architecture and in the documentation of the system. This fact reveals the complementary nature of simulation to other architectural assessment techniques (such

as SAAM; Bass, Clements, and Kazman 1998) that are based on the study of scenarios.

The Architectural Analysis Method

Figure 3.1 presents our approach for applying simulation to architectural models. As already mentioned, the main problems when applying simulation are the cost of producing the simulation models and their accuracy. The approach is based on the use of other by-products of development, different from the architecture but closely related to it (such as the detailed design models). These more specific models can be used for applying simulations if we can relate them to the architecture (a kind of architectural recovery task).

Fortunately this condition holds in the telecommunication domain. There are reported efforts in the use of detailed design models for simulation when they have been described using certain notations—SDL (*ITU Specification* 1993, Olsen et al. 1994) in our case. In this scenario, the effort to produce a simulation model is reduced, and the difficulties that inaccurate models could present are circumvented because the simulation models are more accurate than the architectural models and can also be seen as elaborations of the architectural models. Again the main effort is devoted to architecture recovery because we must allocate to the development view of the architecture not only each part of the code but also the results of the simulation.

In most of the current systems to which the architectural development cycle has been applied (such as the Nokia case study), both the architecture and detailed design models have been available. The reason is related to commercial realities: The architectural processes are applied only to successful systems that have long life spans and for which future adaptations are envisaged. Usually one or more releases of the system have been produced before the documented architecture is developed; therefore the detailed design and implementation products are available alongside the software architecture. In the future, if a system is developed from conception according to the architectural approach, the assessment approach we have presented here may not be suitable.

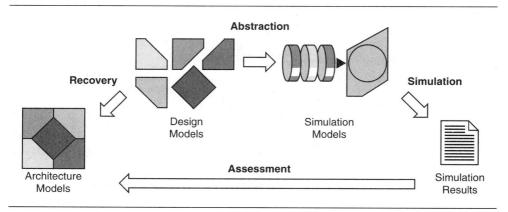

FIGURE 3.1   Method for Architectural Simulation

Tool Support

The performance analysis system takes as inputs the system definition and its operational capabilities and limitations and is able to provide information about the system performance, measured by end-to-end response time, event timing, average and variance time values, and so on. Internally, the tools will convert the external model into one that the simulation engine is able to handle. For the Nokia telecommunication case study, systems are described using TNSDL (Lindqvist et al. 1995), a dialect of SDL, and we used the QUEST tool (Diefenbuch 1997a) that handles SDL models enhanced with the definition of system resources and usage times (Diefenbuch 1997b) by means of the QSDL modeling language.

The initial model must be translated into an SDL model, and then into a QSDL model, by the addition of some information. After the process has been completed, the model can be fed into the QUEST tool, which will provide two different kinds of results: a *message sequence chart* (*ITU Message* 1993) that represents the scenario of system execution, and a *simulation time monitoring* of the internal parts of the system, as seen by user-defined probes. Figure 3.2 shows the phases and by-products in the performance analysis of the system.

Conclusions of Application

Our study of the simulation of architectures allows us to state the following conclusions:

- Simulation is suitable in a reverse architecture framework because it relies on the existence of a model more specific than the architectural model. One valid candidate for simulation is the detailed design model, but its elements must be mapped back to the development view of the architecture.
- Analysis by simulation is suitable only when the models and simulations can be developed at low cost. For this purpose, industrial-strength tools are needed, integrated in the architectural process and able to reuse the same formalisms used for the development and to give the architects the choice to

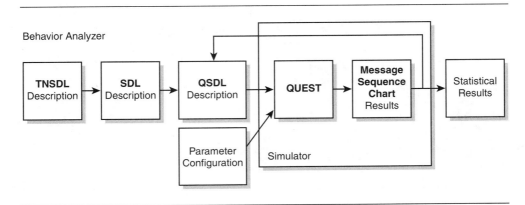

FIGURE 3.2 Performance Analysis

create simulations on the fly, the results of which can be easily traced back to the architectures.

- The difficulties of annotating the architecture with the results of the observations can also be solved by the sensible choice of the architectural description language and tools.

- Simulation, when applied to the software architecture with the scenarios defined for other kinds of analysis, provides objective quantitative and qualitative results.

3.2.3 Response-Time Analysis

We performed two main activities to provide means for the time assessment of software architectures:

- We developed techniques for supporting the analysis of the response time of family products.

- We analyzed multimedia systems at the architectural level, considering multiple resources.

These activities were driven by industrial needs. The main results are presented in the subsections that follow.

Response-Time Assessment for Product Families

The approach taken in assessing response time takes into consideration the fact that a family of products is based on a set of components and ways of interconnecting them—that is, product architectures. We create a new product by selecting some of the available components, either as they are or by making a few modifications, interconnecting them, or possibly adding some new ones. Design decisions have to be made about which components to use or how to connect them to meet the requirements of the new product. In this context, time assessment provides a useful additional criterion by which to discard or select design alternatives: the response time of the system.

This approach requires models for response-time analysis of the components and the interconnections. By connecting some of these components in a specific way, we manually generate a response-time model of a system. We can facilitate and expedite this process by providing means for automatically or semiautomatically generating the model of the whole system, taking into consideration the individual models of the components, their interconnection, and the available resources and their scheduling policies. In the ARES project, we proposed and used an approach for generating global models, and we assessed the approach practically. Two main steps are required:

- **Development of component and connector models.** These models are based on the concepts described in Section 3.1.2. The basic guidelines used in ARES for the extraction of response-time models of components are presented in Section 3.1.3.

- **Generation of the global system response-time model.** This model is derived from the models of the components and their interconnection. Some basic ideas about automatic or semiautomatic support for the derivation of the global model are provided later in this section.

Development of Response-Time Models

One of the required activities is the extraction of response-time models from an available component or architecture. For this purpose we developed the following guidelines:

1. Get the timing requirements of the system.
2. Identify execution modes.
3. Identify meaningful events and complete their relevant information:
   - External events
   - Hardware events (usually interrupts)
   - Internal events (such as alarms)
4. Identify the actions executed in response to events and split them if they use different resources at different times.
5. Merge actions in tasks if they are executed in sequence.
6. Assign priorities to actions. The criteria may be related to the event's deadline, execution order, or priority level. Assigning more urgent priorities to the tasks with shorter deadlines (**deadline monotonic scheduling**) is optimal when fixed-priority scheduling is being used (*ITU Specification* 1993).
7. Consider the resources of the system (including shared resources).

The most interesting problems we faced while developing the models in the ARES project were how to deal with different task-scheduling policies and the notion of execution modes. The existence of several modes of operation is common in most industrial real-time systems. Each mode is characterized by a set of conditions that defines when it is active and by a set of events and associated actions that dictate system behavior in this situation. The functionality of different modes in an application is different and depends on the specific state of the application and the external environment. For example, a fly-by-wire aircraft may have a takeoff mode, a cruising mode, and a landing mode. The mode changes in response to particular external or internal conditions.

The identification of modes of operation is very important for the response-time analysis of the application. There is no point in calculating the response time of an action that is not being executed in certain modes, or in considering the interference of actions that are not executed. The analysis of the time behavior of the system modes is simpler and more accurate if done in isolation. In addition, this approach reflects the current dynamic behavior of the application.

Two types of scheduling policies were used in the industrial case study. The problem is that the system models do not follow the fixed-priority policy, which is the basis of the analysis techniques used in this work. Hence it was necessary to derive models with the same time behavior as that of the original. The first policy can be called **monitor-based scheduling.** The monitor supports a set of priority levels. Higher priority levels preempt lower ones. Each level has an established time period (called simply period) and a set of assigned procedures (tasks). Levels with shorter periods have more urgent priorities. The priority assignment follows the deadline monotonic scheduling method. The procedures associated with a specific priority level are executed in sequence periodically, according to the period associated with the level. The system model consists of multiple periodic events—for example, one for each activity in a level. The level at which the corresponding actions are allocated determines the period. The deadline is equal to the period.

The other model is the classic **cyclic scheduling** policy. The most obvious approach is to model each of the events as periodic, the period being equal to the duration of the major cycle or to the appropriate period if an event can happen in different minor cycles. Individual actions are modeled as actions invoked as logical tasks. Their priority depends on the order of invocation within a cycle.

Composition of Response-Time Models

This section presents the main steps in generating a global response-time model from the models of the system's individual subcomponents. The following steps, mostly part of building the deployment view, are the most important (Alonso, Valls, and de la Puente 1999):

1. Identify the appropriate components.
2. Connect the components on the basis of the events that need to be raised and handled in the components. The connections should reflect the event-handling sequences for the main events—that is, those mentioned in or derived from the specification.
3. Specify a physical model (Kruchten 1995) of the system that identifies the system's resources.
4. Instantiate the partial models, taking into consideration system requirements, execution platform, and management policies for the resources.
5. Model the interconnections based on the characteristics (protocols, communication media, and so on) of the resources used.
6. Assign priorities to the tasks according to an appropriate priority assignment policy, such as deadline monotonic scheduling.

In most cases the connection between models is based on the interconnection of events; that is, one of the results of handling an event is to raise an event in another component. Modeling this scenario requires the following:

- This relation must be reflected in an appropriate table. In some cases the events' entries can be collapsed into one, which is fired by the initial event.
- Because transmission of the event requires some resources, the appropriate activity and the required resources for the communication must be included in the activities table.

The parameters in the models will be generic in most cases. For example, it is possible to know that in a certain component there is a periodic event. However, the concrete period will be known only when the specification of the system is available. The parameters identified will depend on issues such as the following:

- **System requirements,** for parameters such as arrival patterns, periods, deadlines, and so on.
- **Process view of the architecture,** for determining computation time and communication delays.
- **Resource management** scheduling policies, to determine the resources that some of the actions will use, and how they will be scheduled. These policies are part of the deployment view.

The process for extracting response-time models from components (described in the previous section) generates a list of the system events, the elements that handle those events, the sequence of how the events are handled at a high level, and the active components and interactions between the components. The problem is how to derive the global system model from this information. Two main cases were addressed in the context of ARES: centralized and distributed systems.

- **Centralized system.** This system is modeled as a set of interacting components. The connections between them can be described as events raised in one component and sent to the other. An appropriate criterion for merging the sequences is to identify the meaningful events in the system and to base the global model on them. These events are derived from the specification. The actions executed in response to other kinds of events should be merged whenever possible. In this way we obtain the sequences corresponding to the system events.

  The external view of interaction is that of a component executing an action that raises an event in a different component. The question is when an event should be viewed as a continuation of a sequence and when as a start of a new sequence, although in most cases the first choice holds.

- **Distributed system.** The first issue is to consider the deployment view, which determines where each of the components will be executed. In this framework each component must be allocated to a single processor. The resource usage portion of the action table has to be completed according to the allocation information. The procedure for handling the connections that we have described for centralized systems still holds for components in the same processor.

  If the components are in different processors, it is necessary to merge their sequences of actions. A simple concatenation is not sufficient. If two consecutive actions are executed in different processors, it is necessary to add actions that model the communication required—that is, the messages that these components have to exchange in order to execute the appropriate sequence. The basic resources used by these added actions are the communication media.

The communication protocol determines the corresponding message-scheduling policies. Appropriate analysis algorithms are then required. In the literature, different models for TDMA, CAN, FDDI, and other such communication protocols have been proposed.

In this situation, if both processors are scheduled with a fixed-priority policy, it is possible to merge the sequences of actions in both components. The action in the second processor should be executed immediately after the corresponding message is received. If processors are scheduled differently, a slightly different procedure is required (Alonso, Valls, and de la Puente 1999).

Response-Time Analysis of Multimedia Systems

Multimedia systems integrate different sources of information, such as audio and video data. Multimedia systems in consumer electronics handle data from different media to provide the user with adequate information. Such devices are usually mass-produced. To reduce the cost of the final product, engineers working in this area try to include only the resources that are absolutely necessary. To be able to offer the best quality with this limited set of resources, we need to develop techniques to optimize resource usage in the multimedia context.

Multimedia systems have strict time requirements. These requirements are derived from the need to show images with a fixed rate, to synchronize audio and video, and so on. Hence, when developing such systems it is very helpful to have techniques for estimating the response time of the system, taking into account all of the system's resources. Much research has focused on the analysis of scheduling for hard real-time systems, in which the main concern for resource usage focuses on the CPU, data objects, and communication channels. The idea of adding resources such as caches, memory, coprocessors, and buses in an integrated way has received less attention.

Different types of resources can be found in a multimedia system: processors, main memory, caches, coprocessors, buses, and others. This variety leads to different criteria for the categorization of resources, of which the following are the most important:

- **Type of sharing.** Resources can be shared by a *set of tasks,* or they can be assigned and used in a dedicated way by only *one task.*

- **Type of scheduling.** A resource might be accessed in a *preemptive* or *nonpreemptive* fashion. In the former case, the access of a particular task to a resource may be stopped if a higher-priority task is ready to access that resource. Preemptive policies are typically devoted to the CPU, nonpreemptive policies to shared data.

- **Mode of sharing.** Some resources are shared *in time* (CPU and buses), others *in space* (caches and memory). This option is related to the kind of dispatcher or arbiter to be used at run time for handling the resources.

- **Assignment scope.** Some resources are assigned to individual *tasks,* others to *applications.*

- **Necessity.** Resources may be *necessary* or *optional.* If resources are optional, tasks are executed, but with lower quality and/or performance.

- **Blocking effects.** Some tasks free the CPU (allowing another task to be executed there) while trying to access other resources. Others just slow down execution; they increase the task's computation time, though not necessarily the budget.

Industrial Case Study

The case study used for assessing and refining some of the techniques we have presented in this section was the BTM (Balise Transmission Module) of a train control system (TCS), which is presented in Chapter 7. The TCS of ABB Norway is an embedded software system for performing train control operations. The BTM subsystem handles the reception and decoding of reports sent by roadside equipment to the train. Data flows from the roadside equipment through the train antenna and the systems inside the train. Information is transmitted from the roadside equipment, called a balise, to the antenna in the form of so-called telegrams. The BTM, shown in Figure 3.3, is composed of two main modules: TRAN and DECO.

The goal of this work was to develop system models in the architecture of the BTM system in order to assess the response time of the system. These models could be used in the future to quickly evaluate the effects of design changes on the response time of the system. The guidelines presented earlier in this section were used for describing the models. Here we describe how the models of centralized and distributed versions of the system can be obtained.

The scheduling policy used in the BTM is not directly supported by the analysis techniques we have described. Hence it must be adapted. The BTM application is safety-critical, implying that it should be deterministic. Because both the scheduling policies and the models

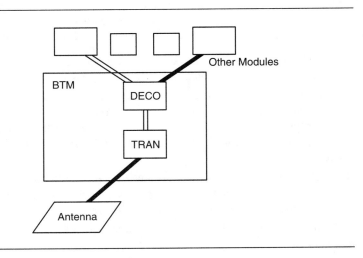

FIGURE 3.3   Overview of the BTM System

in the time analysis framework are deterministic, it should be possible to use these techniques to develop a system model, with a time behavior equivalent to that of the system using fixed-priority scheduling.

The reception of telegrams from the train antenna is probably the most important function of the TRAN subsystem. The train antenna constantly detects signals and converts them into bits. Only the information received when the antenna is over a balise contains telegrams that should be processed. Three modes of the TRAN subsystem can be identified depending on whether meaningful information is being received or has been received: Over Balise, After Balise, No Balise.

Table 3.3 is the event table extracted for the TRAN subsystem. The "Response or Action" column simply lists the actions. The only shared resource is the CPU because actions invoked by the scheduling approach are activated sequentially. Symbolic values are used. Proper timings or estimations, based on the time requirements of a product and on the components used, will be assigned to perform the analysis.

The DECO behavior is simpler than that of TRAN. DECO receives messages from TRAN with a minimum separation of P_1 milliseconds. The messages can contain information about telegrams, antenna tests, errors, and the clock. DECO handles each of these types of information, interacting with other modules located in the same processors. Because these modules are at a lower priority level than the DECO functions, they do not interfere with DECO's response time.

Table 3.4 is the event table extracted for the DECO subsystem. The same considerations that apply for the TRAN event table apply here.

TABLE 3.3 Event Table of the TRAN Subsystem

Event	Type	Mode Name	Arrival Pattern[a]	Time Required[b]	Response or Action
Receive_Bit	External	All	Per[P_1]	P_1	Store_bit
Receive_16_Bit	Internal	All	Per[P_2]	P_2	Store_16_bits → Id_Event
Start_Balise	Internal	No_Balise	Bnd[P_3]	D_3	Change_Mode
End_Balise	Internal	Over_Balise	Bnd[P_3]	D_3	Change_Mode
Detect_Telegram	Internal	After_Balise	Bnd[P_3]	D_3	Get_T → Check_T → Tel_Msg → Send_Msg → Change_Mode
Test_Antenna	Timed	No_Balise	Per[P_4]	D_4	Antenna_Test
End_Test_Ant	Timed	No_Balise	Per[P_5]	D_5	Test_Msg → Send_Msg

[a]Per[P] = arrival pattern is periodic, with period P; Bnd[P] = there is a minimum separation time between events, determined by P.

[b]The response time upon arrival of the event. D = deadline, when different from the period (P).

TABLE 3.4   Event Table of the DECO Subsystem

Event	Type	Mode Name	Arrival Pattern[a]	Time Required[b]	Response or Action
Reception_Message	External	Normal	Bnd[P_1]	D_1	Store_Msg
Message_Present	Internal	Normal	Bnd[P_2]	D_2	Analyse_msg
Train_State	External	Normal	Bnd[P_2]	D_2	Operate_Antenna
Antenna_Status	Timed	Normal	Bnd[P_3]	D_3	Handle_Status
Tran_Error	Internal	Normal	Bnd[P_4]	D_4	Handle_Error
Balise_Tel	Internal	Normal	Bnd[P_2]	D_2	Handle_Tel
Check_Tel_A	Internal	Normal	Bnd[P_2]	D_2	Check_A
Check_Tel_B	Internal	Normal	Bnd[P_2]	D_2	Check_B
Validate	Internal	Normal	Bnd[P_2]	D_2	Valid_Check→ Transmit_Comm

[a]Per[P] = arrival pattern is periodic, with period P; Bnd[P] = there is a minimum separation time between events, determined by P.

[b]The response time upon arrival of the event. D = deadline, when different from the period (P).

Two possible systems were studied:

1. **Centralized system.** Building a global RMA (rate monotonic analysis) model for TRAN and DECO has an additional problem: the fact that the two subsystems follow different scheduling policies. Whereas TRAN consists of a cyclic monitor that executes a series of routines, which can be considered as concurrent tasks, DECO's execution is guided by a monitor with a set of levels, each of a different priority. Various tasks execute in sequence according to their priority level. Thus there is no preemption between tasks from the same level, but preemption does exist between levels.

   When creating a global RMA model that integrates two components that do not follow the same scheduling policy (as with TRAN and DECO), we must find a way to integrate the components. Taking into account the procedure sketched above, one possible way in this case is to connect the two components on the basis of their related events. The connection of TRAN and DECO shows two main dependencies:

   - Detect_Telegram (from TRAN) fires Reception_Message (from DECO)
   - End_Test_Antenna (from TRAN) fires Antenna_Status (from DECO)

   Therefore in the global model, Detect_Telegram and End_Test_Antenna will appear as events, and the responses to Reception_Message and Antenna_Status will be concatenated to the original response to those events. The result will be an enhanced response to the events of TRAN, and the two lines associated with the two DECO events will be removed. However, not only the action sequence or response to some dependent events will be modified. We will have to change other columns in the model to fully consider the effects of the integration of the two components, TRAN and DECO, into a single processor.

In this case we assume that the CPU uses a monitor scheme. The assignment of priorities to tasks depends on the parameters of the events of the components. Because tasks in TRAN have shorter deadlines, they will always take precedence over DECO tasks.

Finally, the arrival pattern might have to be changed to reflect the broader range of integrated events. The same applies to the time requirement, which might have to be modified to show the addition of new actions to the responses to the events `Detect_Telegram` and `End_Test_Antenna`. Table 3.5 is the event table for the global model. As with the event tables for the TRAN and

TABLE 3.5 Event Table for the Centralized System

Event	Type	Mode Name	Arrival Pattern[a]	Time Required[b]	Response or Action
Receive_Bit	External	Normal	Per[P_1]	D_1	Store_bit
Receive_16_Bit	Internal	Normal	Per[P_2]	D_2	Store_16_bits → Id_Event
Start_Balise	Internal	Normal	Bnd[P_3]	D_3	Change_Mode
End_Balise	Internal	Normal	Bnd[P_3]	D_3	Change_Mode
Detect_Telegram	Internal	Normal	Bnd[P_3]	D_3	Get_T → Check_T → Tel_Msg → Send_Msg → Change_Mode → Store_Msg
Test_Antenna	Timed	Normal	Per[P_4]	P_4	Antenna_test
End_Test_Ant	Timed	Normal	Per[P_5]	D_5	Test_Msg → Send_Msg → Handle_Status
Message_Present	Internal	Normal	Bnd[P_6]	P_6	Analyse_msg
Train_State	External	Normal	Bnd[P_8]	D_8	Operate_Antenna
Tran_Error	Internal	Normal	Bnd[P_9]	D_9	Handle_Error
Balise_Tel	Internal	Normal	Bnd[P_7]	D_7	Handle_Tel
Check_Tel_A	Internal	Normal	Bnd[P_7]	D_7	Check_A
Check_Tel_B	Internal	Normal	Bnd[P_7]	D_7	Check_B
Validate	Internal	Normal	Bnd[P_7]	D_7	Valid_Check → Transmit_Comm

[a]Per[P] = arrival pattern is periodic, with period P; Bnd[P] = there is a minimum separation time between events, determined by P.

[b]The response time upon arrival of the event. D = deadline, when different from the period (P).

DECO subsystems, the "Response or Action" column simply lists the actions, taking into account that the only shared resource is the CPU. Because most activities in the model are activated sequentially, data is not considered shared.

2. **Distributed configuration.** The distributed configuration of TRAN and DECO reflects a current operating version. The two systems are located in separate processors and communicate by means of serial links. An analysis of this system reveals that buffering is used. The effect is decoupling of the time behavior; the response time of the system is the same as if the components were isolated. Thus to obtain the end-to-end response time, it is necessary to consider only the worst-case response time of the handling of a telegram in TRAN.

3.3 Quality Assessment Process

As with any other artifact produced during the development process of a software product or service, the software architecture can be either a final or an intermediate product. In the first case, the architectural design phase is considered in isolation, and therefore the same assessment techniques that can be applied to other final products are applicable here. In the second case, which is more important for product families, the software architecture is put in its context, and the evaluation results must refer to the quality of the final product. It is then necessary to establish a common framework for the assessment of software architecture, which enables developers to capture, express, and keep the quality specification of each subsystem consistent with that of the final product throughout the development process. Maintaining this consistency is possible only if quality requirements are specified in terms of a common quality model.

The **quality model** specifies the system properties that must be present. The ISO/IEC 9126 standard (*ISO-9126* 1991) specifies a quality model that categorizes software quality according to six characteristics, which are further subdivided into subcharacteristics. For each characteristic or subcharacteristic, externally observable attributes have to be defined. However, the standard does not cover these attributes or their relationship with the subcharacteristics. Moreover, the available assessment techniques are not yet specified.

To apply the assessment concepts in practice, the evaluation process must be defined. The process is depicted in Figure 3.4 for metric qualities. The starting point for the process is the description of the user requirements; these may be just the architecturally significant requirements, but sometimes there are more requirements. In any case, all stakeholders may have quality requirements for the product. However, the external quality requirements for each relevant quality characteristic of the product should be available. These requirements are represented by a specific set of externally observable attributes (in the same way as response time is used to define the efficiency of a computer system). The developers will evaluate the product against these requirements before delivery. The product must then be evaluated by means of external metrics applied under conditions that emulate the expected conditions of use as closely as possible.

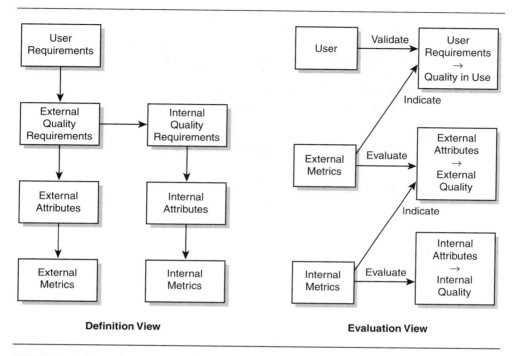

Definition View   **Evaluation View**

FIGURE 3.4   General Quality Assessment Process

The purpose of external metrics is to evaluate the software architecture as a product in itself. External measures depend on the intended use of the software architecture (e.g., for evolution analysis of a product line), so they have to be evaluated as part of an operating environment. The following external metric measures the analyzability of software architectures:

$$\text{Mean time for analysis} = \frac{\text{Sum of times between analysis requests and their execution}}{\text{Number of analyses to be carried out}}$$

A different viewpoint for assessment comes from the internal quality requirements of the product. The specification of the internal quality is composed of value boundaries for the internal attributes of a product, and it must be designed in such a way that the boundaries are met. In the software architecture case, requirements of all stakeholders—that is, the requirements of users, the development organization, and the sponsoring organizations—must be met. The external attributes differ from the internal ones in that they reflect the influence of the environment on the product (related to user requirements). The internal attributes focus only on intrinsic properties of the product (such as modularity and complexity), which are related more to its structure and how it is being built (related to the development organization's requirements). In any case, the specification of internal quality attributes should use the same quality model that is used for the external quality specification, in order to maintain the relation between external and internal attributes.

The internal quality requirements are defined to aid in the selection of the development process, and they may be common to a product line. The internal quality of each product can be evaluated by internal metrics, which measure the internal attributes (which can be used for deciding among several technical options) and can be used as external quality indicators. In addition, internal metrics can be used for the continuous improvement of the process.

Following these general considerations for the development and evaluation processes, the specific process for evaluating software architecture is shown in Figure 3.5. The process (which is described completely in Dueñas, de Oliviera, and de la Puente 1998) contains the following steps:

1. The users and the developers specify the criteria for determining the external quality of the product or system and the external quality of the

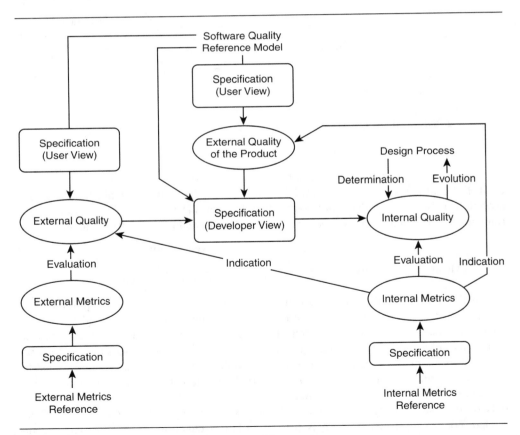

FIGURE 3.5 Quality Model for Software Architecture

software architecture using the quality reference model (*ISO 9126* 1991). The specifications must contain the selected quality characteristics, their values, and the metrics chosen for their evaluation.

2. The developers specify the criteria for determining the internal quality of the software architecture from the external quality of the product and the external quality of the software architecture using the same quality reference model (*ISO 9126* 1991), and they define a set of internal software attributes. The specification must contain the internal software attributes selected for each quality characteristic, their values, and the metrics selected for their measurement. As the process of software architecture development constrains the internal attributes of the software architecture, the measurement result can be used as feedback for improving the software architecture development process.

3. The reviewers evaluate both the external quality of the software architecture using the external metrics, and its internal quality using the internal metrics already defined. The external quality of the product can be estimated by measurement and analysis of the internal attributes.

4. The results of applying internal metrics to the software architecture can be used as an indication or prediction of the presence of certain quality characteristics in the end product, if there are no available specifications.

5. The results of applying external metrics, normalized by internal metrics—such as size or complexity—can be used to compare two or more software architectures.

This model reflects both the current state of the art in assessment of software architecture and an agenda for future work. The ultimate aim of relating internal quality attributes of the architecture to the external quality of the product is still beyond the capabilities of the available tools.

3.4   Final Remarks

This chapter has described the activities of and results obtained in the ARES project with regard to the assessment of software architecture. Our approach has taken into account the abstract nature of architecture and covers the activities performed in the architectural development and recovery processes. We have reviewed some of the techniques that were available before the project started, and we have seen that they were used for assessing not architectures but rather other more mature models, such as detailed design and implementation. We have investigated how these techniques may be used for software architecture. The techniques chosen were structural assessment by means of metrics, timing assessment by means of rate monotonic analysis, and behavior assessment by means of simulation. Their results are integrated in an assessment process specific for each product line.

These are the most important conclusions:

1. Software architecture has a profound impact on the final system quality. Therefore, measuring the quality of the architecture is a good way of forecasting the quality of the final system.

2. Architectural assessment is possible only if suitable models are available; thus the assessment problem becomes a modeling problem. It is important to incorporate as much information as possible—for example, that provided by other phases of development.

3. Architectural assessment, and therefore architectural modeling, depends on and is guided strongly by the purpose of assessment.

4. Because architectural modeling deals with a high degree of abstraction, architectural assessment carries a certain degree of subjectivity. The more concrete the model is, the more applicable are the assessment techniques.

5. Metrics that evaluate architectures can provide results in only the mid- or long term: Only after several products have been developed and measured are we able to correlate the metric results with the measured qualities of the architectures. In this context, metrics are very applicable to software architecture for product lines.

6. Time analysis of architectures is a feasible technique for assessment, suitably applied when predictability and time requirements are important. A set of known techniques has been extended for use with families of products.

7. Behavioral analysis can be applied to architectures when it is integrated in an architectural recovery process; the main task of such analysis is to relate simulation results to components in the software architecture. This type of analysis is especially useful when dealing with dynamic architectures.

8. The decision-making process based on the results of metrics, time, and behavioral analysis is specific to each product line or company.

9. Architectural assessment will be easier when component development cycles are used in the industrial arena. Each component in the architecture must carry information about its functionality, interfaces, and assumptions about other components, as well as about its properties with respect to general requirements, such as modifiability, performance, and so on.

Many issues in the area of software architecture assessment remain open to research. Among them is the relationship between the results of architecture assessment and the quality of the final systems after development. Solving the practical implications of this problem would greatly facilitate the development of complex software.

4

Software Architecture Recovery

Berndt Bellay, Harald Gall, Mehdi Jazayeri

Chapter 2 showed us the importance of techniques for describing software architecture. In Chapter 3 we saw that such descriptions are needed, for example, to perform architecture assessment. For many existing systems, however, architectural descriptions either do not exist or no longer adequately describe the current implementation of the system. For these reasons it is often necessary to describe the architecture of an existing system. The term "architecture recovery" refers to techniques and processes used to uncover a system's architecture from available information.

At the start of the ARES project, many researchers were already talking about software architectures and their importance for the software-engineering process (Garlan and Shaw 1993, Perry and Wolf 1992, Witt, Baker, and Merritt 1994). The term "software architecture," not yet universally accepted, was still ambiguous, used to mean different things. Common to most of these meanings, however, was the idea that the main issue of software architecture is the structure of a system (e.g., blackboard, pipe/filter) without taking other aspects into account. The interpretation that software architecture can be seen from many viewpoints and that many different views are needed to describe a software system completely was only beginning at this time (Kruchten 1995, Soni, Nord, and Hofmeister 1995).

Although the work on software architecture was already well on its way, software architecture recovery was in its infancy and resembled design recovery, but on a higher level. Furthermore, there was no clear distinction between the processes of design recovery and architecture recovery, but more a smooth transition between these processes. For the process of architecture recovery, reverse engineering tools were seen as a good starting point (Biggerstaff 1989, Biggerstaff, Mitbander, and Webster 1994).

Thus our plans for architecture recovery were based on using reverse engineering tools and methods as the starting point (Bellay and Gall 1998b). First we evaluated reverse engineering tools to determine their capabilities for recovering an architectural description of a software system. On the basis of this evaluation we identified the missing information that is needed from the recoverable views to arrive at an architectural description. Such an architectural description should represent not only the structural views of a software system, but also its quality attributes. Through this process we arrived at the formulation of *architectural properties*.

4.1   Architecture Recovery Based on Properties

Each software system is built to satisfy a set of requirements. These requirements guide the design and development of the system. Some of the requirements are reflected in architectural decisions that impose constraints on the design. These constraints are not explicitly part of the design. For example, in the train control system (TCS) that was the main case study for our architecture recovery work (see Chapter 7), one requirement was that the system be fail-safe. This requirement led to the architectural decision of building a redundant system. By examining the design of the system, one cannot see (i.e., recover) *why* a redundant design was chosen. We call such an architectural decision an **architectural property.** We developed the notion of architectural properties for our specific case study and have generalized it for possible application to other domains.

Each architectural property describes a specific aspect of a system (including family aspects). Because a system consists of many system aspects, we recover and describe a particular software architecture as a set of architectural properties. The use of architectural properties originates from the need to recover and describe specific architectural aspects of a single system, to reason about them, and to recover the architecture of a family of systems.

During our investigations of several members of the TCS product family, we recovered architectural properties of a system by identifying strongly related aspects of the systems. For an embedded TCS, one of these aspects was *safety*. From the system documentation it was unclear what kinds of mechanisms were used for safety and how these were implemented. The parts related to safety were often inherent and spread throughout the documentation. Because safety plays an important role in the train control system, we decided to explicitly describe this architectural property in a separate view.

Another important aspect in the TCS case study was *data communication:* The software system is closely combined with hardware, and for many reasons this hardware can change over time (e.g., new sensors, other interfaces, faster CPU). Information about data communication can usually be found in the documentation, but it is often scattered throughout in the documentation. By describing this architectural property, we make the information available in a data communication view that allows identification of the parts devoted to data communication, thereby making it easier to concentrate on and perhaps modify the part and/or the interface.

The architectural properties that we have identified can be divided into the following three categories:

1. **Domain-independent properties.** System structure, system control, data communication, and dynamic structure are found in all systems, although their relative importance may vary. These properties are similar to the views found in Kruchten 1995 and Soni, Nord, and Hofmeister 1995.

2. **Domain-specific properties.** Certain domains require certain properties, such as security or safety. For example, in the safety-critical train control system, the architectural property safety is at least as important as the functionality itself. The domain-specific properties are related to what in the literature is called quality attributes, or critical system properties (Rushby 1994, Barbacci et al. 1995).

3. **Product family properties.** In this category we include properties that are used to generate different variants of the system. The mechanisms for creating variants range from the definition of constants that may change (e.g., the maximum speed of the train, from which all other criteria then have to be derived) to complete parts that are included or excluded during compile time or run time (Cheong, Ananda, and Jarzabeck 1998).

Figure 4.1 illustrates our approach to architecture recovery for product families. We start with some existing systems that are assumed to be members of a product family, A (F_A). From these systems we recover the architectural properties (APs) of each single system. The results are architectural descriptions based on architectural properties AD(APs) of all the individual systems of this product family. This information provides the input to identify the product family architecture, resulting in a family architectural description of program family A.

We use architectural properties as a means of recovering and describing the software architecture of a single system, as well as of a product family. For the recovery of a single software architecture we have designed an **architecture recovery framework.** The framework consists of a recovery process based on architectural properties, architectural descriptions, recovery methods and tools, and the available information sources of the system. We have validated this framework with the TCS study. We have also defined the process of recovering and describing a product family architecture using architectural properties, but we have not yet validated this step. More detail on this step is given in Chapter 7.

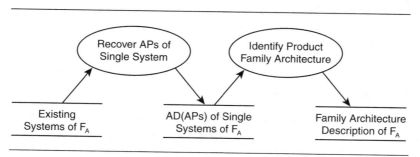

FIGURE 4.1   Recovering a Software Architecture on the Basis of Architectural Properties

4.2   The ARES Approach to Software Architecture Recovery

This section describes our approach to software architecture recovery from the initial statement of the problem through the development of our goals to our solution. The approach we developed is based on one of the ARES case studies, an embedded real-time train control system (TCS), which we will use throughout this chapter as a descriptive example. We expect that the approach generalizes to other domains as well. This case study is the focus of Chapter 7, which describes the ABB experience with architecture recovery.

4.2.1   The Case Study: A Train Control System

Our case study focused on three train control systems (A, B, and C) developed independently by ABB. These systems are embedded software systems that control the speed of locomotives by checking and processing signal information received via the antenna of the locomotive. System A is a railway system, system B is a subway system with the additional functionality of precision stops, and system C is a new subway system currently under development.

The main characteristics of these train control systems are the following:

- **Safety and fault tolerance.** If there are erroneous transmissions that cannot be decoded into useful control information, the train must be stopped for safety reasons.
- **System family.** The TCS should be customizable for different markets and their specific requirements (e.g., signal transmission and train standards).
- **Embedded real-time system.** Hardware components such as sensors, receivers, antennas, and so on have to be checked in predefined time intervals to ensure reliability.
- **Mix of programming languages (C, C++, Assembler).** Software and hardware are closely connected (i.e., the interfaces in C and Assembler to the hardware are essential).
- **Different development and target environments.** For development and testing, a different environment must be used to simulate real-life situations of train control.

4.2.2   The Problem Statement

Our industrial partner ABB identified three train control systems as candidates for a product family. Although at first glance the source codes and the hardware might look quite different, the main functionality and requirements and—as we identified later in our study—many other aspects (e.g., safety) are common. The differences are partly in functionality, but most drastically in the hardware (e.g., two processors versus a single processor, multiple buses versus a single bus, redundancy inherent in hardware versus completely in software), the source code languages (C, C++, Assembler), and the implementation (e.g., monitor with tasks versus monitor with the SDL [Specification and Description Language] run-time system versus real-time operating system). Although some components at the code level and design stages may have been reused, this reuse is not well documented. The documentation was developed for each system individually, and the common parts and common architecture are not described. These situations are typical of development environments that do not use an architecture-centered approach.

Successful industrial systems have to be maintained and extended, and new systems have to be developed for new markets and/or customers. Because each system in this case was developed individually and common parts are not documented, there are maintenance problems. The documentation, which may even be incomplete, is not easy to read, so it takes a long time to understand the system. Furthermore, additional study of the source code to understand some aspects of the system is needed, and worse yet, this information must be studied for each system separately. From the architectural side of the system, architectural properties are not clearly visible, and high-level and architectural descriptions are missing for both single systems and the product family. Error repair and enhancements are difficult because of the insufficiencies in the documentation and the missing architectural description, and they must be implemented and documented for each system individually.

When a new system has to be developed, starting from scratch is often too expensive. Thus an existing successful system that exhibits a certain degree of similarity is often used as the basis for the new system. The problem of this development approach is that because no combined knowledge and experience of prior systems is available, such as an architectural description could provide, each system is developed on the basis of only this single system, and not in an orderly fashion. The result is the same problems of maintenance, enhancement, and development already discussed.

4.2.3 Motivations for Architecture Recovery

The need for architecture recovery is usually based in the recognition of the existence of several systems that have much in common and thus can be seen as one product family. By using the knowledge inherent in these systems we can learn, for example, what the common parts are, what is reusable, what could have been done better, where the differences are, or how we can achieve easy adaptability for future enhancements. As a consequence, we can define a product family architecture.

Recovering the software architecture of *single systems* is expected to be useful for the following activities:

1. **Redocumentation.** This activity is inherent in the architecture recovery process of each single system and is needed for further development.

2. **Reasoning and assessment** (see Chapter 3). Although not required, these activities are nonetheless important for further development. Architecture recovery helps us to gain more confidence in the system at a high level

(e.g., structure, use cases), to verify the fulfillment of requirements, and to identify limitations of the current architecture (e.g., extendibility, safety).

3. **Architecture redesign.** Architecture recovery helps us understand a system at higher levels of abstraction (e.g., basic structure, data flow) and thus facilitates the making of changes in the architecture of the system.

4. **Maintenance.** Architecture recovery helps us understand the system and measure the impact of changes, as well as inherent dependencies.

5. **Evolution.** Architecture recovery allows "graceful" evolution of the system by helping us understand higher- and lower-level changes (e.g., data structures, hardware devices, functional enhancements and additions) when new functionality is being implemented.

6. **Development of a new system, or a successor, from a single system** (for new markets and/or customers). Architecture recovery allows us to reuse concepts, parts, and knowledge recovered from previous systems and, by engaging in reasoning and assessment, to develop a system that meets the requirements better.

Recovering the architecture of a *product family* can be useful for the following activities:

1. **Development of successors.** Architecture recovery decreases the development cost (by allowing reuse from architecture, documentation, and even source code), offers better support of changes (many possible changes can be anticipated from recovered systems and their assessment), and decreases the maintenance effort of systems derived from the product family architecture.

2. **Maintenance of original systems.** By identifying common parts, architecture recovery decreases the effort required for error repair and enhancement and improves our understanding of the overall system.

3. **Development of product families that share requirements.** Architecture recovery enables the reuse of parts (from architecture to source code) of the recovered product family for the development of other product families (e.g., another product family with similar safety or security requirements).

4.2.4 Goals of Architecture Recovery

The goals of architecture recovery process in our case study can be summarized as follows:

1. To analyze the system aspects and family aspects of the train control system and, on the basis of that analysis, recover and describe the architectural properties of the case study

2. To identify and describe common architectural properties to define a product family architecture

To achieve the first goal, we defined a framework for the architecture recovery of single systems (see Section 4.5). To accomplish the second goal, we described ways to get from single-system architectures to a product family architecture (see Section 4.6).

4.2.5 Overview of Our Approach to Architecture Recovery

Our approach to architecture recovery consists of two main steps:

1. Recover and describe the architecture of *single systems* by deriving the architectural properties of the system under study from its system aspects

2. Recover and describe the *program family* architecture on the basis of the architectural descriptions of several individual systems

The architecture recovery of single systems is accomplished through the use of existing reverse engineering tools, which derive (low-level) views of the system. In addition, our process combines the recovered views to achieve higher-level views and integrates human knowledge to raise the level of abstraction to higher architectural levels (Figure 4.2).

The architecture recovery process starts with the recovery of several system aspects in terms of architectural properties. In the train control system we recovered, for example, the architectural properties were safety and data communication. (Architectural properties are discussed in detail in Section 4.4.) Figure 4.3 is a conceptual representation of this recovery process with individual architectural properties ($AP_1, \ldots, AP_n$) for a single software system.

To recover a product family architecture, we have defined a process based on the architecture recovery of the single systems (see Figure 4.4):

1. Recover architectural properties of each system of the product family

2. Analyze the architectural descriptions of family members for commonalities

The architecture recovery process for a product family relies largely on the description of the individual software architectures. Because architecture recovery is based on architectural properties that are common in the product family systems, the results are easier to compare and thus the common parts of the properties can be identified more easily.

4.2.6 An Architecture Recovery Scenario

The architecture recovery of the train control system took place over a period of almost two years. During this time we held many meetings with various product experts, and we examined many documents of the systems. Only over time did the importance of these meetings become clear. We did not start with the available documentation and expect to come up with the architecture automatically. Rather, the process included several analysis steps, starting from informal discussions with the application programmers and designers and leading to tool-supported program analysis and program comprehension. In this section we give an overview of the steps that we expect to be typical in any realistic architecture recovery project.

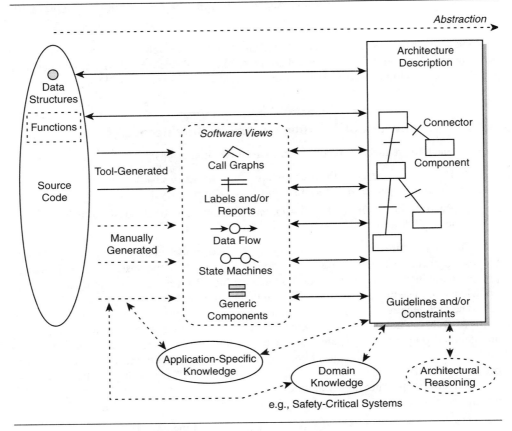

FIGURE 4.2 Architecture Recovery of a Single System

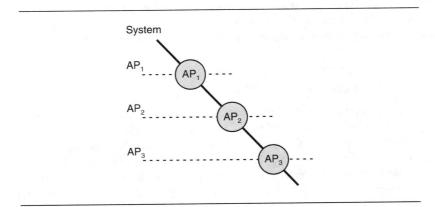

FIGURE 4.3 Architecture Recovery Based on Architectural Properties

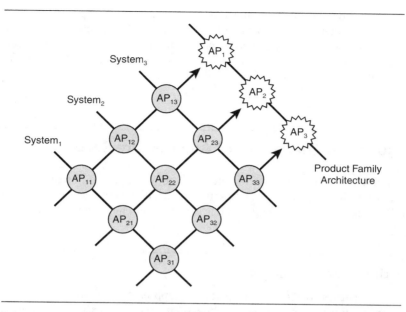

FIGURE 4.4   From Single-System Software Architecture to Product Family Architecture

Discussions with application experts (programmers and designers) and domain experts were, of course, critical. In this step we came up with a preliminary object model representing a program family member in terms of objects and relationships. This step turned out to be important because the application experts were accustomed to a more process-oriented (functional) view of the system. The object model therefore represented a completely different view of the system from that in the existing documentation (although at this stage of the project this new view was not fully accepted by all stakeholders).

We then examined different kinds of requirements and design documentation and developed object models based on different information and abstractions. We first developed an object model based on the design documentation given. We then modified this object model according to the requirements gathered from the requirements documentation and the requirements enumerated by the application experts. This human support of the process turned out to be valuable and essential for achieving a dependable result. On the basis of this (requirements-oriented) object model we developed an architectural object model, much more general than the object model we had developed from the design information. This architectural object model turned out to be a good basis for discussing product family issues and developing a reference architecture later in the process.

We then used reverse engineering tools for program analysis at the source code level. We combined the software views generated by this analysis, such as data and control flows, with the models we had developed in the previous steps.

Note that we did not start our architecture recovery process with program analysis at the source code level; rather we began with analysis at a much higher and more abstract level. For this reason we were not burdened by programming-language issues and details and could concentrate on architectural and design issues right away. We will argue for these initial steps of architecture recovery throughout this chapter.

4.3 Issues and Challenges of Architecture Recovery

Using the problem statement and the definition of the framework for architecture recovery, we can identify the issues and challenges for the architecture recovery of product families. In this section we discuss the key factors in our approach and the issues that the architecture recovery process must address.

4.3.1 Architectural Properties

Architectural properties are the essential part of our approach to software architecture recovery. We therefore must identify which architectural properties exist in software systems. These architectural properties should

- Be complementary
- Describe the complete system
- Be nonoverlapping
- Be incrementally recoverable and describable
- Apply to typical software systems (not only embedded software systems)
- Be based on requirements-related concepts

Each architectural property must be specified in terms of its essential elements, such as components, connectors, relationships, and implementations. For example, timing properties may require descriptions of relevant aspects of a scheduler, state machines, scheduling algorithm, and so on. In addition, we must list architectural description techniques and/or notations that are well suited for describing an architectural property (e.g., state chart diagram for system control). It should also be possible to trace the elements that form the architectural property all the way to the source code.

4.3.2 Architectural Description

Once an architectural property has been recovered, it must be documented in a description. We identify existing architectural descriptions and the architectural properties for which they are suited. We classify architectural descriptions by type (e.g., informal or formal, textual or graphical, design method) and applicability (e.g., target use or target audience).

4.3.3 Information Sources

Before starting any recovery activity, we must be able to determine the kinds of information sources that exist (e.g., source code, source code comments, documentation) and their quality: Is the information dependable or biased? Is it up to date? For example, recovery from documentation is easier because it is less detailed and more understandable, but it may differ from the actual implementation; source code, in contrast, is not as easy to understand, but it is dependable and up to date. Furthermore, the information quality influences the recovery activities. For example, if the source code has no comments, we cannot use certain analysis methods (see Section 4.5.3).

4.3.4 Integration of Human Knowledge

Human knowledge and experience are essential ingredients in the recovery process; they help us raise the level of abstraction of the recovered software views. We have investigated possible processes for integrating human knowledge, especially in terms of tool support and the appropriateness of information sources. This integration must be able to cope with inconsistencies, such as differences between source code and documentation. A common inconsistency is that recovered information from the documentation may not be identical with the actual implementation and thus yields wrong results.

4.3.5 Reverse Engineering Methods and Tools

Because we use reverse engineering methods and tools for the architecture recovery of single systems, we have identified available reverse engineering tools that are useful for our process to generate intermediate and/or architectural views. We have classified these tools according to the type of recovery supported (automatic, semiautomatic, or manual; see Section 4.5.3), the information sources needed (e.g., source code, documentation, application knowledge), and the results achievable (e.g., type and content of recoverable views and documentation). The most important factors to consider are how usable these reverse engineering methods and tools are for our process (e.g., the source code languages supported) and what benefits (e.g., extensibility, ease of use) and shortcomings they have.

4.3.6 Commonality Analysis of Architectural Properties

To recover a product family architecture we use a commonality-based approach. Therefore, we need to find a method for comparing architectural properties (both the description of the architectural properties and the additional architectural descriptions) and identifying commonalities. In addition, we must consider the requirements and difficulties of this commonality analysis. For example, should all properties be documented using the same description method? And how are the different properties related?

4.4   Common Architectural Properties

To develop our definition of architectural properties, let's first revisit the definition of software architecture we gave in Chapter 1: "Software architecture is a set of concepts and design decisions about the structure and texture of software that must be made prior to concurrent engineering to enable effective satisfaction of architecturally significant explicit functional and quality requirements and implicit requirements of the product family, the problem, and the solution domains."

Architecture recovery aims at extracting such architecturally significant requirements from different kinds of information: from high-level (requirements and design) documentation to low-level source code of a software system.

Many of the reasons and constraints leading to a particular design can be expressed in the design documentation, but often much of the design rationale, such as why a shared memory is used for data communication, is missing. The reasons for certain design decisions are found not in the design, but rather in some high-level concepts derived from the architecturally significant requirements, such as safety or security, because they affect both the design and the implementation.

An architectural property represents a specific design decision related to a functional or quality architecturally significant requirement, and that property may be described by means of different architectural notations. Each architectural property consists of a set of aspects identifiable in the software system (e.g., safety methods such as redundancy, hardware tests, time-outs, or checksums for the safety architectural property). For each architectural property different architectural views can be recovered.

In the TCS study we identified a list of important architectural properties for the system. These properties were not explicitly expressed in the design documents. We generalized the architectural properties and completed the list with other related properties not originally found in the case study. Here is our final list of architectural properties:

- System structure
- System control
- Data communication
- Dynamic structure
- Safety
- Variance (product variation)

This list is not complete and might have to be extended to fit the specific case study or domain. Using the categorization presented in Section 4.1, we can group the architectural properties as follows:

- **Domain-independent properties.** System structure, system control, data communication, dynamic structure
- **Domain-specific properties.** Safety
- **Product family properties.** Variance

For the purpose of recovery and description, each architectural property may be decomposed into lower-level properties that we call **architectural aspects.** Graphically, the aspects to recover are shown in a treelike structure, with the root representing the property. These aspects are then decomposed as necessary down to the source code elements and parts that make up this property as the leaf nodes. Any elements that can be identified are described with simple text.

For example, for the architectural property data communication, such a decomposition reveals *components* that exchange data and *connectors* that realize the data exchange. Each connector can be categorized further according to the kind of data that is exchanged and the connector type, which describes the properties of the connector (see Section 4.4.3).

The aspects that we derived from our case study we subdivided as far as we could, but such a list can never be complete. A good exercise for a domain would be to attempt to complete such a list. The list provides a useful characterization of a product family because it captures the design decisions that each family member must face. By describing an architectural property in terms of its architectural aspects, we recover the source code elements and parts that implement the architectural property, as well as the mappings from high-level artifacts (i.e., architectural descriptions) down to the actual implementation, including intermediate views.

To overcome the shortcomings of informal descriptions, we use additional architectural descriptions of the property based on various notations. For these additional architectural descriptions we do not enforce a specific means for description, such as UML (Douglass, 1997), boxes and arrows, textual descriptions, or ADLs. We do not limit ourselves to any particular description method because the description method strongly depends on what is recoverable and on the specific needs and purposes of recovery. Whereas some descriptions can be based on one architectural property, others require the recovery of more properties: The UML deployment diagram, for example, requires both the system structure and the data communication properties. In such cases the description should clearly identify which parts are from which architectural property.

In our architecture recovery process, we describe each architectural property by the following:

- The intent of the property
- Attributive, hierarchical, nonenumerative explanation
- Small example(s) illustrating the property
- A list of suggested architectural notations
- The benefits of recovering the property (overview)

The subsections that follow discuss in turn each of the six architectural properties that we have identified in this section, describing their parts in detail. Each discussion ends with a list of architectural notations that are well suited for describing the architectural property at hand, followed by a list of benefits that are gained by recovery of that property. The kinds of notations that are suitable may change over time as new notations are invented; they may also be dependent on the existing standards of the organization that is involved in the architecture recovery process. The list of benefits indicates what other uses the recovery of the property may have in addition to helping in architecture recovery.

4.4.1 System Structure

System structure gives a high-level structural view of the system and the decomposition of the system, from the viewpoints of both software alone and hardware/software integration. System structure is one part of the static structure of the system; it is closely related to the module structure, one of the architectural structures introduced in Chapter 1. The other part of the static structure is represented in the architectural property system control (see Section 4.4.2).

Often we look at system structure not only in terms of how it is subdivided into its individual parts, but also in terms of common patterns of structural organization (Garlan and Shaw 1993, Monroe et al. 1997, Shaw et al. 1995). Several well-known patterns, such as layered, kernel/shell, pipe/filter, and hardware/software integration (hardware wrappers), exist. The corresponding architectural description reflects not only the overall modular organization of the system, but also structural aspects from data communication and control flow. We treat system structure, data communication, and system control as three separate properties.

The system decomposition (Parnas 1976, Parnas, Clements, and Weiss 1985), which can be based on function, data, or objects, makes a system more easily comprehensible and allows one to describe it at different abstraction levels. For example, at one abstraction level a system may be of the pipe/filter type, while its individual modules are of another type. Furthermore, this hierarchical description can also describe certain architectural properties using higher-level entities, which is beneficial for architectural descriptions.

Hardware/software integration, or the decoupling of the software that is responsible for producing the required functionality from the software that is used to integrate the supporting hardware system, is often accomplished by the use of structural properties. It is of great importance for embedded systems because it must support the easy replacement of hardware components with small overhead in terms of both programming effort and system performance.

As an example, we recovered a hierarchical functional decomposition of the system structure of the TCS. On the other hand, we also identified software parts that have interfaces with hardware and fall into the category of hardware/software integration system structure. Figure 4.5 shows the elements of the architectural property system structure.

Architectural Notations

1. System decomposition
   - Package diagram (UML)
   - Structure diagram down to elemental types (function, data, object)
2. Possible mapping to structural architectural patterns
   - OSI layer diagram
   - Structural architectural patterns
3. Hardware/software integration
   - Deployment diagram (UML)
   - Ellis's onion skin (Ellis 1994)

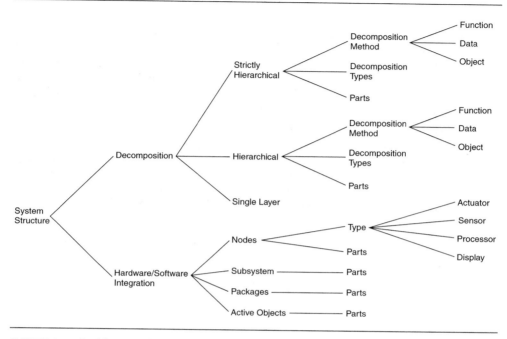

FIGURE 4.5   Architectural Property: System Structure

Benefits

1. Better understanding of the structure of the system
2. Identification of the structural guidelines used
3. Overview of the hardware/software integration
4. Identification of the software parts that have interfaces to hardware

4.4.2   System Control

System control is concerned with the static process structure of a system. It plays a prominent role in the train control system, showing the control flow in the system for both hardware and software. We describe this property on the basis of components and connectors and of system states. To recover this information we group the control flow components into active and passive components. First, we identify active components that have a major influence on the control flow, such as the scheduler and other main functions. Then we describe the passive components—simple functions and functions of special concern, which are not invoked through "normal" calls in the main control flow of the system (e.g., interrupt service routines, remote procedure calls). To enrich the control flow information, we specified the connector type as (1) sequential or concurrent and (2) event- or timer-driven.

An example of an active, sequential control component is a main program. A scheduler can be either a sequential or a concurrent control component, but it is usually considered concurrent. Both uniprocessing and multiprocessing systems may be based on (irregular) events or (regular) timer interrupts. In a uniprocessing system, the main task is normally interrupted by events. The intervals between events must be longer than the time required to process them.

In addition to the control flow, we recover states and state transitions of the system. Using this information, we can create state charts and state transition diagrams, describing the control flow in another form. These views are descriptive, and some commonalities among different systems can be found, although the control flow of the implementation identified might be quite different. Furthermore, such diagrams allow the fault conditions and fault recovery to be expressed. Figure 4.6 shows the elements of the architectural property system control.

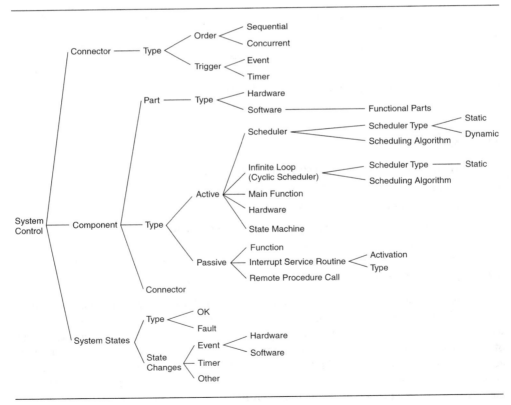

FIGURE 4.6   Architectural Property: System Control

Architectural Notations

1. System structure in terms of active and passive components: custom diagrams
2. Control flow between the recovered active and passive components: control flow diagram
3. System states and transitions
   - State chart table
   - State chart diagram
   - Activity diagram (UML)

Benefits

1. Better understanding of the static control of the system
2. Identification of relevant parts that implement system control
3. Clear distinction between system states
4. Basic understanding of control flow

4.4.3 Data Communication

The architectural property **data communication** provides information on the mechanisms used for data transfer among the different parts of the system, both software and hardware. The communication partners, called *components,* are identified and the data communication they perform, represented as a *connector,* is described.

The way in which components exchange information has great influence on the design and on the roles of the components. Certain forms of information exchange allow the components to run on different CPUs. The use of memory for information exchange, however, normally restricts the software components to running on the same CPU; if the memory is shared among different CPUs, however, the components may run on different CPUs. Thus we divide the types of information exchange into the following three types: memory, data line, or a combination of the two.

Information exchange can be further classified by the type of communication: (1) uni- or bidirectional, (2) 1:1 or 1:n transmission, and (3) blocking or nonblocking. Synchronization methods may also be required for information exchange. For example, shared memory and global variables must be protected when used by concurrent processes.

The components involved in information exchange may play different roles. In the simplest case, they can be either active or passive. An active component with respect to a variable is one that either creates the variable or modifies it. A component is passive for a variable if it does not actively modify the variable (e.g., it transfers it to another component without modification). Components could be specified further as client or server, producer or consumer, and so on.

The exchanged data may be classified according to the type of the data (e.g., time, speed) and according to hierarchies of message types (e.g., the message can be an alarm message or a transponder message). This classification is needed to trace the data flow, as well as composition and decomposition, of specific information in the system (e.g., content of the data sent from a balise to different subsystems). In the process, data dependencies can be identified. Awareness of such dependencies helps us analyze changes in the system that are required when we are introducing changes in the content, length, or source of the information. Figure 4.7 shows the elements of the architectural property data communication.

Architectural Notations

1. General data flow
   - Data flow diagram
   - Message flow (UML)

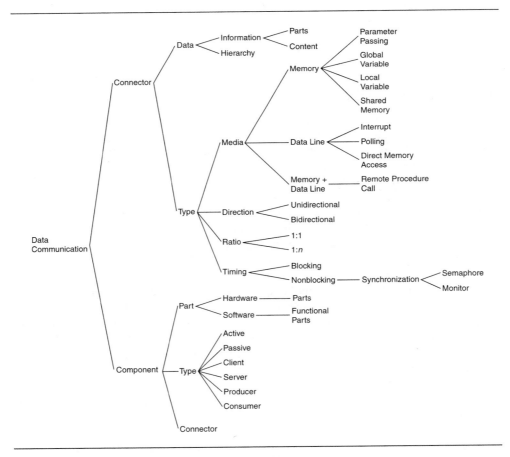

FIGURE 4.7 Architectural Property: Data Communication

2. Data flow between nodes: deployment diagram (UML)

3. Data hierarchy: class diagram

Benefits

1. Overview of data exchanged throughout the system (internal and external)

2. Identification of guidelines for data exchange

3. Traceability of information

4. Identification of data dependencies in the system

4.4.4   Dynamic Structure

Dynamic structure encompasses two main aspects: (1) scenarios (execution structure)—i.e., run-time elements and their interactions—and (2) real-time characteristics.

The architectural properties that we have described so far do not reflect the dynamic structure of a software system completely. Some systems have run-time elements that appear only during execution and can therefore be described only from this point of view. An example of a run-time element is a process: In a client/server system a client process sends a request to a server process. In terms of dynamic structure, the server process could either perform the request itself, or it could spawn a child process to do it. For these two cases there are two different architectural descriptions of the underlying run-time concept. Such architectural descriptions are sometimes referred to as execution architectures (Soni, Nord, and Hofmeister 1995). They can also be used for various performance measurements and simulations of the run-time behavior. Figure 4.8 shows the main elements of the architectural property dynamic structure.

Architectural Notations

1. Execution structure of the system in the context of scenarios: scenario diagrams

2. Active tasks in the system: deployment diagram (UML)

3. Timing constraints in the system: timing diagrams

Benefits

1. Visualization of dynamic dependencies of the system

2. Clarification of the dynamic concepts and constraints of the system

---

4.4.5   Safety

Safety plays an important role in many (embedded) software systems. To achieve the required degree of safety, the designer can use different safety mechanisms, which restrict the design in different ways. The safety of a software system can be described as one of three

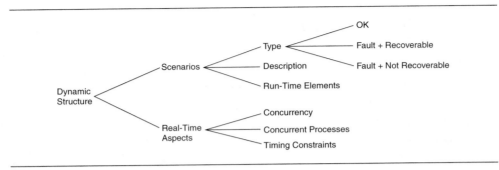

FIGURE 4.8   Architectural Property: Dynamic Structure

types: fail-operational, fail-stop, or, conceivably, none. These types are often directly related to whether the system is a low-demand (e.g., emergency shutdown system) or a high-demand safety-critical system (e.g., flight control system).

Independent of the type of safety are the different safety mechanisms: Examples include redundancy (static or dynamic), hardware tests (during run time or at startup), time-outs, and checksums. Static and dynamic redundancy are common techniques used to achieve reliability, availability, safety, and fault tolerance. There are different ways of implementing redundancy, such as by replicating the hardware or the software, by running the same operation at two different times, or by performing an operation in two different ways. Dynamic redundancy requires that the detection of an error cause a switch to the redundant part. An error can be detected by different methods (e.g., verification process, manual interference, watchdog timer). Static redundancy uses n versions of a component with a voter component that chooses a result returned by a minimum of m components as the correct result. This technique requires *diversity* among the components..

Software diversity can be realized by n-version programming, using different methods to create different versions of the same software component. For example, the versions could be written by different people and use different algorithms to achieve the same task. Further, we can categorize software by how its different versions are executed (e.g., serially, in parallel). Figure 4.9 shows the elements of the architectural property safety.

Architectural Notations

1. Visualization of the effects of safety efforts: scenario diagram
2. Visualization of safety mechanisms (dependent on mechanism)
   - Static redundancy: enhanced data flow diagram
   - Time-outs: scenarios
   - Checksums: data flow diagram

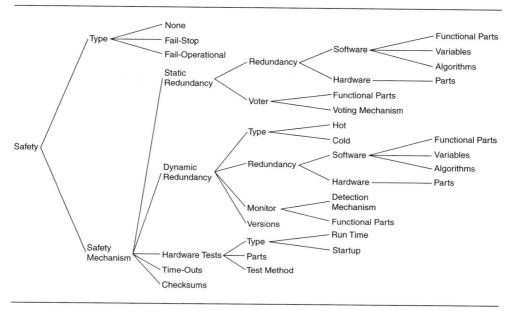

FIGURE 4.9   Architectural Property: Safety

Benefits

1. The gathering together of all safety aspects (ease of understanding and communication)
2. Separation of safety from functionality
3. Better understanding of safety needs and influences of system changes

4.4.6 Variance

The aspects of **variance** deal with the impact of product variation. Variance can be imposed by the need to address different markets or to run on different hardware platforms. Thus it can be divided into the following types: customer needs, standards (international or national), and hardware platforms. For many companies, national and international standards regulate parts of the software, ranging from consumer electronics to railway or subway control, as in the TCS case study. These standards substantially influence the architecture of the software. The structure of the system must enable easy replacement of parts, adaptation of country-specific parts, or addition of new features based on user requirements.

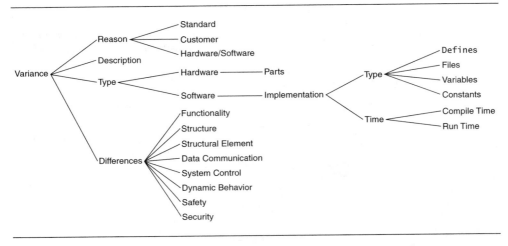

FIGURE 4.10 Architectural Property: Variance

Variance can be incorporated into a software system by different implementation methods (e.g., `defines`, files, variables) and at either run time or compile time. The implementation of variance has a strong impact on the software system (e.g., its maintainability, such as the introduction of new functionality or, especially in embedded software systems, changes in hardware). Furthermore, variance plays an important role in the recovery of the architecture of a family system: The existence of many differences in the individual systems shows how well the design accommodates changes from the family architecture viewpoint. Figure 4.10 shows the elements of the architectural property variance.

Architectural Notations

1. Identified implementations of variance in the software system: textual and tabular description of the implementations
2. Differences of the identified versions of the software system: individual architectural notations depending on the types of the differences

Benefits

1. Overview of all variants in one place
2. Clear identification of the reason, implementation, and points of difference among the various properties

4.5   Architecture Recovery of Single Systems

In this section we describe an architecture recovery process for single systems that is based on architectural properties. This process is part of a framework based on the experiences gained from recovering the architecture in the TCS case study.

The framework consists of five parts: the software system (i.e., the information available on the software system under study), architectural properties, architectural descriptions, architecture recovery methods, and an architecture recovery process. The first four parts influence each other and limit and guide the architecture recovery process (see Figure 4.11).

4.5.1   Architectural Descriptions

During our work on the TCS case study, we confirmed the general experience that no single architectural description is optimal for all concerns. Different architectural descriptions are better suited for describing certain aspects of a software system in terms of architectural views (see also Chapter 1). The lack of a single description is the reason behind solutions proposed by Kruchten (1995) and Soni, Nord, and Hofmeister (1995). Prevalent notations are Rumbaugh's OMT object/functional/dynamic model (Rumbaugh et al. 1991), Booch's model (Booch 1994), component/connector models (Magee et al. 1995, Shaw and Garlan 1996), behavior-centered models such as OCTOPUS (Awad, Kuusela, and Ziegler 1996), layered models, or just boxes and arrows.

To support the creation of different architectural views, we allow the use of different notations for each architectural property if necessary. We roughly classify architectural descriptions as follows:

- Informal or formal
    - Informal: boxes and arrows, architectural notation, textual description
    - Formal: architectural description languages (ADLs) (see Chapter 2)

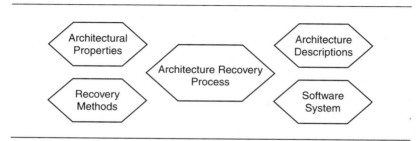

FIGURE 4.11   Components of the Architecture Recovery Framework

- Textual or graphical (Garlan 1995, Kazman et al. 1994)
- Design method (Booch 1994, Rumbaugh et al. 1991)
- Static (modular or object-oriented structure) or dynamic (simulation-, behavior-centered model) (Awad, Kuusela, and Ziegler 1996)
- Domain-independent (e.g., pipe/filter, kernel/shell) (Garlan and Shaw 1993) or domain-specific
- Hierarchical (properties at different abstraction levels) or flat (all properties at the same abstraction level)

The architectural property data communication, for example, can be described by an informal type of notation, such as a component/connector description, or a formal one, such as an architectural description language.

An important issue in determining which type of architectural description to use is the intended purpose of the description: the target use and the target audience. Target uses may be formal verifications, gathering of knowledge, or assessment. Target audiences may be customers who are interested in functionality and safety, management interested in development, hardware engineers interested only in hardware interfaces, software developers who need to know the system structure, and third parties who may not be shown confidential information but are interested in the system.

Textual descriptions are an example of a generic architectural description type; they can therefore be used to describe any architectural property. They are, however, not suitable for either formal verification or day-to-day handling by system designers. For example, information exchange can be informally described by textual descriptions or boxes and arrows, but to verify, for example, that there are no covert channels in a system, one would need a more formal description.

Hierarchical descriptions are a suitable way of describing the relationship among architectural concepts and properties that cannot be represented at the same abstraction level. Some properties can be found at a high abstraction level but also need some lower-level descriptions. For example, a static redundancy mechanism to implement the safety architectural property may be found at a high level because a whole subsystem may be implemented this way, but it may be necessary to trace the property down to the function level, or even to the source code level, to identify or verify its implementation. Hierarchical descriptions are thus helpful for human understanding, although it is often quite difficult to ensure consistency among levels that would enable formal verification.

The best-suited description of an architectural property is system-dependent and must be determined by the system architect for a particular architectural property.

4.5.2 Software System

The software system in our architecture recovery framework is defined by the type of the system (application domain) we are recovering, along with the information sources and their content that are available for the architecture recovery process.

At the outset we can differentiate whether the information stems from domain knowledge or originates from the system, the so-called application-specific knowledge (e.g., source code, documentation). The domain knowledge provides a preliminary overview of what is interesting for a system and what type of architectural elements can be expected or are usually used. For example, in the domain of safety systems, the architectural property of safety is important, and one might expect elements that implement redundancy, checksums, and watchdogs. The application-specific knowledge gives detailed information about the implementation of these general concepts and those that are not so common in the domain.

Application-Specific Knowledge

The source code represents the system "as is" and does not contain all the architectural information about the system. Additional information sources are needed to recover the software architecture of a system. For example, the reasons behind design decisions are not present in the source code and have to be recovered with the help of additional information.

We distinguish among different application-specific information sources and their classification, which for our case study are as follows:

- **Source code.** Dependable, incomplete
- **Executable system.** Not available
- **Documentation.** Informal, incomplete, undependable
- **Architects and designers.** Dependable, biased

We discuss each of these sources of information in the subsections that follow.

Source Code

The source code of a software system represents the current state of the system: Because it represents the latest data, it is the ultimate arbiter of what the system is. Although other information sources of the application may be easier and faster to understand, the information recovered from them often must be verified on the basis of the source code because other information sources tend to be out of date or biased in some way. To be useful for the recovery process, the source code must be available in electronic form.

Important for the recovery process are the programming languages used for the implementation, as well as the quality and quantity of the source code. The programming languages influence what tools are available and what results can be achieved with these tools, as well as which additional tools are required. These factors have a large impact on the effort and time needed for the recovery. Resource requirements for architecture recovery vary significantly depending on whether an existing tool can be used as is or adapted, or a new tool must be developed.

The quality of a source code can be evaluated by two main criteria. The first criterion is whether the source code is compatible with certain standards (e.g., ANSI C, FORTRAN-90) and how much platform independence it has. Source code tools are more likely to be available for standard programming languages on common platforms. The second criterion of source code quality is how well the programming-language concepts, which constrain the recoverable views and their quality, are applied. For example, if the C++ class construct is systematically used to implement domain concepts, then recovering the domain concepts is more tractable.

The quantity of the source code indicates whether the source code is complete and available. The source code is made up of different files, such as source files, header files, make files, and additional configuration files, and all are needed for architecture recovery. In our case study, we had access to the latest version of the TCS. The source code of the system is based on a mix of different programming languages: C, C++, and Assembler for the three individual systems. C and C++ recovery tools were available, but we had to write a customized program for the Assembler source code (see Section 4.5.3). The quality of the source code was fairly good, and most changes required were due to the differences between the development platform (MS-DOS) and the recovery platform (UNIX). The transformations required to parse the source code were adaptations from the platform (e.g., file name length, upper and lower cases, platform-dependent header files) and minor changes to adapt to language standards. These transformations were performed in a preprocessing step to make the code acceptable to the recovery tools.

The information available was limited to one subsystem (only part of the overall system) including all source and header files, some make files, and some configuration files. Although most information was provided with these files, it was not evident from the source code how the implementation is generated.

Executable System

An executable system allows knowledge of the system to be gathered at run time. If the system also can be compiled with debugging and profiling information, the recovery of additional run-time information is possible. For example, reaction to specific input or failure events can be observed. This information can help recover views that otherwise cannot be generated (Jerding, Stasko, and Ball 1997), and it can be used to verify the information provided by architects and designers.

Because our case study focused on a train control system, we were not able to test it in real-life situations. Whereas developers have a test environment available to them, this environment was not available to us.

Documentation

The documentation of a software system provides detailed information about the application using different notations. Although this information is more readable and thus allows faster and easier understanding of the software system than the source code does, it is also often not in sync with the actual implementation or is out of date because of recurring maintenance. Thus the views and information recovered from the documentation have to be verified in some way.

The documentation is usually divided into different structural parts that are expected to reflect the structure of the system. It is usually provided only in printed form, but electronic form would be more useful. An electronic format would allow the documentation to be searched and views to be recovered from it automatically. Automatic recovery of views also requires that some kind of standard is used for the documentation or that some parts of it are represented in a formal way. Typical documentation does not conform to standards and is usually informal (e.g., custom diagrams).

The documentation can be classified similarly to the source code. For quality, the use of standards and formal representations is important. The different documentation types available—for example, system documentation in textual form, SDL diagrams, or comments in the source code—attest to the variety in documentation.

Although the documentation available for our case study was limited to the single subsystem, this documentation also included an overview of the whole system. This overview does not provide in-depth documentation of the entire system, but it does provide valuable information about the rest of the system. The documentation is structured into a subsystem description and two block descriptions. This description is informal, but a formal description for one block is also available in the form of an SDL description. The documentation is available only in printed form. Additional documentation is provided by the comments in the source code, which can be found in the source and header files and provides information about the content of the files, a description of each function, and essential variables and constants.

Architects and Designers

Architects and designers play an important role as information sources in our recovery process and in general. First, they are dependable, and most importantly, they know the overall system and the design decisions behind it, which makes them the ultimate source if the needed information cannot otherwise be recovered. Although their importance varies depending on the other information sources available, their usefulness in providing views on the system is somewhat limited because this information is usually biased (e.g., hardware and software architects see the system from different viewpoints and thus describe it differently).

In addition to providing additional knowledge for our case study, architects and designers were needed in our recovery process for three other reasons:

1. The complete system was not available, so the boundaries (interfaces) and the complete picture were unresolved (e.g., interfaces defined in other parts not known to us, no complete hardware knowledge).

2. The system was not executable (either in a test environment or as the real system). Thus dynamic information was not recoverable, and details that we could have grasped by running the system were not available to us.

3. The background behind some decisions could not be recovered from the source code and was also not included in the documentation.

To understand these issues and categorize them accordingly, we need the knowledge of an architect or designer. An example from our case study is a hardware implementation of a cyclic redundancy check for the input stream. The reason behind such a choice is rather interesting: Is this a required safety standard or a safety requirement specific to the system? Why was it integrated in hardware—for additional safety or for performance reasons?

These questions are important for several reasons. First, they categorize the particular decision, thereby improving our understanding of the system. For example, it makes a difference if the hardware realization is done for additional safety or for performance; the former is an architectural property, the latter an implementation issue. Second, these questions help us assess a system. For example, could the function of the system be accomplished better in software with less communication overhead? This knowledge is most important for family systems: to qualify the system accordingly in the reference architecture, and to anticipate variation in different individual systems that make up the family system.

The information available about the software system, including its quality, affects architecture recovery by limiting the following parts of the architecture recovery framework:

- **Applicable recovery methods and tools.** For example, reverse engineering tools require a parsable source code.
- **Recoverable information and architectural descriptions.** For example, is a tool applicable or is manual recovery possible? Are architects and designers available?

and by influencing the following:

- **Effort required.** For example, what methods and tools can be used? Is the documentation up to date or is verification against the source code required?
- **Amount of additional knowledge required.** For example, is the source code or the system documentation complete or sufficient?

Domain Knowledge

Domain knowledge provides information about the domain(s) behind the application—that is, more general information that is valid for many applications in this problem area. Domain knowledge can be obtained from several sources:

- Domain information (e.g., papers or books about the domain)
- Domain standards (e.g., railway system standards in our case study)
- Domain experts

This knowledge is valuable because it provides information about generic concepts such as architectural elements, implementation methods, or architectural styles used in the problem domain. For the train control system, there are three domains of primary interest: the domain of railway systems, and the domains of real-time and safety systems. Standards and books are available for all three domains.

Integration of Human Knowledge

The integration of human knowledge is an important ingredient in our architecture recovery process because it complements the descriptions recovered from the available information, such as source code and recovered views.

Human knowledge is especially required in the analysis of system documentation, application-specific (undocumented) information, and domain standards. The following section includes examples of how we integrated human knowledge in the recovery process in the TCS case study.

4.5.3   Architecture Recovery Methods

A specific architecture recovery method may be appropriate for one or more specific architectural properties. Furthermore, an architecture recovery method may be appropriate and well suited for one system but not for another system. For our architecture recovery framework we give examples of methods for some architectural properties.

The tools and methods, as well as the results they can produce, are limited by the available information on the software system being studied (see Section 4.5.2). Furthermore, the time and effort that are needed and the results that can be achieved depend directly on the type of recovery applied. There are three types:

1. Manual (e.g., browsing, code reading)

2. Automatic (complete recovery by a tool)

3. Semiautomatic (tool-supported, but with the help of an engineer)

Manually Recovered Views

Manually recovered views have the advantage that often the engineer filters only the relevant information out of the available sources of information in the process. The recovered views are therefore easier to understand, focus on the point of interest, and represent the relevant information available. Manual recovery requires knowledge of both the application and the domain, and sometimes additional tool support.

The major disadvantages of manually recovered views are: Their recovery is time-intensive; they cannot be reproduced because of the biased viewpoint of the recovering engineer; and the process is error-prone because of human fallibility. Additional usability problems are that the recovered views are usually not available in an electronic form that can extend their usefulness (e.g., in a reverse engineering tool) and that not all parts are covered (e.g., parts that are of no interest at the time of recovery). Manual views are therefore rarely useful for subsequent processing; for example, errors may be propagated into subsequent views, and biased views have a large influence on further results or have to be transferred into electronic form. In their typical form, manually recovered views are useful primarily for knowledge transfer.

To be useful for architecture recovery, manually recovered views should be recovered in electronic form from the beginning and entered in an appropriate tool that can verify the consistency of input from an early stage.

Automatically Recovered Views

Automatic view recovery uses tools such as reverse engineering tools. Although some human intervention is necessary, the views are recovered automatically. As a result, the recovery is usually fast, but the time required for preparing the input, such as parsing the source code, has to be taken into account because it may represent a substantial portion of the overall time, even though often the input must be prepared only once. In terms of error, automatic view recovery has some major advantages over the manual approach: It is not as error-prone, and, if susceptible to errors, the limitations are usually known; in addition, the sources of incorrect results can be traced. Despite these advantages, however, correcting any errors that do result is not a trivial process. Further benefits are that the results can be reproduced and are available in electronic form (which makes them browsable, cross-referenced, and so on) and thus can be used for subsequent processing.

Although automation is beneficial, it does not integrate human knowledge in the recovery process (e.g., special knowledge about the application cannot be applied). In addition, the results of automatic view recovery are voluminous and cannot be focused on the interesting parts without human intervention. Further, the advantage of speed is valid only when the sources are available in a specified form (e.g., source code in a programming language, documentation in a "standard" format). If not, the tools have to be adapted, a process that requires time and may introduce new errors. Furthermore, subsequent processing usually requires conversion of the recovered views because different tools provide different formats and no standard formats exist.

Semiautomatically Recovered Views

Semiautomatic view recovery is also often referred to as interactive recovery. It is a hybrid of manual and automatic view recovery, sharing their benefits but also some of their problems. An engineer guides the recovery process, but the view itself is generated automatically by a tool. Human knowledge is integrated through the guidance of the engineer, thus enhancing the process. The engineer's guidance also focuses the recovery on a specific point, narrowing the results to only the aspects of interest. Because the view is generated automatically by the tool, semiautomatic view recovery is less susceptible to errors than manual recovery, and it shares some other advantages of automatic view recovery.

The major disadvantage of the semiautomatic approach is that the benefits rely on the input of human knowledge, which is susceptible to error and bias. The other shortcomings are identical to the ones we outlined for automatic view recovery.

4.5.4   Recovery Methods Applied to the TCS Case Study

For the architecture recovery of the TCS we applied the following tools:

- Manual and tool-supported code browsing
- Reverse engineering tools to recover different software views (Bellay and Gall 1998b)
- Custom tools `ImagParse`, `RefineParse`, and `ParDsp`, which we had to build to recover specific information from other sources (Bellay and Gall 1998a)
- View integration and combination to generate extended and new views from recovered software views (Bellay and Gall 1998a)

The subsections that follow expand on our experiences with these tools and techniques. We also developed a technique, called hot spots, for combining reverse engineering tools and application domain knowledge. This technique is described in Bellay and Gall 1997. Another custom tool we developed was the ESPaRT tool for recovering similar string patterns in the source code. This tool is described in Knor 1997 and Knor, Trausmuth, and Weidl 1998.

Manual and Tool-Supported Code Browsing

Code browsing is one of the most commonly used methods during maintenance because the engineers already have a general understanding of the software. This general understanding is essential for recovering information manually by code browsing. For architecture recovery, manual code browsing is usually not applicable, but it is important for verifying information recovered by other means, as well as assumptions made on the basis of unreliable sources such as documentation. Manual code browsing is time-consuming and suffers from other problems, and it can benefit from tool support.

Benefits

1. Knowledge already acquired, such as domain and application-specific knowledge, can be used and integrated in the recovery process.
2. The information used is always up to date.

Problems

1. The process is time-consuming.
2. Without tool support such as conditional compilation, syntax highlighting, search functions, and cross-references, this process is not really applicable.
3. The quality of recovered information depends on the engineer and is prone to errors.

For recovery of the TCS case study we used manual code browsing sparingly. Most of the time we used Imagix 4D, with its capabilities for code browsing (e.g., cross-references, highlighting of syntax, and point-and-click movement from views to source code). In general, we used code browsing primarily to gain knowledge about the system, to verify views recovered by other means, and to verify assumptions. In only a few cases did we use it to recover views manually.

Reverse Engineering Tools

Reverse engineering tools help software engineers analyze and understand complex software systems during maintenance activities. The size and complexity of commercial software systems require automated reverse engineering support to facilitate the generation of textual and graphical reports (e.g., function reports, call trees) of the software system under study. Several commercially available reverse engineering tools provide different capabilities and support specific source code languages.

The ability of reverse engineering tools to generate different views of software systems automatically and to help improve our understanding of a system, as well as their availability for many programming languages, makes them a good starting point for architecture recovery. But reverse engineering tools can automate the process only in part: Design recovery or architecture recovery activities still require the expertise of a human engineer (Biggerstaff 1989, Biggerstaff, Mitbander, and Webster 1994). The views generated by reverse engineering tools usually are too low-level and thus do not represent architectural views per se. They do provide a good base from which to recover architectural information and to help improve our understanding of the system.

Although reverse engineering tools provide many benefits to architecture recovery, they also suffer from some problems.

Benefits

1. They gather knowledge faster than code browsing does.
2. They recover many software views (automatically or semiautomatically).
3. They browse code interactively and recover additional information.

Problems

1. Parsing the source code requires application-specific knowledge (e.g., macros for generating different versions of the software under study) and domain knowledge (e.g., safety-critical systems) for many tasks during reverse engineering (e.g., parsing the source code, generating useful software views), making it not as simple as it may seem.
2. The size of the system under study can be difficult to manage (e.g., confusingly large representations, insufficient layout algorithms, clustering, unreadable labels, time-intensive to create).
3. Reverse engineering tools are insufficient to provide a comprehensive picture (e.g., they are unable to parse all source languages, client/server code cannot be related to each other automatically).
4. Multilanguage support is required for most real-world applications.
5. It is almost impossible to focus on essential elements across views.

After investigating many reverse engineering tools, we applied two different tools to our case study. Refine/C (by Reasoning Systems) we used mainly to generate function, variable, and type reports. In contrast, Imagix 4D (by Imagix Corporation) we used (1) to generate different views of the software system, as well as automatic documentation to support understanding, and (2) to browse through the source code to validate assumptions or otherwise recovered views, or to recover views manually. Both tools lack mixed language support (Refine/C is only for C and thus applicable to only one system; Imagix 4D is only for C and C++) and thus were able neither to parse the Assembler source code nor to integrate the views. The result was incomplete views of the system. In addition, because these tools did not enable us to combine different views, only low-level views could be recovered and no integration of knowledge was possible.

Custom Tools

Custom tools are used usually when other tools cannot be customized or customization requires too much effort. These tools are often small tools for just one purpose for a specific application and thus are faster to program than full-blown tools for individual systems (Johnson, Ornburn, and Rugaber 1992). Often programs like Perl or grep are used for these custom tools to analyze different parts (e.g., source code, results of other tools, documents) in electronic form and gather new results. Although implemented for only one specific application, with slight modification custom tools can also be used for other applications.

Like all other architecture recovery methods and tools, custom tools have both advantages and drawbacks.

Benefits

1. They can usually be implemented quickly.
2. They can produce results in a short time.
3. They are tailored for a specific problem.

Problems

1. They often apply only once for a specific problem.
2. They may be error-prone because users do not spend much time validating the results.

We implemented several custom tools in the TCS case study. Two of these, `ImagParse` and `RefineParse`, are used to parse the results of the reverse engineering tools—`ImagParse` for the documentation and `RefineParse` for the tabular output—to recover the file and function relations in a form usable by other tools, such as the Relational Calculator. These tools naturally can be used for other applications and are limited only by the versions of the reverse engineering tools.

A third tool, `ParDsp`, was needed because no tool was available to parse the Assembler code. Although we could have used a reverse engineering tool like Software Refinery (another Reasoning Systems product) to define the grammar and then parse the source code, this approach did not seem worth the effort because the result could be used only for the specific type of Assembler code. Instead, we chose to implement a small tool in Perl that is able to analyze the Assembler source code, taking into account the conditional compilations, to recover the file and call relations of the functions.

These three custom tools were the basis for our recovery of complete views of the TCS application, as will be shown in the next subsection when we discuss how to combine different views.

Integration and Combination of Software Views

View integration and combination are powerful means to generate new abstractions for a system. These views provide new, more complete, or higher-level information such as architectural representations. The benefits of view integration are that it documents the current state of a system, which is essential for many tasks, and that the integrated views provide new insights and inspire more confidence in the recovered views.

Tool-generated views, also based on the results of different tools, can be used together with manually recovered views. Most important is the integration of additional information such as domain knowledge and system documentation.

In our case study we saw that we can generate many interesting views by integrating or combining just a few simple views with additional information. We can generate new views by combining views of the same type or of different types. And we can generate many additional views by combining other basic views of the system (e.g., data views) with already integrated or combined views.

For the TCS case study we integrated and combined many views intensively, mainly to cope with incomplete views (e.g., mixed languages, systems running on different processors) and to integrate human knowledge. Figure 4.12 shows an example of view integration and combination based on source code, system documentation, and domain knowledge to recover a so-called module uses view. We distinguish among three kinds of views:

- **Basic views,** such as call graphs or file views, are generated by reverse engineering tools.

- **Integrated views** are put together from many views of the same type. In our case study, a complete call graph is the integrated view of the call graph of the C part and the call graph of the Assembler part of the TCS.

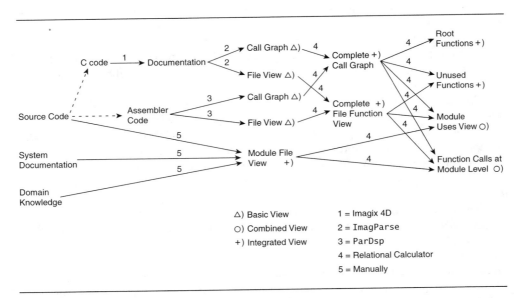

FIGURE 4.12 Integration and Combination of Software Views

- **Combined views** are put together from different types of views. For example, the module uses view of the case study was generated from the complete call graph, the complete file function view, and the module file view.

The tools that were used for the integration and combination of software views were Imagix 4D, ImagPars, ParDsp, and the Relational Calculator. Still, some views, such as the module file view, were generated manually because of lack of tool support.

Our conclusion is that integration of human knowledge is essential because basic views are insufficient for architectural descriptions. Combined or integrated views are useful architectural representations, but current reverse engineering tools do not support such view manipulations.

Other ways of providing additional information are to use different representations of the views (e.g., different layout algorithms for graphs), to use one tool for generating and visualizing all views, and, of course, to generate new views using other tools (e.g., similarity analysis of files).

The techniques of combining and integrating views have both advantages and drawbacks.

Benefits

1. They are powerful methods for generating new abstractions for a system (e.g., simplifications, integrated or combined information content).

2. They are based on recovered views (both manually recovered and tool-recovered views) and thus are independent of source code.

3. They enable the integration of human knowledge.

4. They can create more reliable views on the basis of different views with identical context.

Problems

1. They depend on the correctness of primary recovered views.

2. Views that are to be combined may be inconsistent, incomplete, and semantically mismatched.

4.5.5   Architecture Recovery Process

The architecture recovery process part of the recovery framework consists of guidelines and a process. We present both in this section. The guidelines are generally applicable to any architecture recovery project and should be taken into account in the planning stages. The process is more specific and can be seen as a recipe for how to recover a certain software system. Both the guidelines and the process definition were developed on the basis of our experiences with architecture recovery of the TCS system.

Guidelines

Architecture recovery should follow these guidelines:

1. Identify and state the recovery purpose clearly.

2. Identify and classify the individual information sources that are available for the application, as presented in Section 4.5.2.

3. Identify the domains that are relevant for the application and the associated information that is available for them.

4. Using the information obtained in step 3, identify special architectural notations, relevant architectural properties, yet unidentified architectural properties or aspects, general applicable domain information, and so on, for each domain.

5. With the information obtained in step 2 and the information provided in Section 4.5.3, identify the recovery methods that are applicable.

6. On the basis of the information obtained in steps 1 and 3, choose appropriate notations and description methods for the additional architectural descriptions. See the suggestions given for the individual architectural properties in Section 4.4 and the categorization and discussion of the notations in Section 4.5.1.

7. Recover the architectural properties using the architecture recovery process that is presented next.

Process

The detailed steps of the architecture recovery process are as follows (italics indicate corresponding labels on Figure 4.13, which depicts the process):

1. Select candidate architectural properties to be recovered:

   a) Identify architectural properties (*APs*) that are of interest for the recovery process.

   b) Use the categorizations of the APs to identify aspects associated with them.

   c) Select candidates for architectural properties and related architectural aspects on the basis of system information on the system under study (*Software System*).

2. Identify architectural properties in the system (*Identify AP (X)*).

   a) Choose an appropriate method (*M*) for each architectural aspect to identify it in the system on the basis of the available information.

   b) Using the recovery methods, search for the architectural aspects that represent the architectural properties.

   c) Add additional architectural aspects that are found directly in the system and were not originally candidates.

   d) Add identified and recovered architectural properties to the set of architectural properties of the system (*AP (X)*).

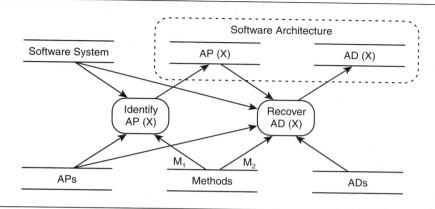

FIGURE 4.13   Architecture Recovery Process

3. Choose appropriate additional architectural description(s) (*ADs*) for the architectural properties.

4. Recover the architectural descriptions of the architectural properties identified (*Recover AD (X)*).

   a) Choose appropriate methods (*M*) to recover the missing descriptions of the architectural aspects identified.

   b) Document the architectural aspects that make up the architectural properties, thereby documenting the architectural properties themselves (*AD (X)*).

5. Build the additional architectural description(s) from the architectural description of the properties (*AD (X)*).

The recovered architectural properties (*AP (X)*) and architectural descriptions (*AD (X)*) are denoted as the software architecture of the system X.

4.6   From Single Systems to a Product Family Architecture

Applying the architecture recovery framework presented in Section 4.5, we are able to recover an architectural description based on architectural properties of single systems. By applying this framework to the presumed members of a product family, we should be able to recover architectural descriptions that, when combined, should represent the common parts as well as the variances of this product family. But although the development of a product family may be based on this architecture, it has shortcomings because it is based only on existing members and does not take into account future family members. Therefore, the recovered family architecture needs to be refined so that it can provide an architecture for product family development. We call this refined architecture a **reference architecture for product family development.**

There are two steps in recovering an architecture for product family development. The first step is the recovery of a product family architecture from the individual single systems that make up the family (this can also be seen as an initial reference architecture). The second is the building of an ideal reference architecture for the development of a product family.

Why are two separate steps required? The most important reason is that these two steps require completely different approaches and yield distinctly useful outputs. Whereas the first step may be automated to some extent, the second can, at most, be interactive—if not completely manual—because it relies largely on human knowledge. The additional benefit of having a product family architecture of the systems that are already successful is also of great importance. Furthermore, the aspects that are identified as variations in the recovered product family may result in a common part in the reference architecture.

Although we think that these two processes can be supported with interactive tools, we are currently doing them manually and have not yet completed our validation experiments and therefore the detailed development of the processes. Thus they are subject to change, and we can present only the general approach here.

The key issue in recovering a product family architecture is to identify the common and diverse parts of the individual systems that make up the family (DeBaud and Girard 1998). We do this by analyzing the commonality of the architectural properties recovered for the individual systems (see Figure 4.4). For this we take the architectural properties as they are, without evaluating them or reasoning about them.

To be able to recover a product family, the available systems and our process must meet certain requirements having to do with the following:

1. **Number of systems required.** The recovery of the product family architecture is based on our framework for recovering the software architecture for single systems. Although we can use as input different versions of the same product, the differences among versions are usually minor, so these would not validate the representation as a product family. As a result, at least two individual systems within a family should be available to make possible the recovery of a product family architecture, although this requirement is, of course, subject to the individual systems and their differences, as well as the kind of product family. As such, the decision of the number and choice of systems required to recover a product family depends on the engineer and the engineer's experience.

2. **Human recovery.** The fact that the recovery of the software architectures of the single systems requires human expertise poses a potential pitfall for the commonality analysis. The reason is that humans are biased and the recovery process is thus prone to individual interpretation. Thus individual systems should be recovered either by one person or by one group and, if possible, the human information sources should also be the same.

3. **Ambiguities of parts.** One problem of our architecture recovery framework is that some parts can seem, or be, ambiguous (e.g., the issue of performance versus safety in implementing a part in hardware). The engineer has to decide to which architectural property a particular part best fits. The chance of thus not identifying common parts can be minimized to some extent if we let one person recover all systems.

4. **Recovered architecture.** The descriptions of the architectural properties originally chosen as candidates for recovery, as well as those of the additional architectural properties recovered, must be documented in ways that allow them to be compared.

5. **Outputs.** As output, we want to identify the common and diverse parts on all levels of an architectural property. This action is required because some aspects may be different (e.g., voting mechanism, different redundancy used) while the overall aspect may be common (e.g., the safety mechanism static redundancy). In other cases, commonality may be found down to the actual implementation of an aspect, and locating commonality at this level requires comparison of the source code.

6. **Grade of difference that distinguishes a common part from a diverse part.** The definition of this grade represents one of the essential challenges for the whole process, and it is one of the reasons why we do the recovery manually. The problem is that this grade can be quite different for different architectural properties and is influenced from the actual implementation up to the individual aspects of a property. As an example, consider a scheduler of the architectural property system control that should require that the scheduled components and their order are identical. The problem here is that the components might have different names but identical functionality, or that two components may have been integrated into one. In addition, if this requirement is satisfied, is the scheduler a common part if it uses a different scheduling algorithm?

To recover common parts, we can take any of various different approaches to commonality analysis. For an example, see Chapter 7.

4.7 From a Product Family Architecture to a Reference Architecture

A **reference architecture** (defined in Chapter 1) is a generic architecture for applications in a given domain. Inventing reference architectures is a difficult task. One of the potential uses of a family architecture is as input to the process of developing reference architectures. Application and domain experts may use the recovered individual architectures and the recovered product family architecture as input for generating the reference architecture.

The required effort, of course, is strongly related to the requirements of future systems. The requirements that were not part of the original system development have to be identified by application and domain experts. The quality of the generated reference architecture—that is, its ability to accommodate changes based on these future requirements—depends on the ability of the engineers to anticipate this future development and to derive an appropriate architecture. To derive such an architecture, we use as input the assessment of the architectures of the individual systems (see Chapter 3) and the product family architecture.

From these perspectives we have derived the following steps for recovering the reference architecture for a product family:

1. Identify future requirements. That is, identify probable variances of future development that were not already taken into account in the recovered systems (e.g., new markets, changes of standards), as well as limitations of the recovered architectures that are limitations for future requirements (e.g., performance, safety issues).

2. Evaluate, and reason about, the recovered product family architecture. Questions such as the following should be investigated:

   - Is the current architecture sound (e.g., are there performance bottlenecks or safety loopholes)?
   - Does the architecture accommodate the variants of the recovered individual systems and future ones in a graceful manner?
   - Can future requirements (such as better performance needed to handle faster data transmission or larger data volume) be satisfied with this current architecture?

3. Evaluate, and reason about, the architectures of the individual systems. The product family architecture should include only common parts that can be identified in all systems. The reference architecture, on the other hand, must take future development into account. Therefore, if one of the recovered systems departs from the general family, a property that is not common is now a requirement. From this viewpoint the recovered architectures of the individual systems should be assessed in the same way as the product family architecture.

4. Generate the reference architecture:

   - Create an initial reference architecture, which is based solely on the product line architecture.
   - Refine the initial reference architecture by repeating steps 2 and 3.
   - Reevaluate the reference architecture to verify that the common parts are sound for all future developments anticipated and that variations can be accommodated in a graceful way to derive the individual systems.
   - Refine the reference architecture until the requirements outlined in step 3 are satisfied.

The result of this process is a reference architecture composed of common parts, a design that can accommodate future requirements, and possibly a repository of reusable parts for the development of new systems.

4.8   Final Remarks

In this chapter we have described the architecture recovery approach that we developed on the basis of the TCS case study to be discussed in Chapter 7. Several important aspects of the TCS led us to the definition of architectural properties that describe aspects such as the following on an architectural level: safety and fault tolerance, hardware/software integration, embedded systems, and so on. We used the TCS to identify and describe architectural properties and completed their description with aspects taken from other systems.

Architectural properties simplify the understanding and effective communication of software systems. They are manageable units for architectural reasoning and help recover the software architecture of a system incrementally. Architectural properties influence each other in many ways and impose a certain recovery order and dependence. In deriving a family architecture, architectural properties facilitate the identification of commonalities.

Reverse engineering tools help us recover information from a system, but the views they generate are not sufficient for architecture recovery. These views need to be integrated and combined to produce architecture-level views, but such integration and combination capabilities are not supported by current reverse engineering tools.

The recovery process is highly dependent on the information available about the system and its application domain, as well as the quality of this information. The integration of human knowledge is an important factor for dependable results in architecture recovery.

From the modeling view, different architectural notations and models, architectural description languages, software views, and recovery methods or tools are required for the recovery of architecture and the description of different architectural properties in a real-world setting.

5

Experiences with Family Architectures for Mass Electronics

Frank van der Linden

In this chapter we describe the experiments that Philips performed within the ARES project. These experiments were concerned with mass electronics development. The main focus of the experiments was architecture description. However, recovery and assessment were also important for Philips; in fact we used these techniques to gain information about the systems we were building. We describe what we did to solve our problems and what experiences we gained from using software architecture for building product families. The ARES approach is a topic-based, top-down approach. Our problems originated from the bottom up within an actual development organization. We had to select relevant problems and map them to the topics addressed by ARES.

Because ARES was meant to use product development as an experimental workbench for our architecture research, we had to define experiments that:

1. Made progress in solving our problems

2. Involved the architects in the product division and promised short-term benefit to those architects

3. Gave us the opportunity to measure (qualitatively or quantitatively) the results of the experiments

We report here on two main experiments—one small, one large. The small experiment dealt with the management of diversity information, an important problem that we encountered. The solution for this problem is given in Sections 5.5.3 and 5.5.4. The large experiment was concerned with finding a solution for many of our problems, addressing point 1 above. To tackle these problems we decided that choosing which tools and languages to adopt and use would be a good starting point toward finding solutions. The rationale behind this decision was to make it difficult for developers and architects to make certain classes of errors; that is, we wanted our tools and languages to support the right decisions, thereby helping to address point 2. We used the ideas underlying Darwin and our own requirements to build a language and tool called Koala (for more information about Darwin and Koala, see Chapter 2). We describe how Koala solved our development problems in Section 5.5, which addresses point 3.

The chapter is organized as follows. We first sketch the context of our experiments. In Section 5.1 the problem domain is more fully described. Next, in Sections 5.2 and 5.3, we describe the context of our experiment in terms of the architectural problems we encountered during product development, and in Section 5.4 we outline the best architecture practices we know.

5.1   The Basics of Mass Electronics Systems

Mass electronics systems are (mainly stand-alone) devices that are bought by a large audience, in most cases for personal use. Philips produces a large variety of these systems that are aimed primarily at the personal entertainment market, such as televisions, video recorders, and audio equipment.

Although most of these products are internally controlled by a microcontroller, most users do not view the equipment as a computer. Only a selected functionality is expected from the equipment, and software replacement is currently not an issue. In this chapter we take the television as an example of a mass electronics system. However, most of our observations and conclusions also hold for other consumer electronics equipment.

A television transforms incoming antenna signals into images and sound. Figure 5.1 is a schematic representation of the signal flow within a television. Signals may come from diverse sources, such as an antenna or a SCART.[1] Sound and images may be displayed on various devices. A large collection of software features is available to enhance and facilitate the user interaction. Examples of such features are picture-in-picture (PIP) and teletext. Most software in a television is used to control the signal stream.

Televisions display a large amount of variation, originating from three sources:

1. User interface diversity
2. Differences in transmission standards
3. Differences between low-end and high-end products

The first two sources of variation are related in part to geographic diversity. Different countries have adopted different transmission standards—e.g., PAL, NTSC, and SECAM—each of which has several variants. Cultural background influences the user interface requirements and the way in which the user views the equipment. Cultural differences originate partly

---

[1]A SCART (Syndicat des Constructeurs d'Appareils Radiorécepteurs et Téléviseurs) is a bus that can be used to interconnect audio and video devices. It may carry both signals and commands.

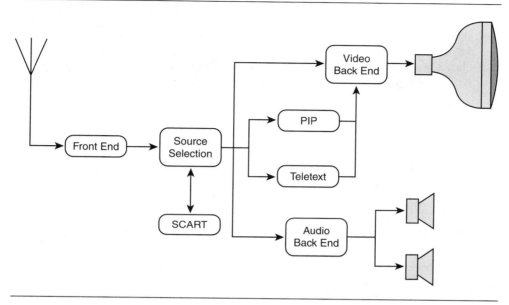

FIGURE 5.1   Signal Flow of a Television

from geographic differences. However, cultural differences may also be related to age, so they can also occur within a single geographic segment. Differences among television sets are expressed by the availability of commercial features, which are the criteria by which televisions are sold.

A television is a reactive system. Its reaction to events coming from peripheral devices depends on its internal state. The events have to be serviced in a timely manner. A user may be disturbed when a reaction to events is not fast enough. Note that not all events come from the user; certain events—for example, characteristics of the input signal—come from other sources.

There is a collection of peripheral hardware units, each acting with its own timing requirements. The central processor must regulate the peripheral hardware, but it usually cannot influence the timing behavior. The processor can communicate to the other devices through an I2C bus.[2]

Hardware costs are crucial for a mass electronics system. Each piece of unnecessary hardware in a design is multiplied by millions in production and will result in a loss of large amounts of income. Therefore we have to consider several resource restrictions—for instance, that the processor must be of limited capacity (certainly not the state of the art in

---

[2]An I2C (inter-IC, where "IC" stands for "integrated circuit") bus is an internal bus, used within consumer electronics equipment.

the case of PCs; price is the main criterion of choice). At present, an 80C51-XA processor is used in high-end televisions. This is a 16-bit version of the 8051. Low-end systems still have 8-bit processors. Televisions also have severe memory constraints. For instance, the ROM size ranges from 32K to more than 1MB. For RAM we consider sizes from 256 bytes to more than 32K (the current high end), and the sizes will be even greater in the future.

To conclude, televisions represent a system family characterized by:

- A short time to market
- A high degree of diversity
- Severe resource restrictions
- Severe time requirements, bordering on real time

5.2 Current Practice in 1995 and How We Worked

In 1995 we developed television software with SPRINT, a formal method designed for the development of control software for audiovisual (AV) systems. SPRINT stands for for *spec*i-fication, *pr*ototyping, and *r*eusability *int*egration; it covers the entire software development cycle except requirements engineering (Jonkers 1993). SPRINT addresses both the development view and the process view, treating the two separately.

In the development view, the fundamental unit of design in SPRINT is the *component*. Because a complete TV system is regarded as the only unit of deployment, each SPRINT component is not necessarily a unit of deployment and therefore not considered to be a "real" component as defined by Szyperski (1997). However, a SPRINT component is a unit of abstraction, analysis, compilation, extension, and maintenance. That is, all hardware and software parts of the system, the system itself, and environmental entities such as users and television stations are viewed as components.

SPRINT components are essentially state transition systems. In our projects, SPRINT components were specified in the formal language COLD (Bergstra and Feijs 1992, Feijs 1993, Feijs and Jonkers 1992, Feijs, Jonkers, and Middelburg 1994, Jonkers 1991, Wirsing and Bergstra 1989). Low-level components were implemented in C or Assembler. Higher-level components were specified in PROTOCOLD, an executable subset of COLD (van Vlij-men and Wamel 1993). A PROTOCOLD compiler compiles PROTOCOLD to efficient (low memory usage) C.

In the process view, all components are seen as state transition systems. Each compo-nent has an interface consisting of a collection of functions, which are classified as follows:

- **Command.** A command is used to trigger a state change within the component.
- **Observer.** An observer is used to query the internal state of a component.
- **Event.** An event is used to inform external components that the component is in a specific set of states. As the scheduler detects events, the listener is awakened and does explicit polling. In reply the listener is informed whether the event is

(still) enabled or disabled. When an event is enabled, the corresponding state change will be executed; otherwise the state change will not be executed.

- **Step.** Each step corresponds to an internal state change. Typically, the run-time environment has a scheduling strategy for determining the order in which steps are executed.

Moreover, each component can have a collection of input and output ports. Input ports are used to model incoming (media) streams that are to be processed by the component. Output ports determine outgoing streams. Examples of such streams are antenna signals and video and audio streams in several formats.

In the development view, connections are made via usage relations. In the process view, connections are made via the design of the run-time environment. This environment determines when enabled commands, observers, events, and steps are executed. The two different means of making connections lead to separate designs in the process and development views.

In the development view, a component A may use another component (B) in two distinct ways (see Figure 5.2):

- Component A may **import** B; that is, component A may call or execute commands, observers, and events of B during its (A's) own state changes. Component B is regarded as residing outside of A. State changes of B do not necessarily imply state changes of A, so B can be imported by many other components.

- Component A may **include** B to implement part of its behavior. In particular, state changes of B imply state changes of A. A component (like A) that includes other components (like B) is called a *compound component.* Component B is not visible outside of the compound component A. Instead, B is regarded as residing inside of A. A component can be included in only one other component. Component B can be imported only by other components

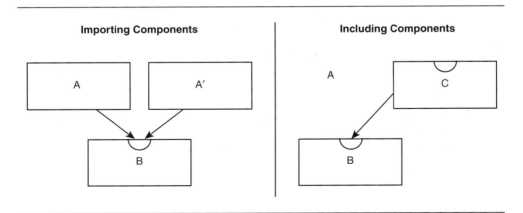

FIGURE 5.2 Importing and Including Components

that are included in A. To make multiple inclusions of B possible, COLD has a mechanism that copies components, resulting in several distinct instances.

The development view of the television architecture consists of eight layers. A **layer** is a logical grouping of components and is itself not considered to be a component. Because of distinct structuring principles, components can be elements of more than one layer. However, layers are used to define dependency restrictions between components. Calls from one layer to another have to be made according to predetermined layer dependencies. In televisions we recognize the following layers:

1. The **hardware layer** contains the hardware components of the system.

2. The components in the **drivers layer** provide a first abstraction of the hardware by lifting the hardware functionality to the software level.

3. The components in the **AV functions layer** turn the hardware functionality provided by the drivers into logical functionality as required for a proper software design.

4. The components in the **AV components layer** are compound components consisting of an AV functions component, a driver component, and a hardware component.

5. The components in the **system control layer** deal with two main things. First, they rearrange, combine, abstract, and extend the functionality offered by the AV components layer in such a way that it matches the functionality needed by the user control layer. As such, the operations offered by this layer correspond to the basic functions from the point of view of the user interface. Second, the components in the system control layer coordinate and control the behavior of the AV components. To this end, the system control layer components contain tasks that handle system-related events.

6. The components in the **user control layer** deal with the interaction process between the end user and the television set.

7. The **resources layer** contains two categories of components. The first category supplies generally applicable services that may (in principle) be used by all components in the system. Examples of such generally applicable services include operating system services, nonvolatile memory services, and communication services (e.g., I2C). The second category controls rather than supplies certain central functions in the system. Examples of such central system functions include initialization and refreshment of the hardware. The components of the first category are often referred to as *resource suppliers* and those of the second category as *resource controllers.*

8. The components in the **domain layer** define the data and signal types that play a role in the application domain.

These layers and the allowed usage relations among the layers are depicted graphically in Figure 5.3. Each component is assigned to at least one layer.

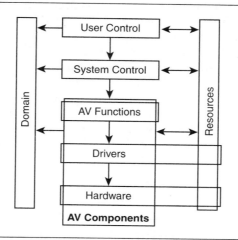

FIGURE 5.3   Layered Architecture

5.3   Architectural Problems

Several problems in television development were caused by the fact that although SPRINT supports components, no component implementation model was available and the developers lacked sufficient awareness of the idea and use of components. In particular, in this model, the following aspects were not clear about a component:

- What it was supposed to be
- What its boundaries were
- What it should capture
- What should be hidden by its border

One of the problems was that no explicit component architecture was available below the layer level. The architecture was available only in the minds of the architects, which meant that in practice it was impossible to conform to the architecture. In the end, the architecture only provided hints with respect to the implementation structure, and it was, for instance, certainly not adequate for training new software engineers. The development architecture was tracked through tool support that visualized the module architecture of developed code (Feijs and van Ommering 1996). Human inspections were used to compare this with the intended architecture, making it possible to correct architecture deviations, but it was not always clear how the result was to be compared with the intended architecture.

The development process was organized through a *specify* → *design* → *implement* cycle. Nobody was clearly responsible for any given part of the software architecture; different groups of developers were responsible for different parts of the system. But in fact everyone shared the overall responsibility for the software architecture. In addition, the developers did not fully realize that software could be constructed as a family. Diversity was incorporated in macros and compiler flags, none of which were limited in application to only a (small) set of components. Moreover, the macros and flags appeared everywhere in the code, making the code hard to read and obscuring the architecture such that no clear overview of the implications of a specific variant could be obtained.

The process architecture was not considered in much detail. Because of resource restrictions, only a few processes were available. Because timing requirements were only informal, it was impossible to design the process architecture well in advance. The timing behavior of the systems that had been built was observed in practice, and fine-tuning was performed afterward.

5.4   Software Family Architecture Considerations

To solve many of the problems we have mentioned, we investigated architecture and development process support. Developing software for a product family requires a conscious decision concerning the boundaries of the family. One approach to family software with which we are acquainted is the building-block approach (van der Linden and Müller 1995a). It is based on a construction set of software components (building blocks) from which a subset must be selected to build products. Many of the considerations we present in this section are based on the building-block approach. These considerations are also the basis of improvements in the software development process for televisions.

5.4.1   Components

If system components and their mutual interfaces are recognized at an early stage of development, the different components can be developed simultaneously, with the work being distributed among many persons at an early stage. In addition, system documentation may be distributed to the system components. All the relevant information of one component can be kept together. Developers need to know only the information relevant to their own component and several closely related components. Thus the amount of communication necessary in large projects is reduced.

We investigated available component models to support component-oriented architecture. Because the component support that can be obtained on the market (COM, CORBA) was too demanding of resources, we invested in creating our own component support targeted at our particular problem domain. To facilitate a switch to commercial component support as soon as it becomes feasible, we took into account the ideas present in external component model support. In addition, the language we developed is based on the ideas underlying Darwin (see Chapter 2). This language is called Koala (see van Ommering 1998 and Chapter 2).

The Koala language is designed to make components self-contained: Everything that is logically connected to a component belongs to the component. But of course, a component cannot be constructed completely independently of the other parts of the system.

5.4.2   Levels of Information

Development of a large system involves a large amount of information—too much for a single architect or developer to maintain control over. To make it possible for an architect to maintain intellectual control over a system, *levels* of information have to be created. The development process is not defined as a process of stepwise refinement; instead it consists of tasks that work on several layers, where higher-layer tasks may guide multiple tasks in lower layers.

Each layer of the development process is assumed to proceed in stepwise refinement from abstract to concrete. In the case of layered processes, a lower-layer process may receive input from a higher-layer process. The higher-layer process determines the architecture to be implemented by the lower-layer process. As the higher-layer process determines components, the lower-layer processes develop these components. Although it may also be necessary to influence the higher layer from a lower one (i.e., through feedback), this is not considered to be the preferred direction. However, such influence may be necessary to maintain consistency among the layers of development.

By assigning the role of software architect to a small group of engineers in our organization, we introduced a development process consisting of two levels. However, more levels may be necessary in the future. An example of such a process is depicted in Figure 5.4. The

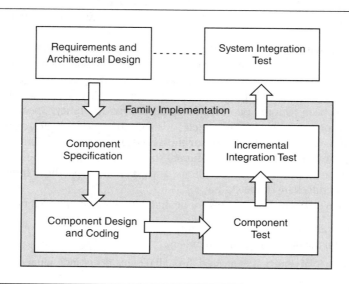

FIGURE 5.4   Layered Development Process

higher layer encompasses requirements and architectural design, family implementation, and system integration testing. The lower layer encompasses component specification, design, coding, and testing; and incremental integration testing.

Another example of such a layered structure, also with two layers, can be found in Jacobson, Griss, and Jonsson 1997. Application Family Engineering (AFE) is the highest layer. The lower layer consists of Component System Engineering (CSE) and Application System Engineering (ASE). The AFE process provides inputs and guides the CSE and ASE processes.

In line with the previous point, the development team should be organized in a way that is consistent with the product family to be developed. In particular, each person in the development organization should be able to act properly with only a limited view of the system. For instance, the layered development process is reflected in the following organization: separate architects and separate development groups for each main component determined by the architecture. Moreover, separate departments may exist for separate concerns (e.g., testing, dynamic aspects, configuration).

5.4.3   Diversity

Components can be made reusable only if they are heavily parameterized (consider, for example, the long property lists of Visual Basic components). Traditionally, such heavy parameterization results in components using lots of RAM and ROM. When addressing resource-constrained systems in Koala, we can parameterize our components heavily because we have tool support that removes undesired flexibility when we are inserting the component into a configuration. The parameterization is necessary for the family of products, and not for individual products. Diversity parameters are implemented outside of the component.

We can deal with diversity only if we recognize it at the architecture level. Different pieces of functionality may be similar to a certain extent. When such similarity is recognized, it is preferably factored out. Such separated functionality is called **generic functionality.** The remains of the different pieces of functionality from which the generic functionality has been factored out are called **specific functionality.** Specific functionality may have the form of parameter lists, which is called **parametric diversity,** but it may also take form in optional components (**structural diversity**). Each product family member consists of the generic functionality, with additional specific functionality. The generic functionality embodies what is common for all its corresponding specific expressions, and it determines the middleware of the system.

We have two different mechanisms for dealing with the two different types of diversity:

- **Structural diversity** is expressed through components that may or may not be present in the different family members.
- **Parametric diversity** is expressed through parameters of individual components.

In the first case the generic part is captured in the structure; in the second case the generic part is captured in the parameterized components. Note that there may be degrees of genericness.

Certain pieces of functionality are common to all members of the family; others are common to only some members. In the latter case we still have generic functionality, but on a smaller scale.

Koala addresses diversity by first separating structural and parametric diversity, and then integrating support for them through the use of diversity (requires) interfaces and switches. The diversity interface is an interface for accessing diversity parameters for the component.

Koala treats structural and parametric diversity in the same way. Structural diversity expresses itself in the presence or absence of components in a configuration. Because each configuration is regarded as a compound component, the configuration may be selected via diversity parameters of the compound component.

5.4.4   Configurations and Diversity Management

As we deal with the architecture of a product family, we must combine components into many configurations, and we must introduce support for dealing with diversity. For each product of the family, the configuration information includes the collection of components that are used. In addition, it determines the parameter values of parameterized components—for instance, by specifying a property list.

To ensure flexibility in future configuration adaptations, requirements must be traceable down to the implementation. When the system has to be updated, it will then be easy to find the implementation components that implement the affected behavior. If the implementation components show one-to-one correspondence with components in each development phase, it will be easy to follow the trace from requirement to implementation.

In addition, a mechanism for updating configurations must be available. Such mechanisms range from reloading or reinitialization to run-time updating facilitated by a broker (Adler 1995). Koala is intended to support various component configurations by:

- Enabling explicit descriptions of configurations in terms of components
- Providing facilities for binding components into configurations in various ways.

Although diversity within a product family is desirable, it may also have a negative impact on the product development. The main reason is that the more diverse the requirements are, the more complex the software will become, which in turn leads to a longer time to market and/or higher development costs. The fact that the product family evolves over time further complicates matters. Although the diversity of the entire product family is not known during the development of the first member of the family, it is expected that new features can be added to subsequent members of the family without a significant amount of the existing software having to be rewritten. However, it is not easy to add new features unless the software was initially designed with these features in mind. In the past such unanticipated addition of features has led to large amounts of the software being rewritten each time a new member of the product family was required.

We can neither simply wait and see and hope that the software architecture is flexible enough to cope with future requirements, nor design the software in such a way that it can cope with all eventualities. In the first case the software may not be flexible enough. In the second case, the problems inherent in the first can hopefully be avoided, but the initial development time is greater because all the eventualities must be considered, however unlikely they may seem. If all the different possibilities are considered, the software produced is likely to be very large and/or complex, which will mean more maintenance.

Abstraction and Configurations

To keep track of the possible and actual configurations, we must manage diversity explicitly. We need to abstract from details (Batory and O'Malley 1992, Jackson and Boasson 1995, Kramer, Magee, and Sloman 1992, Leary 1995). In any situation there may be several sources of abstraction. For our purposes we can identify two:

- **Component abstraction.** Component variants that perform similar functionality have the same abstract component.
- **Interface abstraction.** Interfaces that provide similar functionality have the same abstract interface.

In diversity management we analyze the product family using *abstract components* and *abstract interfaces*. Abstract components and interfaces describe the stable part of the product family architecture—that is, the framework within which all members of the product family should fall. They hide the diversity. Component and interface variants, on the other hand, describe the diversity that is currently foreseen within each abstract component, and consequently within the whole family.

Abstract components provide the means for generating overviews of the product family, either in general terms or in terms of the supported diversity. Obviously it is not possible to foresee all diversity initially, and therefore family evolution has to be taken into account. We design and implement the component variants using the Koala component model. The order in which abstract components, component variants, and Koala components are identified is not straightforward.

In a given configuration, each abstract component corresponds to a collection of component variants, and each abstract interface corresponds to a collection of interfaces. The notion of *relationships* is even more abstract than that of abstract interfaces. In fact, it is not an interface abstraction but an abstraction of a binding. Connections between the abstract entities are consistent with connections between the components and interface variants. An **abstract binding** is an artifact introduced to describe bindings between abstract interfaces.

Because the large number of component variants gives rise to an even larger number of potential configurations, it is necessary to explicitly manage the architecture of the product family and how the individual configurations fit into this architecture. We propose managing diversity through three different kinds of documentation within the development view:

- **Structure** describes the family architecture in terms of abstract components. In such a representation the abstract components and their (abstract) relationships are determined. This is a representation of everything that is fixed within the family; that is, all the family members must be consistent with this architecture.

- **Flexibility** provides an overview of the diversity in the entire family. We describe flexibility using component variants and interfaces. The following aspects are covered:

  - The variants of a given abstract component, including which abstract components are optional
  - The possible ways in which the variants of all the abstract components can be combined

- **Configuration** determines which combinations are actually used to build family members.

Not all the diversity for the entire product family can be documented at one time. However, if foreseeable effects of diversity are considered at an early stage, it is possible to minimize the risks of a poorly designed software architecture. Furthermore, as the product family evolves, there will be changes to the family architecture. New features may become important, or other implementation options may occur. Therefore the family architecture has to be updated to allow for such changes. Updating the family architecture means updating the structure and flexibility, and possibly also the configuration documentation. Of course, the structure, flexibility, and configuration must be kept consistent with each other. For instance, when an actual configuration does not conform to the structure or the flexibility, depending on the situation the structure, flexibility, and/or the configuration should be adapted. This is all part of the management of diversity.

Each product family has usually only a single structure and only a single flexibility, but many configurations. The structure and the flexibility determine the extent of the family, and together the structure, flexibility, and extent determine the **family architecture.** The flexibility and configuration both deal with diversity information. Therefore they constitute the **family diversity.**

In theory, any collection of variants of the abstract components of the family configuration will give rise to a configuration. In practice, however, this cannot be assumed, for the following reasons:

- In many cases variants of abstract components can be combined with only specific variants of other abstract components. This limitation may be dictated by both functional and quality requirements.

- Certain abstract components do not have to be instantiated in all the configurations because the functionality is not necessary, or because in certain cases it may be provided by other components as well.

- Not all combinations will yield sensible products, as is the case with combinations of low-end and high-end features.

For each kind of interface abstraction we introduce the following views:

- The **relationship view** shows only the relationships between the (abstract) components.

- The **abstract interfaces view** shows abstract interfaces between the (abstract) components.
- The **interfaces view** gives the interface variants.

Hierarchy

Since we are dealing with a hierarchical system, our abstract-component models should allow subcomponents. The fact that we are dealing with a hierarchical component model is a complicating factor but not a problem (van der Hamer et al. 1998). It means that the abstractions must also be hierarchical. However, the level of abstraction of the components and their subcomponents may differ, as we will demonstrate. If we define these levels correctly, we will automatically end up with a layered development process

In a hierarchical system each component variant may have a substructure consisting of subcomponents, as Figure 5.5 illustrates. We provide here a relationship view, so no directions and cardinalities are assigned to the interface connections. At the top level is one abstract component: A. Once this component has been identified, we can create structure and flexibility diagrams. The top left-hand side of Figure 5.5 shows the internal structure diagram for A. On the right-hand side we have a flexibility diagram for A (arrow 1). Each of the elements in this flexibility diagram—B_1, B_2, C_1, and D_1—have their own structure, described

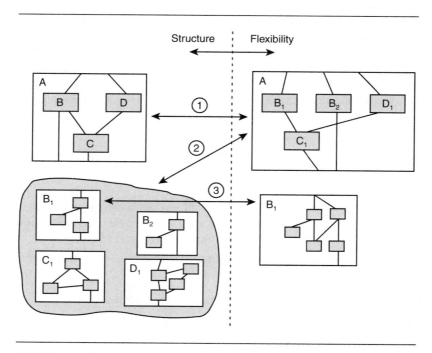

FIGURE 5.5   Abstraction and Hierarchy

in terms of abstract components (arrow 2). Flexibility for these elements may be available recursively, as is shown for B_1 (arrow 3).

Let's consider the possible steps in designing a component—say, A—that has substructure:

- An (abstract internal) structure may be determined (see Figure 5.5, top left).
- The structure may be refined:
    - More relationships are added—for example, a connection between B and D in the structure diagram.
    - An abstract subcomponent may be replaced by a configuration of others— for example, D by a configuration of components (say, E, F, and G).
    - The flexibility may be determined or adapted according to the refinements at the structure level (see Figure 5.5, top right), leading to (more) variants of the higher-level component;
    - An abstract subcomponent may be designed in more detail or adapted according to the adaptations of the flexibility of A, leading to (more) variants of itself—for example, the introduction of B_1 and B_2 at the location of B.

Note that the diagram in Figure 5.5 does not specify an order in which actions have to be taken. In a top-down way we may proceed from high-level structure, via high-level flexibility (arrow 1), to low-level structure (arrow 2) and low-level flexibility (arrow 3). In a bottom-up way we may proceed from component instances and a flexibility diagram, via an abstract structure (arrow 3), to component instances and flexibility at a higher level (arrow 2), to a higher-level structure (arrow 1). In an actual situation, both top-down and bottom-up activities may be performed, meeting somewhere in the middle. In an actual evolution scenario, initially only partial flexibility diagrams may exist, which may be adapted later, resulting in a need for new structure diagrams at a lower level. Technology evolution may lead to new low-level components that can be put in flexibility diagrams, which may affect structure diagrams at that level, resulting in new flexibility diagrams at a higher level.

5.4.5   Standards and Tool Support

Of course, the architect does not only decompose the system into components. Another important responsibility is to determine rules, guidelines, and standards for the design (and implementation) of all the components. Many issues can be settled in standards determined by the architecture. Emergent properties of the system require low-level design considerations on an architectural level. These considerations restrict the design freedom of the component designers. To avoid the repetition of these considerations in the component specification, they are not stated there but are used as direct input for the component design.

The development of single components follows the standard that is set by the architecture. In this way a coherent system is designed, and the conceptual integrity of the system is guaranteed. Standards may

- Reduce the number of unexpected problems. A single solution (or a few) is (pre)determined to deal with a set of anticipated problems.

- Prescribe design patterns (Gamma et al. 1994) to solve selected design problems. In this way similar design problems will be solved in similar ways.
- Make possible automation and CASE tool support. For example, standard code fragments can be generated automatically.
- Lead to the generation of designs and documentation.

To address these issues, we concentrated on language and tool support in the experiments we did within ARES, leading to the Koala tool and language. The Koala tool is a CASE tool that generates a lot of standard code fragments. For instance, it recognizes several patterns for which code generation is automated. Components (and configurations) are described in a component description language (CDL). Interfaces are described in an interface definition language (IDL). These standards enforce similarity of the descriptions. The description of a component contains a description of:

- External interfaces
- Internal component instances and internal code modules
- Interface connections

The description closely resembles hardware parts and net lists.

Because of resource constraints, components are implemented in C. We have a large amount of experience in writing resource-efficient C code, and this knowledge is not easily transferable to other languages, such as C++. In the build plane, a component is a set of C and header files in a single directory, which may freely include and use each other but may not refer to any file outside of the directory. This is an architectural rule that must be obeyed and is easy to check. The consequence of this rule is the enforcement of using the `requires` and `provides` interfaces as provided by the architecture. All intercomponent communication is handled through interfaces. The Koala tool uses `requires` interfaces and the collection of internal interface bindings to generate the right header files for internal use within the component. It uses `provides` interfaces to generate header files for external use. This mode of operation is similar to the GenVoca approach of software generation (Batory and O'Malley 1992).

For identification purposes, each component has a globally unique identifying type name (**long name**). Moreover, for usage within source code, each component type has a globally unique **short name,** consisting of, say, four characters.

A function f in a `provides` interface p of a component C with short name c is implemented in C as `c_p_f`. A function f in a `requires` interface r of a component is called as `r_f`. A call of `r_f` in one component arrives at `c_p_f` in another component through a `#define` statement:

```
#define r_f(...) c_p_f(...)
```

These statements are generated by the Koala tool that reads CDLs and IDLs and produces the appropriate header files to be included by component implementations. Note that the name `c_p_f` must be globally unique (hence the use of c), but the name `r_f` has as scope only the calling component and is unique within that scope. We find this technique very useful in our current applications, which include up to a million lines of code.

Our tools support a number of binding strategies for components. In the next four subsections we discuss how different kinds of components may be connected together at different binding times.

Late Binding

The trend in binding techniques is to shift the moment of binding from compile time to link time to initialization time to run time. Our model supports various forms of late binding, but to explain them, we must introduce another timescale relevant for the development of embedded software.

Consider the binding and instantiation decisions that have to be made to develop a running system. Some decisions can be made in the *design plane,* when the component is designed. As we strive for configuration-independent components, a potentially large number of decisions must be postponed to the *configuration plane.* Even in this plane, not all decisions can be made because it is common to generate a single ROM mask to support a variety of products. Option bits in a nonvolatile memory (set in the factory) can then be used at the *restart plane* to complete the binding decisions.

The strengths of our approach are (1) that binding in the configuration plane will not necessarily mean link-time binding and (2) that the component designer need not know beforehand whether non–design plane decisions are made at the configuration plane or at the restart plane. We achieve this flexibility as follows:

Each diversity parameter is defined by a C macro within the component (following our binding implementation conventions). A component designer may treat such a parameter as a normal function and write, for instance:

```
if ( div_param() ) { do_something(); }
```

The parameter may be set to false at configuration time. The system can then be (re)compiled, and the compiler will throw away the "do something" clause, resulting in optimal code. The parameter may also be defined as a run-time function, thereby causing diversity to be resolved at run time.

Note that `requires` interfaces that contain diversity functions are called **diversity interfaces.** In the model, however, diversity functions can be (and are) freely intermixed with normal `requires` functions. The mechanism used here can also be applied for other `requires` interfaces.

Because most compilers are not able to remove unused variables and unused local functions, a second feature can be used by the component designer to aid the compiler. A special macro is generated if the diversity parameter is assigned a constant at configuration time. This macro can be used to guard certain constructs with `#ifdef` statements.

Function Binding

The diversity interface is connected by its tip to perhaps other interfaces, but ultimately through a chain of such bindings to a module. The module may implement the function in C, in which case the Koala tool has no knowledge of it and cannot optimize. Alternatively, the function can be implemented in a CDL in a subset of the C expression language, using constants, operators, and functions available through other interfaces. This option allows the Koala tool to perform optimizations such as constant expression folding.

This mechanism enables a convenient treatment of diversity parameters. We can calculate diversity parameters of inner components by using expressions that contain constants and outer diversity parameters (the flow of information is usually inward). In other words, we obtain an object-oriented spreadsheet of diversity parameters, which allows us to express diversity in different terms at different levels of aggregation.

An interesting side effect of this spreadsheet approach is that the Koala tool can calculate certain design properties, such as memory usage at configurations, if basic components export this information through provides interfaces and compound components perform the correct calculation and export the information again.

Switches

Our binding tool for Koala knows about switches. If a switch is set at configuration time to a certain position, the other component is removed from the configuration (if it has no other connections), and the connection to the remaining component is the same as in the case of static binding (with zero overhead). If the switch setting is not known at configuration time, some form of code is generated (e.g., a set of `if` statements or a VTable technique) to connect the interfaces, and all components are included in the configuration. Naturally this process is executed recursively for compound components.

In normal cases the switch for the searching tuner in Figure 5.6 is set at configuration time. Then only one of the components—hardware-searching tuner or software-searching

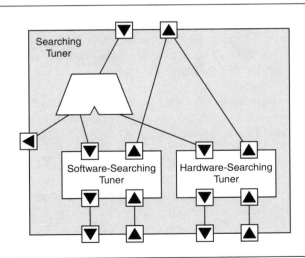

FIGURE 5.6 A Koala Switch

tuner—is incorporated in the code. In a very advanced situation an additional simple tuner may be available to enable graceful degradation. When the hardware-searching capabilities of the tuner fail, software searching may take over. In this case the configuration parameter can be changed at run time, and code for both components should be included in the product.

Optional Interfaces

An optional interface has an implicit extra function called `iPresent`, which acts as a Boolean diversity parameter. It is `true` if the tip of the interface is connected to a nonoptional interface, `false` if the tip is not connected at all, and defined within the module if the tip is connected to a module. If the optional interface is connected to the base of another optional interface, the `iPresent` function inherits the value of the corresponding function in the other interface.

At the base side of the interface, the function can be used to establish whether the other functions in the interface may be called at run time. Koala will generate the necessary stubs for dangling interfaces to ensure that the software compiles and links correctly.

In our example, the new interfaces may be connected to a new module, and `iPresent` of the `provides` interface may be equated to `iPresent` of the `requires` interface. If the component is used without connecting the optional `requires` interface, the optional functionality is not available.

5.5   Dealing with the Architectural Problems

In the following sections we describe how we dealt with the architectural problems we encountered. We will focus on the following issues:

- Compound components
- Software architecture visibility
- Diversity parameters
- Resource restrictions
- System dynamics

5.5.1   Compound Components

Compound components are an important ingredient in television development because they make it possible to build components recursively out of other components. Compound components form part of the SPRINT method, as well as the Koala language.

Because they lacked a proper understanding of components, the developers were not always sure whether they were dealing with a compound component or with a subcomponent. This confusion can best be illustrated by the example of Chapter 2. Refer to Figure 5.7, which presents two views of so-called AV components of the television. In this particular case we will consider the tuner component.

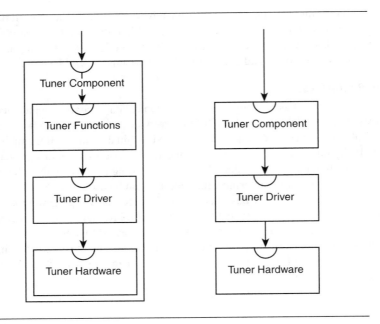

FIGURE 5.7 Compound Components?

On the left, the tuner component is regarded as a compound component that is subdivided into a hardware component, a driver component, and a component providing tuner functions. On the right, the tuner component is regarded not as a compound component, but as a component at the same level in the "part-of" hierarchy as the hardware and driver components.

In television development these two views were used interchangeably and were assumed to be equivalent because they both carry the same interface. Thus the difference between tuner functions and the tuner component was not clear. Although this difference may seem innocent at first glance, it is actually a crucial mistake. The reason is related to encapsulation. For instance, on the right-hand side of Figure 5.7 other components may access the driver component and leave it in a state that is not expected by the tuner component. The result, in turn, may be unexpected errors.

Compound components are supposed to encapsulate their internal components in a way that is similar to how noncompound, or basic, components encapsulate their state variables. That is, the internal components of a compound component may not be used directly by components at a higher level in the "part-of" hierarchy. Because of this confusion, this principle was violated in a rather dramatic way in the television, in particular in the system layer.

By using the Koala component model, we solve the problem through the following features:

- The differentiation between component instances and component types
- The control of component access completely through interfaces, which is enforced by the Koala tool
- The use of `provides` and `requires` interfaces

Within the Koala component model, all the component *types* reside at the same level. Each type encapsulates only its internal structure, which may contain *instances* of other components. Access to these instances is completely regulated by the component's own interfaces. External components cannot have direct access to the encapsulated instances. When the functionality of the encapsulated component is needed, external components can only `require` a particular interface providing that functionality. Different components cannot access an instance within a compound component. Instead, they can only use another component providing the same interface, or *another instance* of the same component. A component may provide interfaces already provided by an internal component, either by forwarding or through a special implementation.

To summarize, in the Koala component model:

- Component borders are more visible to the developers.
- Unauthorized reuse is made impossible.
- Configurations of components are guarded by higher-level designs.

5.5.2   Software Architecture Visibility

The software architecture for televisions was not visible, in part because the software structure was originally simple and could be shared with all developers. When the development group expanded, it became impossible for both the new developers and the experienced developers to grasp all the details of the architecture. Specific people were made responsible for different parts and/or views of the architectures, and no consistent overall view existed. Moreover, there was not enough documentation specifying the architecture.

During development, architectural problems were solved locally by changes that violated unwritten rules about the architecture. Even though these changes were not consistent with the intended architecture, or with the beliefs of the other developers, it was difficult to detect such violations. Tool support was used to obtain diagrams of actual components and their relationships. However, this information could not be checked through comparison with the intended architecture because the architecture was not documented.

The Koala component model solves this problem in the following ways:

- There is a top-down hierarchy of four layers of constituent components.
- There are people (architects) who are responsible for certain components at a certain level in the hierarchy. These people must configure and glue lower-level components in order to develop their own component. They are clients of lower-level component developers.

- Component types and interfaces are laid down in specifications. Component builders can trust the specifications of other components and interfaces. A change request procedure is in place to deal with changes in component or interface specifications.

- Simple configuration management support is available for dealing with different versions of components. Each component has its own directory. It may not refer to anything outside of its directory, nor does it need to, because the Koala tool support generates the right header files.

- Tool support is still used to obtain views of the actual situation. However, we can compare the actual with the intended situation because the actual situation is documented.

5.5.3 Diversity Parameters

Diversity was incorporated in macros and compiler flags, with applicability over all components. Because of the large number of such diversity parameters and their lack of structure, there was no clear overview of the variants within the family. Parameters were used to modify the internal workings of components and/or to modify dependency relationships. There was no way of determining the consequences of a given setting, except by inspecting all code files. Such an inspection was, of course, infeasible. Neither was there any overview of the feasible combinations of the parameters.

We have unburdened the component developer by making it unnecessary for him or her to decide whether binding and instantiation can be realized at configuration time, link time, initialization time, or even run time. Instead these decisions are postponed to the level of the configuration that contains the instances of the component. This postponement is realized via the uniform mechanism of diversity interfaces of Koala and the tool support that recognizes constants at compilation time.

Each diversity parameter either is a constant at compilation time or is a function to be evaluated at run time. In the case of a compile-time constant, code optimization will be performed. If the parameter is defined as a run-time function, we rely on run-time diversity resolution. All the code necessary for this situation is available in the compiled code. This means that the code is larger but more flexible. Because of the direct feedback on compiled code size, the developer who configures the system may consciously trade flexibility for code size, selecting an optimum for the system at hand.

5.5.4 Resource Restrictions

For mass electronics systems, the resource constraint problems are abundant. RAM and ROM sizes are small, and the processor is slow. To deal with these problems, we introduced Koala tool support.

The Koala tool support deals with code size efficiency by taking several optimization actions. In particular, it removes the interfaces at compile time, thereby removing all component borders. Calls that are directed toward interfaces are directed to the place in the code where they can be executed.

The basis for additional code size efficiency is the observation that when there is enough information to configure at run time, this information can be used at earlier stages to obtain less flexible but more resource-efficient configurations (Batory and O'Malley 1992). Note that diversity information of the televisions is resolved at four stages:

1. Compile time
2. Factory time
3. Initialization time
4. Run time

Diversity information that is resolved at compile time gives rise to the greatest code size efficiency. Because the Koala tool recognizes constants and a collection of simple C-like expressions, it can perform partial evaluation. Choices that are resolved at compile time determine pieces of source code that will not appear as compiled code.

Because of factory restrictions, the number of ROM masks in use is limited. Several configurations are put on the same mask. We select any specific configuration by setting the appropriate parameters at factory time. The code size reduction for diversity that is resolved at factory time is less than for diversity resolved at compile time. However, Koala can still do a partial evaluation, which may result in less compiled code.

For the other two stages of resolving diversity, the diversity parameters are set in RAM. Thus the software must be able to deal with all possible values of the parameters. In particular, less code size efficiency is possible.

To achieve the largest amount of code size efficiency, the diversity should be resolved as early as possible. In particular, the decision of which configurations are put on which masks must be considered carefully. Effective diversity management should support this choice.

5.5.5   System Dynamics

In the development of televisions, system dynamics were originally not handled well. It was not recognized that the system dynamics need their own descriptions, providing their own view (Kruchten 1995, Soni, Nord, and Hofmeister 1995). Only after the system is built can observations regarding time restrictions be made. In many cases, however, this is too late. To deal with time restrictions at an earlier stage, we can use rate monotonic analysis (RMA) (see Chapter 3). To apply RMA, we need to have a defined process architecture. To deal with the other resource restrictions, the process architecture must be compatible with the Koala model for the development architecture. Therefore, calls should be made only via requires interfaces.

We have considered adding events, threads, and tasks to the Koala model. An important ingredient of the dynamic architecture view is dealing with events. Instead of defining an event-handling mechanism in our model, we signal events through outgoing (requires) interfaces (as in Visual Basic). A component that uses the services of another component should provide an event-handling interface that can be connected to the event-signaling interface. We are dealing with a multithreaded system. In order not to adapt Koala for dealing with events, we decided to treat event calls as Koala function calls. Functions in event interfaces are thus called on the thread of the component raising the event. As a consequence, the general rule is that the handling must be quick and nonblocking.

Even though the Koala model is capable of supporting event subscription, we have not included it in the dynamic architecture view. In our systems there is usually one (product-specific) destination for events. We implement event subscription at the configuration level through interface binding. In the rare cases that it is necessary, we also implement event multicasting at the configuration level, using glue modules wherever possible.

Our systems consist of many components, but resource constraints force us to use only a few threads. We declare threads not in basic components, but at the configuration level. Each component may implement its time-consuming activities in terms of tasks that are scheduled synchronously by a task manager running in a global thread. To do this, a component requires a thread ID through a virtual-thread `requires` interface, and it creates its tasks on such virtual threads. The component that implements process support provides the thread interfaces. This component, in fact, is implementing the process architecture. In the configuration plane, this component takes the (many) virtual threads and maps them to the (few) physical threads, thus enabling Gomaa's principle of task inversion (also called thread sharing) (Gomaa 1993).

A component may have tasks that operate on different timescales and thus have to be implemented in different physical threads. It then requires two (or more) virtual-thread interfaces, which will be mapped to different physical threads at configuration time. In this case the component must ensure that the different activities are properly synchronized internally.

There are several ways of defining activities. The SDL style defines an activity in event/action pairs. The Ada style defines an activity as a parallel procedure execution triggered by explicit activation. We use an SDL style of programming for simple activities, but for activities for which the Ada style of programming is more appropriate, a thread may be created within a component.

5.6   Final Remarks

Originally our television software development concentrated on quality. To achieve products of high quality, we used a formal method and language—SPRINT and COLD, respectively—for specification and high-level implementation. Architectural concerns inspired the design of COLD to be able to deal with components. Within television development, however, as with the development of many other technologies, the architecture was not well incorporated into the development process. For this reason the COLD components were not embedded in a well-described architecture, and the result was many problems, for instance, in the way diversity was handled.

We began our experiments by analyzing the architectural problems we had encountered during product development. The results of these analyses are reported in Sections 5.2 and

5.3. At the same time we evaluated the best practices of software architects and formulated them to be used for our case. These best practices are described in Section 5.4. In one case we also tried to include an experiment on the introduction of explicit diversity management according to the best practices of hardware diversity management (see Sections 5.5.3 and 5.5.4). Note that this experiment is closely connected to architecture description.

To ensure better support for components, configurations, and diversity, we introduced the Koala component model and tool. Even though we deviated from the use of a formal method, the main ingredients of COLD are now incorporated in the Koala model and tool support. The developers must follow the restrictions established by Koala to build the system. Therefore, high quality is still guaranteed, but by different means. Of course, a good architecture is still needed, and this is a requirement that Koala cannot enforce.

Once the best practices had been described, we determined that language and tool support would be necessary to solve many of our problems. Using the experience of Darwin, we developed our own language, Koala, and tool support. The way in which Koala solves our problems is described in Section 5.5, which shows that many of the identified problems were solved.

The Koala model is currently used for describing and implementing the architecture of future televisions. In particular, diversity and resource concerns are supported by Koala. The explicit `provides` and `requires` (multiple) interfaces facilitate the generation of views of the system and keep views local. Diversity interfaces are an important tool for dealing with diversity. The Koala tool takes the configuration and diversity problems out of our hands. Our main concerns are what the diversity parameters within our system are, and where they should be placed. Compound components may transform the external diversity parameters into diversity parameters understandable by their subcomponents. We have investigated whether we can use an abstraction mechanism that separates diversity from genericness, but we do not yet have enough experience with that to report on it.

Because of the clear component model in Koala, we are able to develop different components separately, and even to outsource component developments. We still use tool support to compare the existing component structure with the one determined by the architecture, but because the architecture is more explicit, we are better able to resolve problems arising from discrepancies.

We use rate monotonic analysis (RMA) for dynamic analysis. We have separate architecture and component development processes. We have started work with architecture reviews, although that work is still in an informal stage. The development managers are now more aware of the need for a separate architecture process and a corresponding organization.

In the last few years we have introduced a defined development process. We have clear roles for architects and developers at different levels in the component hierarchy. We now have a more mature architecture process installed, but we still have to improve it. The Koala model helps us in dealing with diversity coupled to resource constraints. The Koala tool provides efficient implementations. Our component supports the concerns of component reuse.

6

Simple Things That Work: Learning from Experiences with Telecommunications

Anssi Karhinen, Juha Kuusela, Alessandro Maccari, Alexander Ran, Tapio Tallgren, Juha Tuominen, Jianli Xu

One of the responsibilities of the Nokia team as an industrial partner in the ARES consortium was to provide material for case studies in applying architecture-based techniques to the development and evolution of software for product families. In accordance with ARES philosophy, such material was derived from existing implementations of product families. Case studies also exemplified specific business- or development-related problems. Consequently, a major result of our work is the identification and analysis of architecture-related problems that software developers and managers face.

Some of the problems we identified in our systems were known problems for which various solutions had already been proposed, including difficulties in:

- Describing software architectures
- Understanding and analyzing architectural descriptions for qualities such as performance characteristics
- Managing consistency among different architectural views
- Managing conformance of an implementation of software to its architectural descriptions
- Documenting architectural decisions, including the order in which they were made, and tracing architectural decisions to requirements and preceding architectural decisions
- Structuring software to achieve reuse within a product family and support the evolution of that product family

The ARES consortium used the case studies that represented these problems to evaluate and improve existing research proposals for solving the problems. We did not limit our attention to the approaches popular with the software architecture research community. Thus, for example, in the discussion of modeling execution architecture (Section 6.4), we describe our experience in analyzing the performance of software on an architectural level using a Colored Petri Net (*Design/CPN occurrence* 1996, *Design/CPN reference* 1993) simulation tool.

In some cases the approaches we were familiar with did not address some of the essential aspects of the problem. Such was the case with the documentation of architectural decisions. The common approach uses requirements to motivate and explain architectural decisions. We found that in reality many architectural decisions may be understood and motivated only by preceding architectural decisions. The structure of design decision trees (Ran and Kuusela 1996a) addresses this aspect of documenting architectural decisions and dealing with design rationale.

Some of the problems we identified were new to the ARES consortium and possibly to a wider software architecture research community. Such problems did not have ready solutions to try. In these cases we worked on developing and formulating a proposal for a possible solution by:

- Representing in design the variation that exists in the product family
- Dealing with unstructured feature and implementation variation
- Structuring the interfaces of large software components

Some of these proposals we tried out only on small-scale examples, and in this respect they are not different from other research proposals. However, the problems they address were identified in real industrial systems. In this chapter we describe several such research proposals. We see these descriptions as a necessary first step that will enable experiments on a wider scale.

Some other proposals have already been tried in actual product development. For example, our model for describing interfaces of complex software components has been applied to the description of the interfaces of modules in mobile phone cellular system software. As another example, the concept of interface objects has influenced the design of a new Nokia product for communication networks. Others are still waiting their turn.

In the following sections we describe the domain of our case studies for the benefit of readers not familiar with telecommunication. We then give examples of architectural problems identified in the Nokia case studies. These examples should provide an overview of problems of developing software architecture for product families. We follow this discussion with sections presenting research proposals that address problems described earlier and describing our experience in applying some earlier approaches to these problems—some simple things that work.

6.1   The Nokia Case Studies

We had two industrial cases for the purposes of the ARES project. They were used as the source of information on real systems (industry as laboratory) for different research studies and experiments. The two cases were the telecommunication network (switching) product family from Nokia Networks and the digital mobile (cellular) phone product family from Nokia Mobile Phones.

The size of the software in both cases is very significant. These systems consist of millions of lines of code in different programming, definition, and management languages. Support systems, development processes, and development environments for both are necessarily complex. Development and maintenance organizations consist of hundreds of people.

We will include in the following descriptions enough information about the products and organizations to give an idea of the diversity of features and capabilities that the software architectures of these product families need to support.

6.1.1   Nokia Switching Product Family

Nokia Networks has a family of telecommunication network products for public, private, and cellular networks. The product family has grown steadily through the years with the introduction of new application areas and standards. The core network products can be divided into two main domains: fixed networks such as traditional public switched telecom networks (PSTNs), and cellular radio networks such as AMPS (Advanced Mobile Phone Service), GSM (Global System for Mobile Communications), PDC (Personal Digital Cellular system), and PMR (Private Mobile Radio).

A typical switching network has several types of network elements (Figure 6.1). Switching elements, such as telephone exchanges, create the connections in the network. Transmission networks handle the point-to-point transfer of voice and data. Depending on the network type, there can be fixed access elements (called remote subscriber stages) or wireless access elements (such as base station controllers and base transmission systems). A network can also have service elements for specific functionality such as billing (billing centers) or customer care (e.g., Home Location Register).

The whole product family of switching network elements is called **DX 200.** It uses the DX 200 fault-tolerant computing platform, on top of which product-specific functionality is implemented (Figure 6.2). There is also a higher-level platform for switching products in the DX 200 family. It contains functionality that is common to all network elements that perform switching in the network.

The organization of Nokia Networks somewhat reflects the product structure. There are separate departments for the platform and for different DX 200 products. In the subsections that follow we briefly introduce some of the DX 200 products to illustrate how the domains in which these products operate differ and how different their requirements might be. Significant differences in application domains and product requirements make it especially challenging to construct these products as a single family. Our examples of Nokia Networks products are not necessarily the most recent ones, but they serve the purpose of demonstrating the variance in the requirements for different product variants in the family.

Fixed Networks

Fixed networks are the traditional telephone networks, in which the subscriber interface is made of copper wire (Figure 6.3). Originally these networks were completely analog. Today,

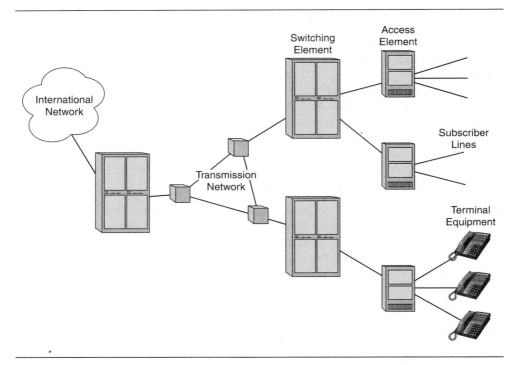

FIGURE 6.1   Switching Network

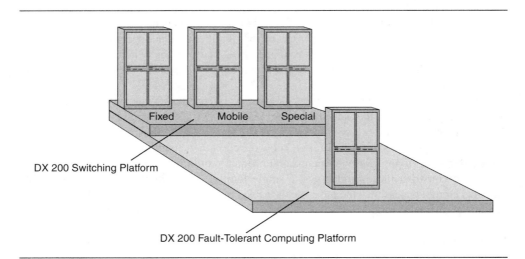

FIGURE 6.2   The Platform Architecture of DX 200

only the last tens of meters at the subscriber end are analog. The transfer and processing of voice and the constantly growing volume of data are digital inside the network. Recently, digital subscriber interfaces such as ISDN (Integrated Services Digital Network) and ADSL (Asymmetric Digital Subscriber Line) have also started gaining popularity.

The range of fixed network products offers a wide scope of service features and capacity levels, covering the full PSTN system. Many special features are available, including the virtual company switchboard (Centrex), IN (Intelligent Network) services, and VPN (Virtual Private Networks). These services are provided for both ISDN and analog subscribers.

The principal products in the DX 200 family for fixed networks have been the following:

- DX 210 exchange, for smaller-capacity fixed local, trunk, and combined networks. It handles 5,000 subscriber lines and 50,000 busy-hour call attempts (BHCAs).

- DX 220 high-capacity exchange, aimed at fixed local, trunk, and combined network applications. It has a subscriber line capacity of 100,000 and a call capacity of 1 million BHCAs.

- DX 200 ISC (International Switching Center), for international exchange operation. It is compliant with the ITU-T signaling system No. 7, No. 5, and R2D.

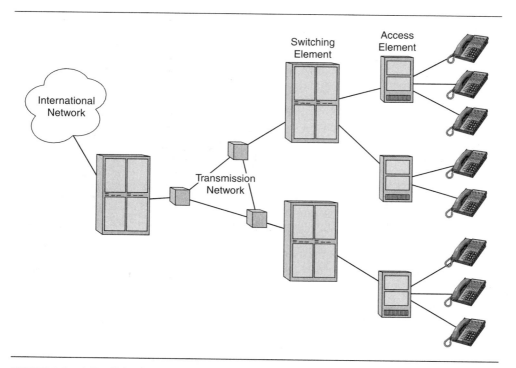

FIGURE 6.3 A Traditional Fixed Telephone Network

- DX 200 RSS (Remote Subscriber Stage), an access node to connect remote subscribers to DX 200 exchanges. It supports ISDN and POTS (*p*lain *o*ld *t*elephone *s*ervice) interfaces. It is available in two capacities, for handling up to 240 or up to 1,020 subscriber lines.

- DAXnode 5000, a concentrating access node that provides open, switch-independent interfaces between the local exchange and the access network.

Cellular Radio Networks

Cellular networks offer mobile access to telephone networks. There are both analog (e.g., AMPS, NMT [Nordic Mobile Telephone]) and digital (e.g., GSM, CDMA [Code Division Multiple Access]) radio access methods. Although the functionality offered to subscribers is very similar to that of fixed networks, the management of mobility of the terminals carries with it special requirements for mobile phone networks. These requirements are satisfied by special network elements such as the Home Location Register.

Nokia Networks business units provide switching and exchange equipment and base stations for both analog and digital mobile networks (Figure 6.4). The main cellular switching products have been the following:

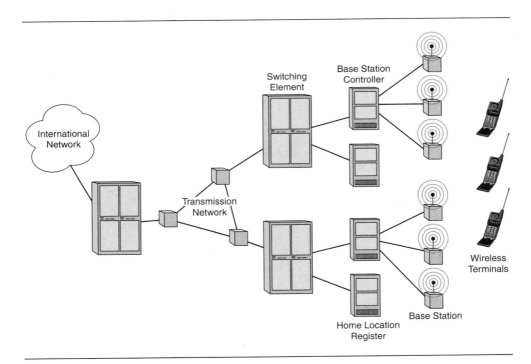

FIGURE 6.4   Cellular Network

- DX 200 MSC (Mobile Switching Center), designed for GSM and DCS 1800 digital networks. It has a capacity of up to 150,000 mobile subscribers with an integrated SSP (Service Switching Point) functionality.

- DX 200 HLR (Home Location Register), for GSM- and DCS 1800–based networks. It handles up to 300,000 mobile subscribers.

- DX 200 BSC (Base Station Controller), accessing up to 128 base stations.

- DX 200 MTX (Mobile Telephone Exchange), operating in NMT-based networks. It has a capacity of 60,000 mobile subscribers and access to up to 2,160 base station channels on 1,024 base station sites.

- DX 200 MTX-C, for smaller, NMT-based networks. It has a capacity of 20,000 mobile subscribers and access to 270 radio channels.

- DX 200 TETRA, for the ETSI (European Telecommunications Standards Institute) standard trunked PMR (Private Mobile Radio) voice and data communication, conforming to the MPT 1327 worldwide open trunking standard.

Cellular radio products have very different requirements. The MSC, HLR, and BSC products are for digital GSM networks; the MTX products are for analog NMT networks. The voice transfer technology in these networks is radically different. GSM networks are digital from end to end; in NMT networks the first leg from the telephone to the base station is analog. In addition, the signaling in GSM and NMT networks is very different.

GSM networks must offer a platform for many value-adding services, such as the IN services. The NMT network is a closed world in this respect.

Private Mobile Radio (PMR) networks are much more primitive with respect to billing and customer features. For example, they are typically half duplex networks, meaning that two telephone users having a conversation cannot talk to each other at the same time. The user must press a special button (tangent) on the telephone when he or she is about to say something.

The primary requirements for PMR products are adequate geographic coverage, reliability, and flexible group communication (conferencing). Typically, officials such as police and rescue organizations use PMR networks, and for them the network is important as a means for easily coordinating large operations by group communication.

Despite the obvious diversity of features and capabilities of different network elements in telecommunication networks, much of the software embedded in these elements is identical. They are developed and managed as a product family. Later in this chapter we discuss some difficult problems that need to be solved to make the development and evolution of this product family more effective.

6.1.2 Nokia Cellular Phone Product Family

The hardware of a cellular telephone consists of a transmitter and a receiver for communication with the network, a user interface consisting of the keyboard and the display, a battery, a microphone, and an earphone for speech exchange (see Figure 6.5). In addition, a telephone has a processor and memory for the software needed to control the hardware. A telephone may also have facilities for some auxiliary services—for example, data communication. As the market has evolved, the telephone has become the center of a distributed system. The software is now running concurrently on a handset, data card, PC, and car control system.

A cellular telephone communicates through cellular networks. Nokia has developed telephones for various network standards—for example, for the analog standards NMT, AMPS, and TACS (Total Access Communication System), and for digital standards such as the Japanese JDC (Japanese Digital Cellular), the American CDMA, and the European GSM. The GSM standard has evolved through different phases; currently features of Phase 2+ are being put into use. GSM is the most widely used wireless network. It is adapted in over 100 countries worldwide. In addition to GSM networks operating at 900 MHz frequency band, GSM-based systems include GSM 1800 (also known as DCS 1800 or PCN 1800), GSM 900/1800 (known as dual-band network) and GSM 1900 (also known as DCS 1900 or PCS 1900). GSM 1800 is in use in Asia and Europe, for example, while GSM 1900, TDMA (Time Division Multiple Access), and CDMA have been adopted in, for example, North America.

For each cellular standard, Nokia provides several telephones for different market segments. These telephones vary in style, functionality, and price. The variation is implemented both in hardware and in software. For example, current GSM products have about 10 series (families) and more than 20 models. They vary according to communication standards (GSM 900, 1800, 900/1800, and 1900), markets (particularly in the Asian and U.S. markets), and telephone capabilities and user interface style. Naturally, these telephones also have different hardware.

Variance domains divide the current software of the telephone into the following components (see Figure 6.6):

- Cellular subsystem for managing the connection to the network
- User interface subsystem that includes applications
- Device control subsystem for interfacing with the hardware

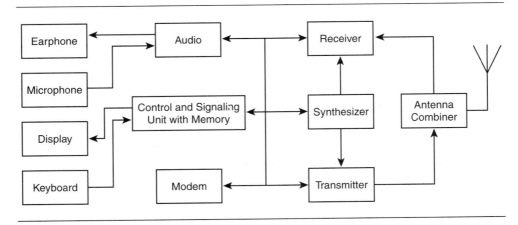

FIGURE 6.5   Structure of a Mobile Phone

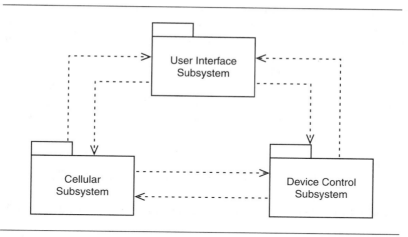

FIGURE 6.6 Software of a Mobile Phone

This system structure will gradually evolve into a new component architecture (see Section 6.4).

The software development organization is geographically distributed. Currently the development sites are in Bochum and Ulm in Germany; Camberley and Southwood in the United Kingdom; Copenhagen in Denmark; Oulu, Salo, and Tampere in Finland; San Diego and Dallas in the United States; and Tokyo in Japan. Each development site bears the main responsibility for some products, but the different sites have to cooperate extensively.

Despite the obvious diversity of features and capabilities of different cellular telephone models, much of the software embedded in these telephones is identical. They are developed and managed as a product family. In the following section we discuss some difficult problems that need to be solved to make the development and evolution of these product families more effective.

6.1.3 Architectural Problems

Good software architecture supports software development in all phases (Rechtin and Maier 1997). The reverse is also true: Deficient architecture will lead to problems that may become apparent all through the software life cycle.

Some problems relate to the capability of developers to understand architectural descriptions and refine them consistently in their designs. If the architecture is incomplete, the designs will be inconsistent, leading to unnecessary repetition of work. In other words, if concerns common to many software designers are not addressed in the architecture, they will be addressed in the designs, albeit in different and possibly inconsistent ways.

If architecture does not address explicitly systemwide properties such as performance or reliability, it may not be possible to meet the corresponding requirements without expensive reengineering processes. When the software system is developed, the software architecture will become more detailed, presenting the problem of managing design complexity and maintaining consistency between the design and the implementation. Finally, maintenance and evolution stress-test the flexibility of the architecture.

It may be insufficient simply to make and document architectural decisions. A process that ensures conformance to these decisions must be present, or the realization of the architecture may fail, defeating the initial effort of definition.

In the subsections that follow we present and analyze a few concrete examples of architectural problems in the Nokia case studies.

How to Make, Understand, and Adhere to Architectural Decisions

Long-lived systems present special architectural difficulties. The first system in the DX 200 family was created in the 1970s. Its high-level structure was radically changed in the early 1990s to reflect the evolution of implementation that took place over 20 years. It is difficult to select architectural components when no one person can understand all the details of the system any longer.

The DX 200 software for the fixed network has six top-level entities. Because of the changes mentioned earlier (see Section 6.1.1), all existing functionality had to be split among these entities. Naturally, many borderline cases did not fit well into any of the categories.

Evolution keeps challenging the existing categories. In the early 1990s, the mobile switching centers did not yet exist. They had eight top-level entities instead of six, to accommodate the special services needed for physically moving subscribers. In the future, there may be yet unforeseen uses for the existing software system. The architecture must be extended to include these as well. Still, the architectural coherence must be maintained.

An especially difficult new feature to implement has been the Intelligent Network. It has a reference model of the call control functions that a switching center performs. This allows the operator to create new services by writing programs for how the switching center should handle call control, based on the reference model. In a sense, IN is an application program interface (API) exposing the internal states of the switch.

Our switching center had been designed before the conception of IN, and the internal states of the switch could match those of the standard-prescribed reference model only by chance. Thus we could not avoid breaking some of the rules of the original architecture and its internal states.

Managing Program Configurations and Designs in the Presence of Variation

Variance means there are several different implementations of similar functionality. This variation causes difficulties in maintaining configurations and program files and in adding functionality or correcting errors. Both case study systems have a large code base to manage, so approaches that work acceptably well in small systems are not sufficient.

Having a large number of related implementations with little structure makes maintaining different configurations difficult. For example, DX 200 has a total of 82 different implementations for a certain feature, including 26 for fixed network switches, 25 for mobile switching centers, 6 for PMR switches, and 4 for base station controllers. No one can keep track of all the dependencies in such a large number of implementations.

When there is only one implementation file, variance is managed at the program file level. A common mechanism for managing variance at this level is compiler switches. This approach is not effective for large product families with multidimensional variance. For example, a 125-line block of code is common to all members of the DX 200 family. This code segment has four different compiler flags: two for functional variation and two to specify the member of the product family. Fifty-eight lines are compiled conditionally. There are seven conditionally compiled parts, the largest of which is 24 lines long.

Even cutting and pasting code can cause problems. In both DX 200 and mobile phones, adding new functionality and correcting errors are more difficult than necessary because so much of the code is copied. When one part of the code is modified, all copies must be manually located and updated. This is a very significant problem; from our studies, we know that typically only 30 percent of the source code lines in most program modules are unique, non-replicated code.

Designing and Describing Interfaces

In a large system, interfaces between components also become large, making the components difficult to use, especially when they are represented by an unstructured list of function or message declarations. Flat interfaces do not help in defining component interactions, often the most problematic part of the system.

The following message list is taken from the interface message specification of a collection of service processes in the DX 200 system:

```
0001    SUPERVISION_MSG_S
0002    SUPERVISION_ACK_S
0003    CHANGE_WORKING_STATE_S
0004    STATE_CHANGE_ACK_S
0005    SET_CHARGING_S
0006    SET_CHARGING_ACK_S
0007    GSM_STOP_CHARGING_S
0008    GSM_CONTINUE_CHARGING_S
0009    GSM_REMOVE_CHARGING_S
0010    GSM_INTERMEDIATE_STATISTICS_S
0011    CHARGING_STATISTICS_S
...
```

The documentation gives the meanings of these messages as the following:

```
0001    The supervision message of processes.
0002    Acknowledgment to the supervision message.
0003    Supervision orders to change the working state.
0004    The process acknowledges a state transition command.
0005    By this message call control sets time charging only in a
        certain process.
```

```
0006    By this message a process acknowledges the set charging
        request.
0007    By this message call control stops charging in the
        process.
0008    By this message call control asks process to continue
        charging.
0009    By this message call control orders process to remove
        charging.
0010    By this message call control asks intermediate charging
        statistics from the process.
0011    Contains information on the charging record.
...
```

The message interface of this process is wide and unstructured, with 127 different messages. Messages are defined in a flat namespace, and there is no modeling of independent interactions or protocols. Although the messages are commented, it is impossible to say which messages belong to which protocol or in which direction the message is sent. The only documentation for the interaction protocols is in code. In the DX 200 system, there may be between 1,000 and 2,000 processes, with the detailed process number depending on different configurations. The interfaces of other processes are generally not as large as in this example, but the same problems are visible.

In the mobile phone software system, the three main subsystems have 286, 170, and 140 interface functions, respectively. There are certain categories in the interface specifications of these subsystems, but in each category the interface functions were specified as a flat list. The largest categories contain 40 to 50 interface functions. The categories are not defined in a systematic way; different subsystems have completely different categories of interface functions. For instance, the call-related interface functions in the user interface subsystem are categorized as follows:

- Common call functions
- GSM call functions
- D-AMPS (Digital AMPS) call functions
- JDC call functions
- Other system call functions

But the cellular subsystem has the following categories:

- Call functions
- Call transfer functions
- Conference call functions
- Harassing call functions
- Data call functions
- Call mode control functions

- Call reestablishment functions
- Call connection parameter control functions

For a category of one subsystem, it is very hard to find its counterpart in the interface specifications of other subsystems. Thus it is difficult for different subsystems to understand each other. In addition, the interface specification does not describe the dependencies among different interface functions.

Interactions and Dependencies among System Properties

Software architecture significantly influences system properties such as scalability, maintainability, performance, and fault tolerance. Unfortunately, often requirements regarding different system properties interfere with each other: Architectural choices made to achieve a specific system property influence other system properties as well. Controlling system properties is especially hard in distributed systems in which concurrency, computation, communication, and state intermix and create synchronization and coherence problems.

For example, consider the DX 200 fault tolerance mechanism. Fault tolerance, high availability, and scalability are essential system properties of the DX 200 product family. Whichever mechanism is selected to achieve fault tolerance and high availability will affect many other system properties. In the discussion that follows, we describe one of the mechanisms used in the DX 200 family. We explain what problems it solves and discuss how it affects, and in particular constrains, other properties.

A telephone exchange continuously processes service requests. The most familiar one is the request to connect a call to a particular number. To carry out the request, the exchange executes several steps, some of which require specialized hardware units such as the switching matrix or a memory unit that contains large in-memory file systems and databases. In this way computing is distributed throughout the system.

For performance reasons, it makes sense to carry out some of the computations in parallel. To provide fault tolerance and high availability, one must maintain the state of this distributed computation. The result of a computational step can always be recalculated, if the state of the whole computation is not lost. The state can be kept in a centralized place, or it can be distributed across several processors. Centralizing the state makes guaranteeing fault tolerance easier. However, maintaining a centralized state can produce a performance bottleneck that limits the scalability of the system. It also makes the system slower when recovering from faults.

The DX 200 system distributes the state of the computation to different processors, each of which is responsible for fault tolerance. This architecture uses message passing for interprocess communication. Such systems tend to couple their components in various ways. Because several processes are concurrently involved in the same computation, they share information. The overall state of this computation is contained in these processes.

Once communicating processes need to know each other's states, their interfaces become modal (protocols). To communicate with other processes via protocols, processes must know about the existence and state of other processes, as well as the different types of messages, including their structure and their content.

Coupling makes distributed systems hard to reconfigure, change, maintain, and develop. It makes independent and autonomous components difficult to isolate and the communication topologies of a system hard to change. In particular, this architecture fails to localize externally visible protocols.

Because the state of the computation is distributed, each process must take measures to protect the state of the computations in which it is involved. This can be done with an active or a passive process. Active fault tolerance means that a spare processor replicates the computation in (almost) real time. The passive alternative implies that the process stores enough information somewhere so that it can continue the computation after a fault. Typically the information is stored on permanent storage such as a hard disk drive or flash memory, but it could also be stored in memory. Permanent storage is slow in relation to processor speeds, so it could be used to store only the most important information. This information would not be sufficient to enable quick recovery from a fault (thus the availability requirement would not be met). Access to memory is much faster, but it does not protect against hardware failures (thus the fault tolerance requirement would not be met).

Replicating the process raises the question of how to bring the replica up to speed. Generally, checkpointing and input synchrony are used. With **input synchrony,** the replica is guaranteed to receive the same messages in the same order as the principal process does. With **checkpointing,** all the relevant information from the process is copied, including the values of most variables, but not incidental information such as memory locations. Thus the information in the process belonging to the checkpoint must be marked. The processes must be able to start running after the checkpointed information has been copied to them.

This checkpointing design has the required capacity and can be easily scaled, while providing the necessary fault tolerance and availability. It is not transparent to the developers and makes the design and implementation of fault-tolerant computations more complex. It increases development and maintenance effort.

This example demonstrates the two kinds of interactions among decisions that are made to address architecturally significant requirements. Architecturally significant requirements related to the same component domain cannot be addressed independently because the structure in each component domain will ultimately determine all corresponding properties. Our example also demonstrates that architectural decisions regarding the texture of software in a given component domain (run time in this case) may influence the properties of another component domain (write time in this case), although this can be regarded as second-order influence.

In the sections that follow we share our experience in addressing some of the architectural problems we identified in both product families. We present two techniques:

- **Design decision trees** are a pattern for making and documenting architectural decisions in the context of requirements and earlier decisions, showing variation and alternatives employed by different members of product families.

- **Interface objects** are a means for designing and describing interfaces for complex software components that solve in a practical way several recurring problems.

Finally, we report what we learned from modeling the execution structure of software in the run-time component domain using an extension of Petri Nets.

6.2   Design Decision Trees

Definite relationships exist among the construction of a product, technology for planning and design, and the knowledge used for planning and design. As products become more complex, advances in productivity and quality require attention to be focused on the enablers: Planning enables production, and architectural knowledge enables planning.

When looking for ways to improve the productivity of the development teams or the quality of the design products, we must address several essential questions: How can a software development team elicit, represent, and share its design expertise? How can we reuse and refine this knowledge in the process of evolution? How can we reconcile the existence of alternative opinions within the development team regarding the best solution to what appears to be the same problem?

Experienced software designers employ architectural knowledge to construct usable, flexible, and gracefully evolving software. They know several alternative approaches toward a solution and they are able to select a feasible approach by its properties. This knowledge is based on experience. It is rarely shared or communicated. It remains tacit, and only other experienced software designers recognize it when they examine the design. Software architecture is often identified with high-level design because it may be the only tangible reflection of shared architectural knowledge in the entire system. The erosion of architecture in long-lived systems is usually a result of these systems being shaped over time by many developers that do not share the knowledge and understanding of the problems addressed and embodied by the original software design.

To improve the situation, designers involved in software evolution and maintenance need to be better informed. They need to know the rationale behind the design decisions. With this knowledge they could evaluate the applicability of their decisions. They would be able to use existing flexibility in the design when the change has been anticipated, and they would be able to understand the consequences of modifying the existing design when the change comes as a surprise.

Existing frameworks for documenting design decisions usually disregard one crucial fact: *Design decisions are taken in the context of earlier design decisions.* As elsewhere in software design, choices are often determined not only by direct problem requirements but also by the context in which the requirements are being addressed. Thus, revising one specific design decision may change the context of and thus invalidate many other design decisions not obviously connected to the former except by following it in time. There are two important consequences of this fact:

1. The order in which requirements are addressed has a significant effect on the eventual software architecture. Therefore the very order in which experienced designers make design decisions is an important (often domain-specific) piece of information that must be recorded.

2. The context of every design decision must be captured, and change-management procedures should support reviewing design decisions once their context has been changed.

We propose the design decision tree as a mechanism for developing and maintaining the information regarding proper ordering of design decisions and alternative choices that exist in every explored context. A design decision tree is organized as a partial ordering of design decisions put in the context of incrementally specified problem requirements and the constraints imposed by earlier decisions.

In the subsections that follow, we describe design decision trees in more detail, show how they can be used in the software development process, and give an example.

6.2.1   Definition

The **design decision tree (DDT)** is an approach to specifying and refining architectural knowledge incrementally in the course of evolution. The DDT orders design decisions, and from this perspective it is similar to a pattern language (Ran 1996). The main difference is that the DDT represents variation and alternatives. To avoid replication when representing alternative solutions to the same or similar problems, the DDT structures architectural knowledge hierarchically into elements that are finer grained than design patterns.

Each element of a DDT includes the following:

- Partial specification of constraints and functional and quality requirements of the problem
- When requirements are sufficiently specified, an approach to satisfying them
- New requirements and constraints implied by this approach
- Reference to further design decisions that refine the specification of the problem and the solution

Each design decision is explained in detail by structured prose, common design notation, examples, and possibly fragments of implementation.

A natural organization of the DDT begins with the more general design decisions and moves to the more specific. This organization allows incremental specialization of context, requirements, and constraints along with the corresponding specialization of the design. As mentioned earlier, however, the ordering of decisions, and thus the organization of the DDT, constitutes domain-specific architectural knowledge. Alternative branches of the DDT explore alternative designs and their distinguishing qualities in the context of the problem requirements and preceding design decisions.

The structure of the DDT should reflect the dependencies among decisions. This arrangement helps us understand designs by following the essential decisions (order, rationale, goals, and alternatives). When change is considered in any given design, decision dependency information and traceability of the design decision to requirements can be evaluated as well.

A useful heuristic for ordering independent decisions made to address given requirements is based on the tightness of the constraints they impose on the design space. Decisions that introduce fewer constraints may be made first because they are less likely to be reversed.

Exploring alternative design decisions in a DDT is essential for verifying the rationale of a specific choice. Design rationale in the form of a logical explanation may be convincing but is often misleading. Justification of a particular design decision is of limited value unless the alternatives are presented and analyzed according to the same criteria.

Despite its name, the DDT is not a tree. Partial architectural knowledge is represented as a forest of several DDTs. Because the ordering rule of taking the least restricting decision first provides only partial ordering for the decisions, a natural organization for a DDT is a directed acyclic graph (DAG), in which several branches can share the same subtree.

It is often beneficial also to show the solution alternatives to a problem that would violate the properties established by an earlier decision. These "illegal" branches would create cycles in the DAG that would force the designer to reconsider earlier decisions. Because a DDT aims to make reversion to earlier decisions unnecessary, we use these branches in the other direction to document the constraints that the decisions place on following solution alternatives.

The DDT is designed to be an evolving organization of architectural knowledge. When a DDT reaches stability, it represents a family of related design patterns. Each pattern is a collection of design decisions that correspond to a path on the DDT.

6.2.2   Incremental Construction of DDTs in Software Design

Essential architectural knowledge is gained with practice. This knowledge may be refined and reused only if it is explicitly represented in a tangible form that is accessible to, and used by, a group of people. To achieve this goal, software designers are required to reflect on their decision-making process. They should explain and document their design decisions in terms of the problems that these decisions solve, the constraints that they satisfy, the qualities that they achieve, and the consequences that they imply.

A development team must take special care to produce a coherent software design. Usable design guidance should strike a fine balance between sufficient generality and sufficient specificity in the information offered. The advice must be sufficiently generic to be useful in a wide range of situations and sufficiently specific to be applicable to a real problem. A DDT addresses this problem by incremental refinement of the requirements and the corresponding design decisions. The specific problems that the development team faces determine the direction of the refinement.

The software development team develops DDTs for itself. Reuse of a generic element in the form of method, process, architecture, and so on commonly requires a significant amount of work on the part of the developer to make that element applicable to the problem domain and then to the specific problem. A DDT increases the probability that a larger part of the problem will be explored and documented.

Strict rules and methods often have a negative effect on programmers' productivity and the quality of the produced software. On the other hand, software development organizations cannot afford to repeatedly start from scratch. A DDT offers a balanced compromise between following the established practice and creating new solutions. Design decisions specified by the relevant DDT should be followed as long as they meet the requirements. If new requirements are introduced, they must be specified and the appropriate branch added to the DDT.

When requirements change, some design decisions must be reconsidered. To safely undo a design decision, a software designer must be able to answer the following questions: What requirements and constraints did this decision address? What other decisions depend on it? What other design decisions were made to address the requirements and constraints that were consequences of the decision being undone?

6.2.3   An Example: A Boot Loader for a Distributed System

This example is a boot loading and initialization system for a distributed software system. A boot loader system is a critical component in telecommunication and networking systems, and it contains many sources of variation. We cover the design decisions mainly at a general level, although our example was derived from a real system, a telephone exchange (Figure 6.7). Different subscribers are attached to the telephone exchange through subscriber access equipment. This equipment is typically located outside of the actual exchange site. The distance from the exchange to the access device can be many kilometers.

Subscribers have different requirements for their connections. For example, common telephone subscribers use an analog connection with either pulse-based or tone-based signaling. A subscriber that operates a wide-area data network needs a fast digital connection (E1/T1) to the exchange. Internet users with heavy demands have a digital subscriber line

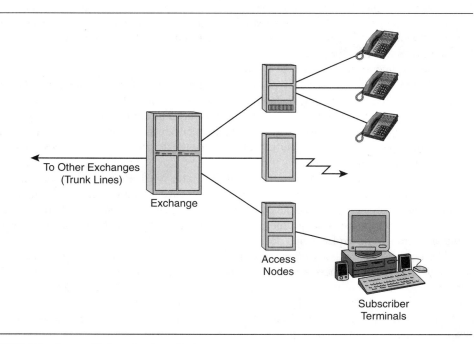

FIGURE 6.7   Access Network of an Exchange

(DSL) connection. Different types of connections need different kinds of interface cards in the access node. The access node connects to the exchange through different lines, depending on the type of the exchange. The topology of the access network is a star, with the exchange in the middle and the subscriber access nodes farther out.

The different services that the access node implements require different software. This software is subject to change as new services are added and defects in the software are detected. The initialization procedure of a software package may change when the software is updated. Similar access nodes are not necessarily all updated simultaneously. Thus similar devices with different initialization requirements may coexist in the system.

Hundreds of access devices can be connected to a single exchange, and their physical locations can be hard to access. For these reasons, their software must be managed in a centralized fashion by the exchange. The exchange operator must be able to download new software packages to the access nodes and initialize them.

At the startup of the network, the software in the access devices must be loaded and initialized according to certain constraints. For example, the order in which the devices are initialized can be important because the initialization may take a considerable amount of time.

The boot loader system is responsible for loading the software into access nodes and initializing them.

DDT for the Boot Loader

In this section we consider design options for a general distributed boot loader system, but we present only the decision path that leads to a boot system suitable for an access network system as described in the previous section. We pay special attention to the potential variance in the system because the ability of a design to absorb change is determined largely by the ability of the system to accommodate variance. In practice, this means making decisions that are likely subject to variance as late as possible.

When variance is already present in the application domain, we can take a modular design approach to managing the variance. This means localizing the variance into certain components of the system. For example, the different interfaces of the initialization hardware in an access node may be localized in a hardware driver module that offers a similar set of abstract initialization services regardless of the node type.

In the DDT notation, each node in the tree represents a design decision. It has an entry criterion that is placed over the arcs leading to the node. The entry criterion is the most general constraint that the decision must fulfill in order for it to be made. Often the entry criterion is used to represent desired system-level properties such as fast performance or robust operation.

Each decision node has three fields. The first field is the design decision currently being made. The second field contains the constraints of the context in which the decision is being considered. The third field contains the implications of the decision.

Though design decisions may be approached simultaneously in a complex process, such an approach would defeat any attempt for formalization or even representation; we therefore commit to decisions in a linear order. Each committed decision restricts further decisions. In practice, then, a decision made early in the process might make impossible a later decision that is crucial to achieving some system-level criteria.

Figure 6.8 shows a DDT for the boot loader system of an access node, based on the real system and the essential design decisions that must have been made while the system was being constructed. The system also reflects the order in which the decisions have been made. The ordering of design decisions allows us to assess the evolution characteristics of the design.

In the first node of the example (see Figure 6.8), a decision to design a booting system is made. This decision may sound trivial, but not every system needs a separate startup system. For example, parts of the system may be started and shut down autonomously.

The second decision is the topology of the boot system. We considered three possibilities: a completely distributed system, a centralized system, and a hierarchical system. There were many factors and tradeoffs for each solution. The sample system we studied was centralized.

A distributed booting system in which the nodes boot autonomously is least sensitive to the capacity of the communication network. On the other hand, it requires that nodes have permanent local memory because the software to be loaded is not retrieved over the network but loaded locally. Local memory in the nodes is not needed in a centralized booting system. On the other hand, a centrally controlled system does not exclude the use of local memory. In this respect the centralized system is more flexible.

A centralized system can be seen as a special case of a hierarchical scheme in which the boot control nodes for a hierarchy and the leaf nodes in this tree each serve a partition of the nodes to be booted. A hierarchical system would have some performance benefits by enabling parallel exception handling and by interleaving the services of different nodes. If the physical topology of the network were hierarchical, a hierarchical booting system would be a natural choice. However, our system has only a single level because only one node is capable of acting as a server.

If the nodes were homogeneous, the boot system node could use simple broadcast to send the same software simultaneously to all nodes. In the system in our example, the software for nodes can be different.

The next decision considers whether the underlying network supports multicasting of messages. If multicasting is supported, as in the sample case, the boot loader node can serve nodes in parallel. Otherwise, the nodes must be served sequentially.

There are two options for initiation of the communication in the boot protocol. The central boot control node can initiate communication after an appropriate period that is needed for the nodes to power up, or the nodes can request the central boot server to supply the loading and initialization sequence. The latter option is chosen in our case because the power-up times of the nodes have substantial variation and this scheme automatically adapts to this variation.

Next, a buffering scheme of the requests in the boot server is considered. The main requirement for the buffering is the ability to combine similar requests into pools that are then serviced using a multicasting mechanism. Because the access devices in our example are independent of each other, we decided to allow arbitrary reordering of request pools.

Sources of Variance in the Boot Loader

The boot loader in our telephone exchange contains many sources for predictable variance. The nodes in the system have different load and initialization procedures. They contain a bootstrap loader in ROM, and there are different variants of this software. The bootstrap loader must be used to load the boot client and initialization program into the node. In addition, the behavior of

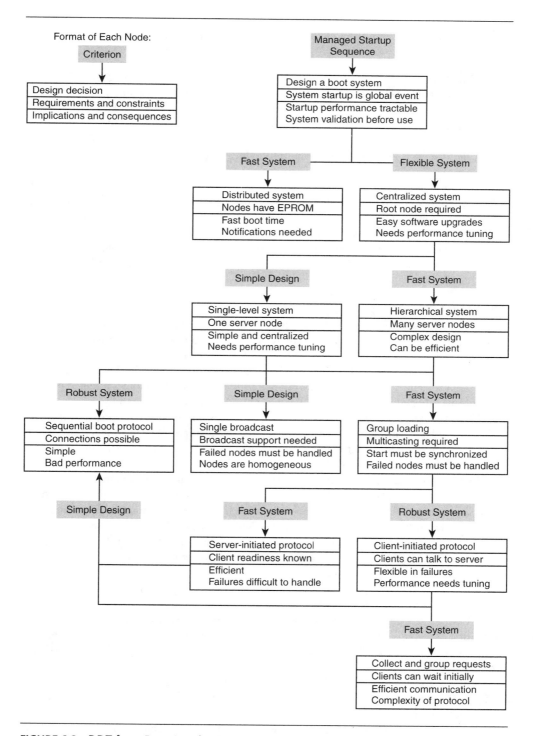

FIGURE 6.8 DDT for a Boot Loader System

the different access nodes varies in the error situations. Some of the latest models contain elaborated self-diagnostic software that can report errors in an itemized fashion; the oldest models just fail silently.

In the future the access nodes may be able to support writable permanent memories (flash memory). At present, the number of nodes ranges from a few to a few hundred. The maximum size of the system is likely to grow in the future. In addition, the number of different devices keeps growing.

The communication channels from the boot loader node to the access nodes use the same technology (PCM—i.e., pulse code modulation) in the current exchanges. However, the speed of the channels may vary from 16K to 64K per second. In the future, radical changes in the technology and the speed of the links can be expected.

The topology of the communication network is a star, with the node controlling the boot load in the middle. Although there is no variation in the topology right now, it could change in the future.

Analyzing Change Requests

The DDT can now be used to analyze the impact of different change requests for our system. In the analysis, only the decisions actually made are taken into account. Alternative decisions are removed from the DDT, thus making the topology of the DDT a genuine tree.

First we locate the decision nodes that the new requirements in the change request affect. Next we select the nodes that are not in a subtree spanned by another affected decision node. Of the affected nodes, these are the ones closest to the root of the tree.

Next we analyze the effect of the new requirements on the selected decisions. If a decision is invalidated, all the decisions in its subtree are also possibly invalidated or are rendered meaningless. The closer to the leaves the affected decisions are located in the tree, the smaller the effect on the design will be.

Invalidation of a decision node does not necessarily result in invalidation of all subsequent decisions. It is also possible that the affected decision node can simply be removed. Such is the case when the decision issue of the node is rendered meaningless. For example, if the system hardware is changed, some architectural options might become impossible.

A change request can also result in new nodes to be added to the DDT. In these cases the decisions below the new node must be analyzed in the context of the new decision. Parts of the tree may be invalidated in this case.

Examples of Change Request Analysis

First let's analyze a case in which the timing requirements of the access devices are changed. In this first example a new line of access equipment is introduced that has a limit for the time it can wait for the boot server to process the request. The limit is hard-coded into the ROM in the devices and cannot be altered.

Our design currently allows the boot server to collect requests in buffers and process the grouped requests in arbitrary order. The result is unpredictable variance in the response time of the boot server.

Now we can locate the design decisions that are affected by the new requirements from our decision tree. It turns out that the design decision that allows the reordering of requests is

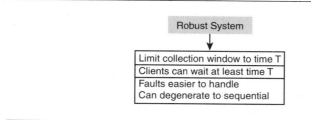

FIGURE 6.9   Additional DDT Node for a Change in Timing Requirements

the last one in our tree. We can immediately see that the impact of the change request on the architecture of the system will not be large.

By adding a new design decision at the bottom of the DDT (see Figure 6.9), we can adapt the system to limit the maximum waiting time for clients. This decision refines the decision to allow the collection and grouping of requests.

In the second example the change request asks for an increase in the capabilities of the access equipment and requires the system to take advantage of these new capabilities. A mass storage module is attached to each node. The storage device is large enough to contain all software that is to be loaded in each access device.

We can locate the decision that is affected by the new requirements in the root of our DDT. The impact of this change request on the system architecture will be very large. The new requirements, together with the constant growth in the number of access nodes in typical exchange configurations, lead us to consider a distributed architecture justified. We decide to aim to maximize performance and future scalability of the system.

We can now analyze the decisions below this node in the new context. It is easy to see that all decisions made in these nodes are rendered meaningless in the new context of a distributed boot system. A new design decision path must be built starting from the distributed boot system node.

We can argue that the decision of whether the nodes have permanent writable storage has been made too early in our sample design. If we could have made the decision later, the impact of adding mass storage to the access nodes would not be so large. Such a system could, for example, facilitate both autonomously booting nodes and centrally controlled nodes.

6.3   Designing and Describing Interfaces

One of the main concerns of software architects is managing the complexity that is inherent in the development and evolution of large software systems. They do this by partitioning software to address essential product and development concerns. To analyze the effectiveness of a given partition, we must understand the interactions that result from integrating and coordinating the parts in the complete system. The dependencies among different parts should be minimal and isolated into concise descriptions of their interfaces. Therefore, descriptions of interfaces and interactions constitute major content in software architecture documents.

Unfortunately, common approaches to specifying interfaces do not scale. Interfaces commonly are flat sets of externally visible elements, such as signatures of callable functions and procedures, or types of messages and signals accepted by the component.

Although it is a common practice to construct larger components by aggregating smaller ones, possibly abstracting and coordinating their functions, interface elements are not structured or abstracted but are simply propagated as such through component aggregation hierarchies. Interfaces of composite, higher-level components are still described as sets of function signatures or message types. Thus composite components may include several hundreds of interface elements. This situation indicates a granularity mismatch between the level of abstraction of components on one hand and their interfaces on the other.

There are other limitations in regarding the interface of a software component as a flat set of names. Such organization offers no structure for encoding information about relationships that exist among different interface elements. Thus possible grouping, ordering, or other relations and constraints among the interface elements themselves or the intended users can appear only as comments. Large components usually have groups of interface elements with strong intragroup and weak intergroup coupling. Often several interface elements in the same group must be accessed in a particular order to accomplish one logical task.

Another limitation in typical interface descriptions is the attempt to specify the interface of a component without specifying the intended user of this interface. Often interface elements are intended for use by an exclusive group of client components. We cannot describe nonuniform visibility of component interfaces without considering the possible collaborators. Furthermore, some of the methods provided by an object should be called by its collaborators only in response to the messages sent by the object itself. Failure to obey such constraints may result in inconsistent states, deadlock, or other undesirable situations. To understand an interface through which two components interact, we need to understand the sequencing of bidirectional service requests that happen during the interaction.

To address these problems we have developed a model for structuring and describing interfaces that is suitable for complex software components. At the heart of our approach is the belief that just as components are structured as compositions of lower-level components, interfaces must be structured as compositions of lower-level interfaces. To achieve this model we apply to interfaces the same structuring paradigm that is used for components: We model interfaces as objects.

Interface objects serve as groupings of interface elements. These elements may be either interface objects or simple interface elements such as function signatures or event types. Interface objects have the state needed to describe (and possibly control) the conditional availability of their interface elements. We use additional annotations to specify collaborator-specific visibility of interface elements. We describe valid interaction patterns between two interface objects by specifying the ordering of bidirectional service access using abstract collaborator classes.

Interface objects are not a new invention. They constitute a common pattern used in the design and documentation of important components of many operating systems. File and socket descriptors, process handles, and timers are all examples of familiar interface objects. However, this paradigm of interface design and documentation is not commonly used in industrial and commercial software. This section documents the ideas necessary to widen the applicability of this useful design pattern in practice.

We demonstrate our approach using an example from the signaling layer of the Global System for Mobile Communications (GSM) (Redl, Weber, and Oliphant 1995): the so-called Layer 3. The GSM Layer 3 interface is supported by components on the mobile station (mobile phone) side and the network side. We discuss the interface of the Layer 3 component only on the mobile station side. We have chosen this example because it is complex enough to demonstrate our approach and still it is not excessively large. However, because the approach targets significantly larger systems than GSM Layer 3, to demonstrate certain ideas we had to stretch both the example and the approach a bit.

We will first present a summary of our model and then explain it in more detail, illustrating the ideas with applications to our example.

6.3.1   Model for Structuring Interfaces

Our model for structuring and describing interfaces uses three main concepts: *interaction domains, interface objects,* and *interactions.*

Large components often participate in several distinct types of interactions. For example, the standard architectural framework for communication systems identifies interactions on data, control, and management planes. A similar partition of interfaces according to different interaction planes is necessary to manage complexity for any large software component. We call the collection of interface objects that are visible through one particular interaction plane an **interaction domain** of the component.

In each interaction domain, we use interface objects to make hierarchical groupings of interface elements related to a specific function or role that the component plays in its interactions with other components. When components are aggregated into composite components, their interface objects may be aggregated in a similar way into composite interface objects.

Let's illustrate the concepts of interface objects using *iterators,* a well-known design pattern for interaction with collections widely exploited in and popularized by the C++ Standard Template Library. Lists, sets, arrays, sequences, trees, and other composite structures must provide iteration service to the clients to obtain contained elements one at a time. It used to be a common practice to mix the iteration interface with other services provided by the composite structures, such as adding or removing an element. Such mixing was problematic in various ways. Iteration service may include several operations, such as initializing iteration, iterating, testing the state of iteration, and so on. How can we separate these operations from other operations supported by a composite structure? Iteration has state—the current element of the composite structure. How do we separate this state and its representation from the state and representation of the composite structure?

Because iterators solve these questions, they became a common design pattern. Rather than providing iteration services, a composite structure can provide iterators. **Iterators** are interface objects that group together and encapsulate state and iteration operations. They can be composed with other interface objects using all available object composition techniques to structure the interface.

Consider an application in which a container (e.g., a list of names) needs to notify iterating clients when a new element is inserted during an iteration process. On the implementation level, the component that implements the container will have to add notification and transaction management services. In the interface objects paradigm, the composite interface would be composed of iterator, notifier, and transaction manager, rather than a flat list of all the services provided by the component. The state of an interface object allows it to specify (and control) conditional availability of its interface elements.

Alternative groupings of interface elements and selective visibility of interface objects to different clients may achieve nonuniform visibility of interface elements to different collaborators. If significant differences exist in the sets of interface elements that are visible to different collaborators, we use alternative sets of interface objects for the same component to specify and control the visibility of interfaces. Otherwise, only annotations for collaborator-specific visibility are used with interface elements. Abstract collaborator classes are used to make these visibility descriptions applicable to several different collaborators.

Finally, we describe the **interactions** of the component with its collaborators as an ordering of bidirectional service access, or a sequencing of sent and received messages. Describing interactions in this way allows us to determine the compatibility of two interface objects better than just by static type descriptions. Interactions also provide another level of grouping for interface elements that belong to the same logical service, thereby helping to manage the complexity of understanding and using interfaces of software components. Figure 6.10 illustrates these concepts and their relations.

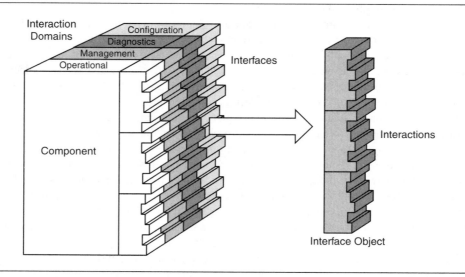

FIGURE 6.10 Structuring Interfaces: Interaction Domains, Interface Objects, Interactions

Our model includes ideas proposed and explored earlier by various researchers and used as patterns of successful design in many existing systems. The unique feature of our approach is the combination of these ideas into a complete and easy-to-use framework for practical application.

In the following sections we discuss in more detail the elements of our model and use an example to demonstrate practical application of the ideas.

Interaction Domains

Large software components often have interfaces that correspond to different aspects of system design. For example, a component may provide interfaces for configuration, management, operation, coordination, consistency maintenance, persistence, reliability, and monitoring. One could say that a component has multiple faces that it presents in different domains of interaction.

Interactions of a component in different domains should be and indeed often are designed separately. However, this separation is often lost at the later stages of design and is rarely used for structuring interfaces. When software designers use a component, they usually need to consider at the same time only one category of services or one face of the component. Filtering important information from unstructured interface descriptions is often hard. Therefore we partition component interface descriptions by domains of interaction in which the component may participate. In each domain, the component has a different face.

Partitioning interface descriptions by domain hides possible interactions between domains from the interfaces. One should analyze these hidden interactions carefully to ensure that interface descriptions provide sufficient information for safe use of the component. Complex interaction between domains may indicate either that separation is inappropriate or that component implementation has introduced unnecessary cross-domain coupling.

Partitioning interfaces into multiple faces, or interaction domains, has several benefits:

- **Separation of concerns.** Organizing interfaces by domain effectively filters information required by a software designer when a component is being used. It is also very effective for the design of interfaces provided by components.

- **Reuse.** A system may include various components that provide a particular category of services. For example, checkpointing may be required for coordinated rollback and hot restart on failure. It must be supported by all components whose state must be consistent with the state of other components. Separating the checkpointing interface from other activities performed by a component makes standardization of this interface across different components easier to achieve. For example, the design of the checkpointing interface may be reused; a component that requires a checkpoint interface for coordinating rollback would work with all components that support standard checkpointing and rollback interfaces.

- **Controlled propagation of change.** The rate of change in different domains is different. Whereas user interfaces tend to change continuously, component interfaces to support reliability may be rather stable. Only interactions that depend on the interfaces where change has occurred need to be revisited.

In our running example, GSM Layer 3 has 48 service primitives. Some service primitives can provide more than one basic service selected by different parameter values. We will attempt to simplify the design of upper-layer applications of Layer 3 by imposing structure on the description of its interfaces.

Layer 3 is not a large component; it is itself a result of decomposition, and it includes only interactions visible through the control plane. The component provides network services of mobile radio interface signaling protocols. However, we can still group interface elements of Layer 3 into two domains: *attachment* and *connection* (see Figure 6.11).

The **attachment domain** includes interfaces for registration services of a mobile station to a mobile network. Only after a mobile station registers itself to a mobile network can it access other services provided by the network (with the exception of emergency call services). The **connection domain** contains all the service primitives used to provide the mobile network signaling services to the subscriber on a registered mobile station, or the emergency call service to any user. Services of the connection domain are call control services for normal and emergency calls, short message services, and call-independent supplementary services.

Interface Objects

Software development is a process of concurrent engineering, sometimes by teams of several hundreds of engineers. Unfortunately, software components are dependent on each other because they must be integrated in, and cooperate in, a single system. To make concurrent development possible, the part of each component that affects the development of other components must be separated and specified precisely. This part is the interface of that component to other components. Interfaces thus serve as contracts between software components, as well as between their developers. To serve their purpose, contracts should be precise and complete. A large and complex contract should also be well structured to make its content accessible and consistent.

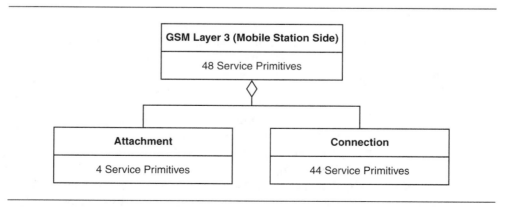

FIGURE 6.11   Partition of Layer 3 by Domains of Interaction

The interface of a software component is most commonly interpreted and specified as a flat set of signatures for its externally callable functions or for types of messages accepted by the component. Unfortunately, such interface descriptions do not fulfill any of the conditions required from a useful contract.

Many researchers have recognized that a set of signatures is an incomplete description of the contract between components because it does not specify, for example, required order and other conditions for accessing interface elements. Later in this chapter we discuss some of the approaches to this problem.

In our scheme, in addition to order and other constraints on interface access, we provide a way to structure simple interface elements into composite entities. This activity is necessary to scale the interface descriptions because large components may have hundreds of basic interface elements. Structuring of interfaces is necessary also for other reasons. Client components are often concerned with only a small subset of interface elements provided by a component. If we explicitly represent these subsets by structuring the set of all interface elements, we can more precisely describe dependencies among the components. Rather than indicating that component A depends on component B, we are able to specify a more precise subset of interfaces of component B upon which component A depends. Some interface elements should not be visible to every client component. It is almost impossible to satisfy these requirements if component interfaces are not structured. Finally, as we will demonstrate later, structuring interfaces helps us provide more precise and complete descriptions of the contract between components.

To keep things simple, we apply to interface elements the same structuring paradigm that is successfully used for components. We model interfaces as objects. Thus interface objects serve to

- Group related services as services provided by one interface object
- Describe conditional availability of interfaces based on the state of the interface object
- Compose higher-level interface objects using object composition techniques

In essence, interface objects isolate and open a part of the component implementation that is relevant for understanding the interactions of the component and thus serve as precise description of the component's interface.

Most large software components play multiple roles even in the same interaction domain. Multiple operations, states, and some abstract behavior are naturally associated with different roles. We use component roles to extend structure interfaces provided by a component. Each role is described with an interface object.

Roles are a useful concept for object design. For instance, Reenskaug, Wold, and Lehne (1996) view objects as a synthesis of multiple roles. We structure interfaces of software components by identifying their roles and representing them as interface objects. Because we rely on roles as the main heuristic for identifying interface objects, we often use both terms to mean the same thing.

We can find the interface objects for GSM Layer 3 by looking for roles it plays in each interaction domain. In the attachment domain, Layer 3 plays the role of a mobile network *registrar.* It is responsible for registering the mobile station to the mobile network. In the connection domain, Layer 3 plays the roles of *call connection, short message (SM) transporter,* and *supplementary service (SS) server.* Figure 6.12 illustrates the result of this decomposition.

Interactions

Programming languages use signatures of callable procedures or types of messages accepted by the component to describe interactions between components. These are the points of contact between different components on the implementation level. From the modeling point of view, however, a procedure call or a message often does not constitute a meaningful unit by itself, but only as a part of a longer interaction, a scenario, perhaps involving several components.

A real contract between collaborating components usually involves several bidirectional service requests and may presume additional conditions, such as availability of certain resources or limited response time. Therefore, we specify the interface of a component as a set of interactions, each accomplishing a meaningful task. The simplest kind of interaction amounts to a single function call or generation of an event. However, usually to accomplish a meaningful task, several different messages must be sent to the component. This sequence of sent messages should correspond to the appropriate sequence of received messages.

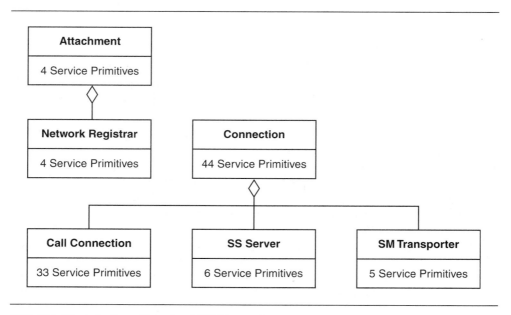

FIGURE 6.12 Interface Objects of GSM Layer 3

Interactions may be described by various means. An interaction diagram (as in UML) is probably the simplest widely used notation that can describe interactions. However, interaction diagrams have well-known limitations—for example, in describing a partial or unspecified order of events. Because interactions happen between interface objects that have state, the composition of interactions may use this state to express conditions for sequencing component interactions.

An interaction diagram describes both sent and received messages. We use such diagrams to validate the interaction compatibility of two interface objects. Two interface objects are interaction-compatible if they play complementary roles in identical interactions. The compatibility of interactions may be formalized. However, because in our work we don't rely on tool support, we used only this informal notion of interaction compatibility.

In our example, the structure of the `Create MO Call` interaction may be described by a message sequence chart that specifies the sequencing of component operations and events. Conditions of access to component operations can refer to the state of the interface object that provides the service. Figure 6.13 describes the interaction of the call connection

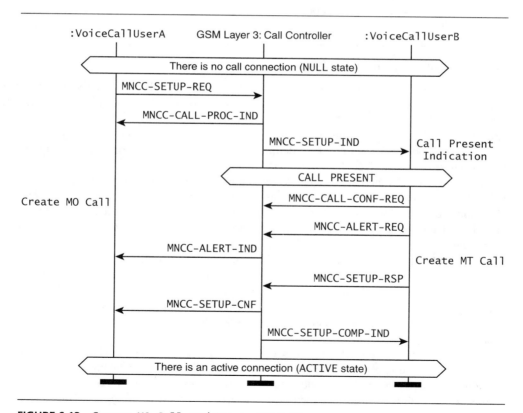

FIGURE 6.13 `Create MO Call` and `Create MT Call`

interface object that creates a mobile-originated (MO) call. This example demonstrates the need for grouping simple interface elements into interactions that describe meaningful services.

The Create MO Call service provided by call connection contains the operations (service primitives) MNCC-SETUP-REQ, MNCC-CALL-PROC-IND, MNCC-ALERT-IND, and MNCC-SETUP-CNF. The Create MT Call Connection service contains operations MNCC-CALL-CONF-REQ, MNCC-ALERT-REQ, MNCC-SETUP-RSP, and MNCC-SETUP-COMP-IND. The interface elements involved in this interaction do not carry by themselves sufficient information. The interaction description, on the other hand, tells us how a call connection is set up when user A at one mobile station makes a call to user B at another mobile station, and user B receives the call (i.e., when we have a mobile-terminated, or MT, connection). Here three interactions—Create MO Call, Create MT Call, and Call Present Indication—are involved.

From the message sequence chart in Figure 6.13 we can identify the service primitives that are included in each interaction, and the right sequence of invocation for these service primitives. We can also check if the corresponding services or interactions match each other according to the signaling standard. Conditions of access to component operations refer to the state of the interface object that provides the service.

6.3.2 Service Visibility

Roles may provide different interfaces to different users or collaborators. Even in programming languages, some basic mechanisms are used to control the visibility of operations provided by a component. Modern programming languages, such as Ada, C++, and Java, provide elaborate mechanisms to control the visibility of services provided by objects and classes of objects. In an interface definition, it is especially important to indicate the intended user of the interface. Specifying intended users by their identity may be ineffective when we are trying to achieve independence among different components. Establishing a fixed classification of possible users for a component is restrictive because rarely is one classification useful in all situations. Therefore, we include in our interface structuring a step to classify possible collaborators. Such a classification can be extended and does not need to be unique.

Each role of Layer 3 also provides different interfaces to different kinds of upper-layer applications. The roles of Layer 3 users and the relations among them are shown in Figure 6.14. Layer 3 applications can be divided into call users, short message (SM) users, and supplementary service (SS) users. Call users and SM users can be further classified, respectively, into voice call users and data call users, and SM-receiving users and SM-sending users.

In this example, a data call user is a specialization of a voice call user, and an SM-sending user is a specialization of an SM-receiving user. A data call can change the mode of the connection to data call connection mode, and hence it can access the services of a data call connection in addition to those of the voice connection. An SM-receiving user can access

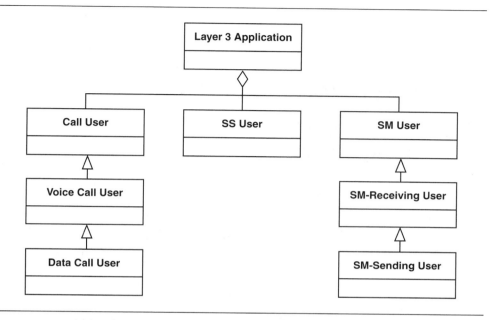

FIGURE 6.14   Types of Layer 3 Users

only the SM-receiving services, but an SM-sending user can access SM-receiving and -sending services at the same time.

6.3.3 Service Availability

Roles (and thus interface objects) may have different states that affect their capability to engage in different interactions. Because interactions correspond to meaningful services provided by roles, one may say that service availability depends on the state of the role; for instance, call connection has seven states that affect the availability of most of its services. It is possible to create an MO call connection only when call connection is not busy (in the NULL state).

A data call user can change the current call connection mode to data call connection only when call connection is in the ACTIVE state. Thus analyzing the states of each interface object, we can specify the conditional availability of its interface elements. An example of a state classification tree for the interface object call connection is given in Figure 6.15. The services listed in each state are available only when the interface object is in the corresponding state. For example, the available services in state CALL INIT are Call SS, Disconnect Call, and Call Reject Indication.

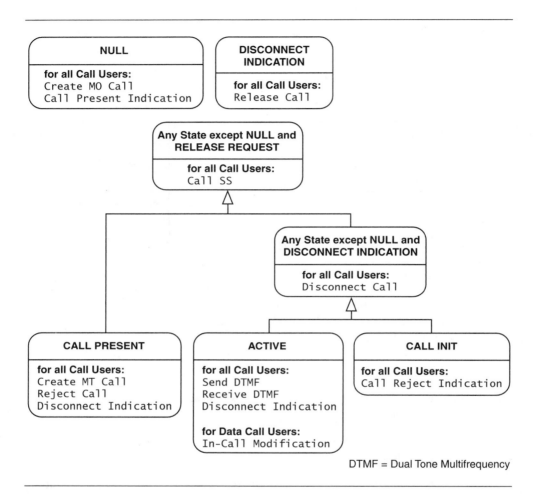

FIGURE 6.15   Grouping the Interfaces of Call Connection by States and Collaborators

6.4   Modeling Execution Architectures

The execution structure of the software in the run-time component domain determines system performance properties. In this section, we show that

- Modeling execution structure is feasible for large industrial-software systems.
- The techniques used are applicable to software performance modeling.

- Validation of the models is feasible and allows behavior predictions for important parameters of the system, as well as performance tuning.

We used Colored Petri Nets to model the execution structure of a mobile phone product family. From these models we gained valuable insights into internal operations of the software. We also could use the models to estimate performance of the software. This information guided us through the early phases of architectural design. We continue to maintain the model and expect it to be a valuable tool in configuring different product family members.

6.4.1   Models for Execution Architecture

To manage run-time properties and predict system performance, the software structure in the run-time component domain needs to be specified. Modeling software execution structure is not currently a common practice. To make such modeling practical for software developers, additional support is required:

- Modeling techniques should be classified according to the reasoning they can support.

- Model templates or examples should exist for different architectural constructs, allowing analysis of different attributes.

- Models should be composable so that the composite model correctly predicts the properties of the composed system.

- Models can be partitioned to overcome computational limitations of model-based analysis tools, but no guidance exists on how to do it.

For various reasons, documented examples of architectural modeling have been restricted to small systems. The example described in this section shows that it is possible to create specific models for analyzing interesting architectural properties of large systems. Several architectural description languages (ADLs) have been developed to model architectures and their properties. Here we demonstrate that general-purpose modeling techniques such as Colored Petri Net and Design/CPN tool can also be applied.

6.4.2   Why Colored Petri Net for Modeling the Execution Structure of Software?

There are many formal languages for modeling system behavior—CCS, CSP, LOTOS, temporal logic, and Petri Nets, just to mention a few. We chose the Colored Petri Net (CPN) for the following reasons:

- A CPN model is an intuitive description of the modeled system that has textual and graphical representation. It can be used as a specification or as a description. CPN diagrams resemble many of the informal drawings that designers make while constructing and analyzing a system.

- CPN supports hierarchical descriptions. That is, we can use CPN to model large and complex systems with a hierarchical structure of simple diagrams rather than one large flat model. Methodologically, the same feature supports incremental specification and description of software.

- CPN has computer-based tools supporting model building, simulation, and formal analysis. Design/CPN has already been used in many practical systems in several application domains.

CPN offers two mechanisms that are of special interest for architectural modeling. First is the flexibility of token definition and manipulation. It is possible to use tokens to model various architectural elements. Second is the concept of subpages, which can be used for hierarchical structuring of models.

Token flexibility comes from the inscription language CPN ML. CPN ML is based on the functional language Standard ML (SML). Each token in CPN has its own value of a predefined data type. Different token types can be used to represent different architectural elements. In our case, components, tasks, messages, events, and even use cases are all described by different types of *tokens*. The value of tokens can be examined and modified by the transitions corresponding to different system behaviors.

Subpages can be used to create a hierarchical system model. The model can be developed either from the top down or from the bottom up. CPN provides well-defined interfaces between submodels, and submodels can be reused. This feature of CPN is very useful in reconfiguring the model to analyze alternative policies and mechanisms. It can also be used as a mechanism to define the dimensions of variation in the product family.

6.4.3 Mobile Phone Product Family Software System

The product family of Nokia mobile phones consists of a large number of products for each mobile communication standard. As the market has evolved, requirements have changed substantially. The telephone has become part of a distributed system with software running concurrently on a handset, data card, PC, or car control system. Image and live video transmission have made the real-time requirements more difficult. New requirements also increase the size of the product family and the variation inside the product family.

A new component-based software architecture has been designed to manage the complexity of the product domain and guide the development of new generations of Nokia mobile phones. This architecture defines software components, message interfaces between components, essential use cases, component grouping, and deployment structure.

Figure 6.16 illustrates the main object interaction pattern that constitutes much of the software texture of the mobile phone family. There are three major parts in this pattern: (1) *system objects,* (2) *utilities,* and (3) *communication and control kernel.* System objects can be client objects or server objects. *Client objects* interact with users to provide them with the custom features of the mobile phone, and they are mostly user interface components. *Server objects* manage and control the functional resources inside the system and provide basic system services to client objects and other server objects.

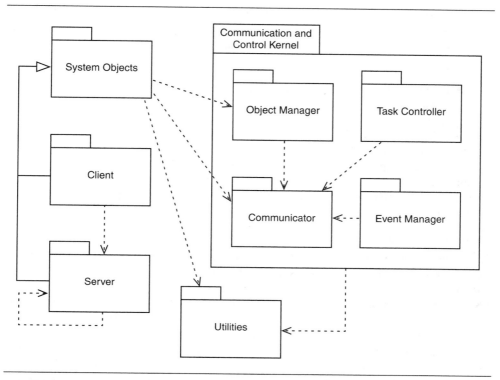

FIGURE 6.16   Texture of Object Interaction in Mobile Phone Software

Examples of resources are call, short message, data call, phone book, window, energy, and so on. During the execution time, system objects are grouped into concurrently executing threads called tasks of the operating system. System objects communicate with each other through the *communicator* in the communication and control kernel. The communicator is responsible for message routing and both local and remote message passing between system objects. It has different policies for interdevice and intradevice communication, and different mechanisms for intertask and intratask communication. The communication and control kernel is also responsible for system object management, task scheduling, and event control.

The communication and control kernel is the infrastructure of the system. The utilities package contains common facilities, such as display and memory management libraries, which can be accessed by all other components. The communication and control kernel is generic to all products in the family. Different products may have different configurations of system objects as a result of different product features and hardware resources.

This architecture supports the need for different product configurations. However, to be able to predict the performance of the system in different configurations before it is implemented, we must develop a configurable and analyzable model of the execution structure.

We used CPN as the modeling language. So far, we have used this model to do the following:

- Specify and verify the task control mechanism
- Specify and verify the task communication mechanism
- Evaluate different task divisions and allocations
- Simulate typical use cases
- Estimate the message buffer usage and message delays

We started modeling the software execution architecture just after the principal texture of the run-time component domain in the new software architecture had been outlined, and modeling continued along with the component architecture design and detailed system design. The CPN modeling iterates over three main steps: creating or modifying the model, simulating, and analyzing.

Creating the Model

Before starting to create the CPN model, we spent about one and a half months preparing for the real work, including learning CPN and SML, learning how to use the Design/CPN tool, and doing small case studies with the Design/CPN tool. The CPN model was created on the basis of the structure and properties of the object interaction pattern presented in the previous section. Figure 6.17 shows the top page of the model. The model contains data objects of devices, functional components (described as client or server), tasks, messages, message queues, and events. Interactions between objects, task scheduling, and message transmission mechanisms are described using CPN structure and inscriptions. This structure makes it possible to describe the allocation of components to tasks, component interactions, space and timing properties of message transmission mechanisms, and task control.

The mapping between the elements of the object interaction pattern and the elements of the CPN model is as follows: Client and server objects are mapped to client and server type tokens. Object manager, task controller, event manager, and communicator modules are mapped to subpages Configure Objects, Task Schedule, Event Handle, and Transmit Msg. The interactions between system objects are modeled by subpage Object Interaction.

Since we are not interested in the detailed internal behavior of client or server objects in the architectural modeling of interaction, client and server objects are abstracted by CPN tokens, which can be reconfigured with different initial markings. The object interaction pattern does not have components corresponding to subpages Generate Events and Generate Requests. These two subpages are added to generate input (use cases) to the CPN model for simulation.

To support the development of an entire product family, the model must be a generic abstraction of the family, and it must be flexible enough to represent different device, component, and task configurations. In our model, data variables and initial markings describe the part that has to be reconfigured and changed because of differences in different products. We can easily change parts without affecting the overall structure of the model. For instance, different initial markings in the place Device Table represent different hardware configurations,

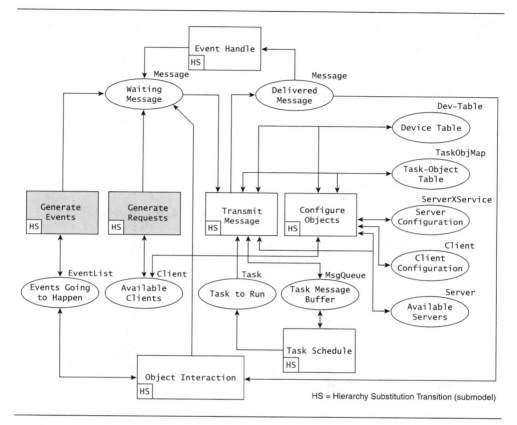

FIGURE 6.17   Top Page of the CPN Model

different initial markings in the place Task-Object Table give different task divisions, and different initial markings in the places Client Configuration and Server Configuration describe different client and server configurations. The generic part of the model is its CPN structure, which represents the properties and mechanisms shared by the products in the family.

The basic system elements (such as client objects, server objects, tasks, devices, service types of each server, and messages between system objects) are defined by types of tokens. Basic token types are composed to describe higher-level tokens, such as configuration tables and use cases.

The list that follows shows the most important token definitions taken from the global definition node of the CPN model. The use cases have been classified into two categories and defined by Usecase_C and Usecase_S, respectively. Usecase_C represents the use cases initiated by clients when a mobile phone user starts to use a certain feature—for example, makes a call, answers a call, sends a short message, or checks a phone number. Usecase_S represents the use cases started by the system (by server or hardware events), such as indicating an incoming call, indicating a short message received, or indicating a low battery. Selected use cases of both types are described as initial markings in subpages Generate Requests and Generate Events before we simulate the execution of them.

```
    color Resource = with NONE | CALL | SMS | PNB | WIN | ENG | DATA |
KEY | DISPLAY |…;
    color DeviceType = with HandSet | PDA | DataCard | SIMReader |
PC | …;
    color Media = with XBUS | YBUS | RS232 |INFRD| ANY|…;
(* communication connections between devices *)
    color DeviceState = with Active | Deactive | Busy | Not_available;
    color DeviceID = int;
    color Device = record d_type: DeviceType * d_id: DeviceID;
    color Dev_Table = product Device*DeviceState * Media;
    color ObjectID = int;
    color Object = record res: Resource * dev: Device * obj_id: ObjectID
timed; (* for a client object res=NONE, for a server object res shows
the resource it controls *)
    color Client = Object;
    color Server = Object;
    color Service = with Create_Call | Answer_call | Release_Call |
Send_SM | Receive_SM | Read_PN | write_PN | Create_Win | Destroy_Win |
…; (* important service functions and event functions provided by
servers are defined here, about 50 items. *)
    color ServerXService = product Server * Service;
    color TaskID = int;
    color Priority = int;
    color Task = record dev: Device * t_id: TaskID * pri: Priority;
    color TaskObjMap = product Task * Object;
    color MsgType = with REQ | RESP | CONF | IND;
    color MsgID = record res: Resource * msg_fun: Service * msg_type:
MsgType;
    color MsgLength = int;
    color Sender = Object;
    color Receiver = Object;
    color SubBlock = MsgID;
    color Message = product Receiver * MsgID * Sender * SubBlock *
MsgLength; (* when necessary more field can be added, like a field of
data content. *)
    color Event = MsgID;
    color MsgList = list Message;
    color MsgQueue = product Task * MsgList;
    color EventList = list Event;
```

```
color ServiceReq = product Resource * Service;
color ReqList = list ServiceReq;
color Usecase_C = Product Client * ReqList;
color Usecase_S = EventList;
color …;
```

Figure 6.18 shows a simplified example of subpage `Generate Requests`. In this sub-page a user may send a request to the system in every `UserReqTime` instance based on a certain probability distribution. The distribution function and the value of `UserReqTime` are based on observations of use patterns. In the time description associated with the arc @ + `UserReqTime` * `NextReq()` on the output arc of transition ReqCheck, the ML function `NextReq` is used to determine, on the basis of the probability distribution, when the next user request will come. An available client will send a service request to a server when a user request comes. The service request is taken from the use cases predefined in the initial

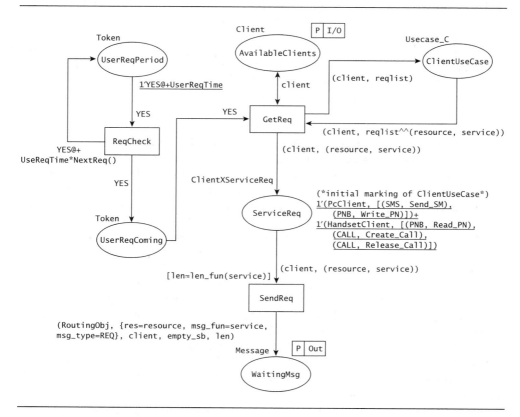

FIGURE 6.18   Example of Use Case Description and Initiation

marking of place. The initial marking of the place `ClientUseCase` describes the following two use cases:

- A client on a PC (`PcClient`) will send a short message and then add a new item to the phone book in the handset.
- A client in the handset (`HandsetClient`) will get a number from the phone book, make a call by that number, and finally release the call.

The service request is converted into a message and is sent to the corresponding server. Message routing and transmission are carried out in subpage `Transmit Msg`. After the server receives the request message, it will perform the request and send a response message to the client. While the server is processing the service request, it may exchange a few more messages with the client. These client/server interactions are modeled in subpage `Object Interaction`.

Similar methods are used for describing and generating the `Usecase_S` type of use cases (in subpage `Generate Events`) and hardware signals (in subpage `Wait Signal`).

In subpage `Object Interaction`, in order to focus on architectural properties, we modeled to any degree of detail only the most important interactions, such as call handling and short message handling interactions. We have abstracted other interactions just as request/response or indication/confirmation pairs.

The CPN model is hierarchical and modular, as Figure 6.19 shows. Subpages (submodels) in the hierarchy can be replaced or reconfigured. The first model has evolved significantly as a result of simulation and analysis. Now the model contains 16 pages, about 100 transitions, 160 places, and more than 60 color sets.

Simulation

Deep understanding of the system and experience with CPN are required to develop a correct model of software execution structure. As a starting point, we used an object interaction pattern that identifies roles and their interfaces. We structured the model by grouping the roles into subpages. Each subpage corresponds to a certain class of actions (interactions between roles) and a group of actors (roles) defined in the pattern. This structural correspondence helps in validating the model.

Once the communication and control kernel part of the model was ready, we ran several use cases. On the basis of the system specification, we knew how the system should behave in each use case and we could debug our model. The Design/CPN simulator provides interactive simulation, so we could run the model step by step, watching the state change and token flow for every step. During this early stage of simulation we found many inconsistencies. Because this is our first real application of CPN, most of the inconsistencies were errors in the model, but we also found several problems in the original architecture.

After the model was stable, we added time parameters, including message delays on different message links, task-switching time of the operating system, and event-processing time. We also defined necessary statistical variables and computations to be updated to yield quantitative results. We created the input parts (subpages `Generate Requests` and `Generate Events`) of the model to automatically generate the streams of user requests, events, and

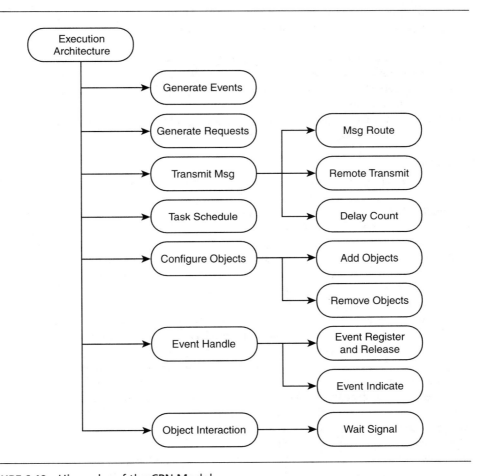

FIGURE 6.19 Hierarchy of the CPN Model

network signals according to different probability distributions. Using these estimates, we could compute the following:

- The message buffer usage in the worst case
- Minimum, average, and maximum message delays (total values)
- Number of task switches needed for each transaction

Simulation allows us to compare the performance and timing properties of different communication mechanisms and control policies. By simulating many typical use cases and some extreme use cases, we estimated the maximum size of message buffers and the average transaction-processing time. Estimated results are based on the actual timing properties of the existing system components and the assumed timing properties of new components to be developed.

Through simulation we found some potential problems of specific components in task allocations and task configurations. In some cases, communication was the bottleneck of the system, in others there were too many task switches, or too many steps in event handling. Description of potential problems, together with quantitative analysis of their impact, is valuable feedback for the system architect. If these problems emerge in the later phases of implementation, the cost of handling them may be much higher.

Conclusions

We succeeded at checking the requirements placed on the system using the CPN model of execution structure. A very important factor for the success of this experiment was the choice to model object interaction patterns. This pattern is used uniformly in the new architecture for interaction among components. The pattern itself is simple enough, but its uniform use in the system increases its influence on system performance and other run-time properties. We could evaluate alternative communication mechanisms, object-to-task allocations, and task configuration using our model. We have found potential problems in specific design alternatives. Simulation of an executable model provided valuable feedback for development of the architecture. The Design/CPN tool has greatly supported our work in designing the new architecture; CPN and Design/CPN tool are suited to this application area quite well.

We have demonstrated that architectural models can be built for industrial systems, and general-purpose formal modeling techniques can be applied to architectural modeling. Modeling can provide quantitative results to be used as a guide in developing the system further. Existing tools have limited analytical power, but simulation can be used in practice.

The model of execution structure also demonstrates the important benefit of architectural modeling. Our main problem was the lack of guidance on using CPN for modeling software execution structure. We had to figure out how to model different constructs, where to approximate, how to model the input to the system, and how to monitor the behavior. We have now applied the same technique also in modeling another system, and it turned out to be a lot easier and much more effective than in the first case. We hope that the documentation of our positive experiences will make architectural modeling of execution structure a more widespread practice.

6.5   Final Remarks

Reading through design documents and source code of software that has evolved over a period of more than 15 years, that exists in many variants, and that has been continuously shaped by thousands of programmers may leave you with a feeling of complexity that exceeds any possibility of understanding. In the systems we have examined, we could identify remnants of various techniques that were applied to design and implementation of the software for a period of time and then abandoned, leaving their characteristic imprint on the scarred body of software. It looked as if people working on these systems were constantly searching for new solutions and finding nothing that seemed to work. How, then, can we hope ever to find the solution?

The old wisdom says that for every complex problem there is at least one simple solution . . . and it is wrong. Our experience seems to fully confirm this idea. Although in this chapter we have been concerned primarily with what may seem to be technical problems and have discussed only technical solutions, in no way are we under the impression that these or other techniques alone can make a difference to complex software development over an extended period of time.

On the contrary, we believe that the most important factor determining the success of an organization in developing complex software is the culture of the organization, including the policies of hiring and rewarding people for their work, values of professional excellence, cooperation and open communication, shared models of success, and system thinking. Understanding the problem is invariably more important than knowing an extravagant solution or using a new tool. Only simple approaches seem to survive over time, and because the problem is indeed complex, we must be able to solve only small parts of the software development puzzle, relying on many simple things that work.

7

The TCS Experience with the Recovery of Family Architecture

Wolfgang Eixelsberger, Håkon Beckman

To benefit from software assets for the development of product families, it is necessary to understand and evaluate the architecture of existing software. The software architectures of existing systems are often not documented or have changed in the evolution process. In many cases it is not only the architectural description of product family members that is missing, but also the description of the family architecture or even a reference architecture.

The reference architecture represents generic architectural information that is valid for all members of the product family. The product family architecture describes the common architecture of the family members and also their variances. Chapters 1 and 4 discussed the relationship between a product family and its reference architecture. The reference architecture of an existing product family could support architectural assessment and forward engineering of new members of the product family, as well as the recovery of a family architecture. At Asea Brown Boveri, as at many other industrial companies, product families have lacked reference architectures. Therefore the task of developing and implementing technologies for the recovery of the family architecture in our case study was challenging. (See Chapter 4 for basic information about software architecture recovery and recovery techniques.)

In this chapter we describe the experiences of using software architecture recovery methods, as described in Chapter 4, applied to a case study at ABB. The case study represents a typical application in the field of product families of embedded systems. Section 7.1 presents the case study system, part of a train control system. Section 7.2 gives an overview of the recovery of a product family member. Examples of the recovered architecture are presented in Section 7.3. The commonality analysis used for recovery of a reference architecture for the case study system is described in Section 7.4. And Section 7.5 presents our experiences with architectural description languages.

As a result of our experiences in this project, we expect significant quality improvements and savings when developing additional family members of the case study. A well-defined and well-described family architecture allows the software architects to reason about the properties of existing family members and about family members currently under development. One important observation is that software architecture recovery is closely interrelated with other architectural technologies, such as description and assessment, as described in Chapters 2 and 3. Only the combination of these techniques will result in complete and correct descriptions of software architectures.

7.1   The Case Study

The case study system we chose at ABB is the Balise Transmission Module (BTM) subsystem of a train control system (TCS). The TCS is an embedded real-time software system for controlling train movement. The TCS represents a product family of systems delivered to various railway companies around the world.

7.1.1   The Case Study System

The BTM handles the reception and decoding of intermittent balise information. The BTM subsystem can be used in systems for controlling high-speed train movement and precision stops in metros (subways). Figure 7.1 shows an overview of the BTM system and its environment. Data flows from the track-side equipment through the train antenna, the transmission equipment, and the BTM to the Automatic Train Protection (ATP) system inside the train.

Information is transmitted from the balise to the antenna in the form of a cyclically amplified or frequency-modulated telegram. The balise gets the energy to transmit the information from the antenna, so the balise will send information only if a train with a powered antenna is passing by.

The BTM receives balise data, protected by the CRC (cyclic redundancy check), when an antenna passes the balise. The data must be analyzed and decoded by software that is implemented in two different versions to achieve safety requirements (two-version software). The safety concept is based on one processor unit with two software implementations of the same software specification, called A and B. The B programs use tables with the index going in the reverse order, as well as bit-inverted values. At certain points in the execution the results from A and B are synchronized and compared.

The decoded telegram information is sent to other subsystems in the TCS. One subsystem ensures that the current speed is within the permitted limit, and it controls how the train responds to signals it encounters along the track. When the train approaches a red signal or its speed is too high, its brakes will be applied. The balises can also be used as reference points for precision stops of the train, as they are with metro lines for stopping at a station.

The case study product family consists of three members, developed for different railway companies in different countries.

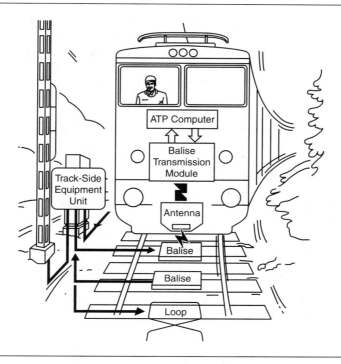

FIGURE 7.1   Overview of the BTM and Its Environment

7.1.2   ABB Status and Expectations at the Start of the Project

At the start of the project, architectural descriptions of the systems in the case study were available in the form of box-and-line diagrams representing components and connectors. Such diagrams give an intuitive picture of the system while leaving many open questions. Do boxes always represent components, and if so, do they represent a set of related functions or processes or files? Do lines representing connectors describe control flow or data flow or both? Are there time limitations associated with the exchange? Does software or hardware implement the represented functionality? Despite these questions, box-and-line diagrams are the prevalent method of documentation, primarily because of their simplicity.

The architectural descriptions in the TCS case study often were incomplete, inconsistent, and described with notations that changed from document to document. It was not possible to check the descriptions by using predefined syntactic or semantic rules, nor to simulate the system's behavior. A description of a reference architecture was not available at all.

At the beginning of the project we (naïvely) expected that we would be able to apply an architecture recovery process and tools to the existing systems to derive the architecture of these systems represented in a form that could be used by ABB engineers. We expected the recovery process to deliver a correct, complete, consistent, and unambiguous model of the structure of the system.

The architectural recovery process must identify and represent common (generic) structures within a product family; that is, it must produce a reference architecture. The architectural representation must be verified and accepted by system and domain experts. The graphical representation of the architecture must be based on clear semantics, supported by browsers and viewers, and integrated with the design documentation. The architectural representation must be easy for both old and new members of development teams to read and understand. The introduction of new team members in development and maintenance projects is often a challenging task, and clear and precise documentation, including architectural information, is vital for addressing this challenge.

Our expectations were similar to those of our colleagues at Nokia who undertook the telecommunication case study (see Chapter 6). Ran and Kuusela (1996b, 148) suggested that different architectural views may be required by a software architect in order to answer different questions. "For example, in order to reason about portability of software, its layering structure and interfaces supported by each layer might be the most essential architectural view, while to assess the performance of a reactive software a view on its process structure and dependencies, scheduling and control mechanisms, policies of allocation of shared resources, as well as information of the external event sequences, processing time, and communication delays may be required."

Timing constraints, safety and reliability, and quality in general are the most critical aspects in the high-level design process for real-time systems. The recovery process must be able to identify these critical aspects, to extract the relevant information, and to express them in architectural models.

The recovery process must be developed as a generic process that can be applied to other systems in different domains. Tools supporting the architecture recovery process must be identified and tested.

7.1.3   Architectural Problems

We identified four distinct architectural issues that the systems in our case study had to address:

1. **Safety.** The main architectural issue for the case study system is the ability to model safety concepts. Whether the safety concept is based on diversified software on the same platform or on redundant hardware, it must be possible to describe and discuss safety issues at the architectural level. The safety inspectors can then be involved at an earlier stage of the development process of a new train control system. The current practice is to specify the system and block levels from a functionality point of view, without focusing on safety issues—an approach that results in software changes in system composition late in the development process.

2. **Hardware evolution.** The hardware of the BTM evolves over time with increased processing capacity. The processing power of future systems will enable higher data transmission speeds for performing CRC checks and deciphering incoming telegrams. The software architecture must allow hardware modules and their controlling software modules to be replaced with new modules. Describing the processing requirements and timing limitations at an early stage would help detect capacity limitations.

3. **Railway standards.** The evolution of the BTM is forced mainly by upcoming railway standards proposals. The essence of these proposals is to enable higher data speeds and longer telegram formats. In addition, the evolution is driven by the need of the railway authorities to run a train through several countries and thereby deal with different telegram formats and data speeds, without exchanging the locomotive or its ATP system. The current interface and component descriptions do not reflect the ability to develop composite BTMs, capable of handling several telegram formats and speeds.

4. **Upward compatibility.** The BTM is sold as an upgradable unit. A customer who buys a BTM that handles today's telegram format should be able to upgrade the software later to handle future telegram formats. The current software architecture does not easily handle upgrades.

7.1.4   Input to the Recovery Process

Software views are documents and source code files containing information about a software system that can be used for reengineering and redesigning the software architecture. The software views of the TCS case study can be divided into the following categories: document views, SDL views, and source code views.

Document View

The **document view** is a report used by software developers in the analysis, design, and implementation process. Documents are either application-specific or of general use; programming conventions are an example of the latter.

The following types of documents were available for the TCS case study:

- **Subsystem description** is the top-level document for a subsystem and is used as the main input for writing block descriptions and block test specifications. It provides information about the subsystem itself, the blocks of the subsystem, and the communication among blocks. These documents contain some diagrams, such as an overview of data flow in the subsystem and a message sequence chart describing a startup sequence. The documents contain general information about the subsystem (also hardware-specific information) and requirements for the application developer.

- **Block descriptions** provide information on requirements and design. Design information, for example, includes the definitions of data fields and modules.

- **Program descriptions** describe how blocks are to be implemented. Each block has two program descriptions, one for the A software and one for the B software.

- **Interwork descriptions** describe the interfaces between subsystems—that is, the classes, functions, and variables of a subsystem that are accessible from other subsystems.

- **Safety standard descriptions** describe safety standards that are valid for all product development processes and for all kinds of safety-critical software. These documents contain information that software architecture must take into consideration.

- **Architecture specifications** provide a short system description, interface and safety descriptions, and system decomposition information. Included is hardware- and software-relevant information, but not the complete system structure or architecture.

SDL View

The **SDL view** represents the analysis and design models written in SDL-88 or SDL-92. SDL (Specification and Description Language) (Braek and Haugen 1993, Olsen et al. 1994) is a specification language with concepts for describing reactive and discrete systems. SDL was originally specified as a language for telecommunication systems, but it is not restricted to telecommunication. It is generally useful for specifying real-time and embedded software systems that follow stimulus-response types of behavior.

The SDL view describes the dynamic behavior of the system with state machines. The view is sometimes expanded by the use of message sequence charts, block diagrams, or object models used for decomposition of the domain into smaller pieces.

SDL diagrams from the case study can be divided into two categories:

1. **Design specification models,** which provide an overview of the processes identified, the connections among the processes, and the behavior of the processes represented by SDL state machines. Some of the SDL state machines are incomplete because the transition activities are described in plain text for documentation purposes. The state machines thus provide an overview of the process states, the input and output signals, and candidates for procedures.

2. **Documentation models,** which resulted from a reengineering process and are intended to document existing source code and simplify the maintenance process. The inputs are C source code files and implementation knowledge from the programmers. SDL documentation models are built from state machines that cannot be found directly in the source code. The programmers' input is very important for identifying states and signals.

Source Code View

The **source code view** contains all source files of the case study. This view represents compressed information from all other views. Source code views are therefore of major interest for the architecture recovery process, especially when other views are incomplete or inconsistent.

A source file—in C++, C, or Assembler language—usually contains a module as seen in the block description. Each source file has a corresponding header file. Classes, functions, and variables used by other subsystems are found in a subsystem header file. The classes, functions, and variables are described in the interwork description.

The source code is the implementation of the program description, and it adheres to an in-house programming standard. Libraries from compiler vendors are usually not used, and needed library functions are developed in-house. All source files are kept in a version control system. The files are inserted into the version control system when the software developer has performed an accepted module test. After the module test, a block test is performed according to the block test specification. After an accepted block test, a subsystem test is performed according to the subsystem test specification. After an accepted subsystem test, a system test is performed according to the system test specification before testing starts at the customer site.

The code size of the TCS case study system is approximately 150,000 lines of code. The BTM software is implemented as state machines as described in the SDL specifications. The time-critical parts are implemented in Assembler language, the rest of the software in high-level languages. The code is not automatically generated from the specifications. The software execution is controlled by a software monitor that schedules the implemented state machines and the basic hardware (RAM, ROM, CPU) testing.

7.2   Recovery of System Structure

Chapter 4 describes the methodology that we developed for recovering architectural information from legacy systems (Eixelsberger et al. 1997, 1998). The methodology is a stepwise approach to the recovery of distinct architectural properties. It specifies the steps starting from identification and preparation of input data to representation of the reference architecture. Chapter 4 contains a comprehensive description of these steps in general. In this section, we describe some specific experiments we performed, primarily to recover structural properties of the train control system.

7.2.1   Component and Connector Identification

Because many definitions of software architecture define it as consisting of components and connectors, we considered recovering the system structure properties in terms of components and connectors. Various definitions exist for the term "software component." Components are "such things as clients and servers, databases, filters, and layers in a hierarchical system" according to Shaw and Garlan (1995) or "primary computations of the application" according to Abowd, Allen, and Garlan (1995). A source code–oriented definition says, "Components can be small pieces of code (such as modules) or larger chunks (such as stand-alone programs like database management systems)" (Kogut and Clements 1994).

Identifying what in our system constitute components is not as simple as it might look. There are several sources of this information:

- **File structure.** Files contain definitions of functions and data structures. The reason for collecting functions in a file is often functional dependence. Files may therefore be considered as candidates for components.

- **Coupling.** Coupling is the measure of interconnection among functions in a software system. A high degree of coupling between two functions could be an indication that the functions belong to the same component. A low degree of coupling could accordingly indicate that the functions belong to different components.

- **Diversified software.** The TCS of our case study is a safety-critical application, and *n*-version software is used for handling safety aspects. All safety-critical parts of the system are implemented in two versions. Functional units formed by the safety elements are candidates for components.

- **Design documentation.** Box-and-line diagrams are found in the design documents of the case study. Boxes in such diagrams are candidates for components. Additional indicators are chapters or subchapters of the documentation because components are often described in specific chapters or subchapters.

- **Monitor.** The execution of the case study at run time is controlled by a software monitor. The monitor tasks encapsulate functionality that must be completely performed within a specific time frame to ensure correct behavior of the system. Monitor tasks can therefore be seen as candidates for components.

These different sources of component candidates were discussed with system developers. The consensus was that each one had a distinct value for component identification and none should be excluded.

We started the recovery work by analyzing the design documentation. Box-and-line diagrams indicated that the overall system was built as a hierarchy of components. The box-and-line diagrams and the document structure with subchapters clearly identified components on the highest level. The components at the next lower level were identified mainly by analysis of the monitor. The monitor schedules tasks that divide the components into nonoverlapping subcomponents. These subcomponents were again divided into lower-level components identified on the basis of the diversified software principle. These components are on the lowest level of abstraction that seemed to be useful for our approach. The component identification process was an iterative process with multiple processing loops and feedback rounds that involved the system experts and system developers.

The connector and interface identification process is part of the component identification process. Each component is analyzed with respect to its interactions with the environment (i.e., other components) and with respect to interaction protocols. Services provided and required by the component become part of the component interface. The transport media for data and control between interfaces are the connectors.

7.2.2 Tool and Manual Recovery

We applied four commercial reverse engineering tools to the TCS case study (Bellay and Gall 1998b): Refine/C, Imagix 4D, Sniff+, and Rigi. Typical views that are generated from such tools are call graphs, data flow diagrams, and cross-reference tables. We found these reverse engineering tools helpful in our case study because they generated higher-level abstractions of the source code.

But the tools had severe limitations. The complete views of the system were rather cluttered and unreadable. Many of the generated views were incomplete because the tools were not able to analyze an application that uses multiple programming languages. The tools lacked a functionality for the engineer to augment the automatically recovered view with additional information, such as domain or application-specific knowledge. The reverse engineering tools therefore did not directly support the identification of components and connectors from the source code, but they provided a starting point.

We had to generate additional views manually either by directly examining information sources or by combining already available views. Data flow and state transition views are of special interest in manual recovery. Specifically, we performed manual analysis to recover the interface and data flow views. Because the interfaces to other subsystems of the case study are based mainly on shared memory and interrupt functions written in Assembler language, the reverse engineering tools failed to provide the interface information. Manual code analysis provided all necessary interface information, which was a precondition for the data flow analysis. Data flow analysis has been performed for important instances of data flow through the case study system.

7.3 The Recovered Architecture

By using the views described in Section 7.1.4 and the component candidates described in Section 7.2, we tried to describe the system structure of the systems using the Darwin ADL (described in Chapter 2). Figure 7.2 shows the highest hierarchy level of the system. The diagram shows two important points: Components contain subcomponents and are related to different hardware platforms. The DECODE, SELECT, and LOCO_INFO components are related to the same hardware platform; the TRANSFORM component is related to another hardware platform. The hardware platforms are connected through a serial link.

Components of the TCS case study play different roles. The TRANSFORM component works as a server for the DECODE component. The DECODE component, acting as a client, sends commands through the O_channel and receives data through the I_channel from the server TRANSFORM. Toward the SELECT component the DECODE component plays the role of a producer; the connections between them are based on shared memory and function calls. Toward the LOCO_INFO component, DECODE plays the role of a server and LOCO_INFO is accordingly the client.

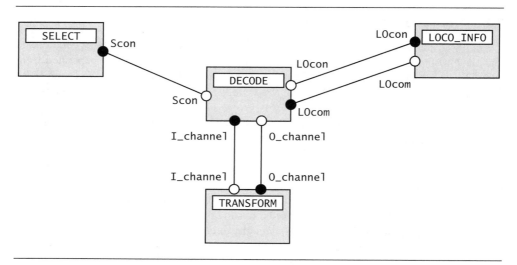

FIGURE 7.2 Components of the TCS Case Study

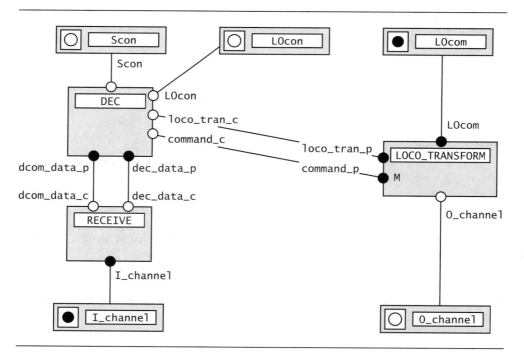

FIGURE 7.3 The Subcomponents of DECODE

Figure 7.3 describes the subcomponents of the DECODE component. The DEC and LOCO_TRANSFORM components are scheduled by a monitor that was developed in-house; the connections between them are shared memories. The DEC component is a fail-safe component with three subcomponents: A, B, and C. The DEC component therefore has A and B inputs and outputs. The A and B parts of DEC control the TRANSFORM component through the LOCO_TRANSFORM component.

The results of the component and connector recovery process are promising. While recovering architectural information, we identified problems in the overall system structure that will be avoided in future products. Another important discovery was the identification of typical communication patterns in the train control system. We plan to analyze these in the future to find ways to improve system performance and verify timing constraints.

7.4   Commonality Analysis

Section 7.3 described the components that we identified in the TCS case study system. As described in Chapter 4, the most important step in deriving a family architecture is to identify the common aspects of the family members. To do this for the TCS family, we developed a method at ABB called **commonality analysis.** The main inputs to commonality analysis are the system structure descriptions of the family members.

Commonality analysis focuses on components and tries to identify components from different family members that appear to be similar. The inputs to the process are the components of the family members to be analyzed. We performed the commonality analysis manually, although tool support is possible and desirable. In this section we describe the commonality analysis approach in general and the results of its application to our case study.

Commonality analysis consists of three steps:

1. **Select components in each family member.** For this process we defined the following selection criteria: (1) component role, (2) component group, (3) component safety, and (4) component type. The numbering of the commonality factors matches the selection sequence. After each selection step the number of valid components that fulfill the selection criteria is reduced. The order of the selection criteria has no influence on the resulting component sets, but it is very useful to choose the criteria with many components first. In this way we reduce the number of components at every level.

   Figure 7.4 shows the generic selection tree. The name of the created component set indicates the original selection group (e.g., S_1), the selection step (e.g., 1), and the selection attribute value (e.g., A). After the last selection step, selection 4, the number of components in the selection group will be small (between 0 and 10). Figure 7.5 shows the selection tree of the Bilbao member of the TCS case study. Bilbao is one of the members of the family of train control systems.

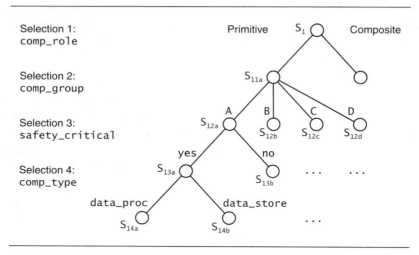

FIGURE 7.4 Selection Tree

2. **Analyze the selection tree.** A human expert analyzes the leaf component sets of the selection tree (e.g., S_{14a}) against the same component set(s) of other family members (e.g., S_{24a}, S_{34a}). Components that provide similar services and therefore similar functionality are selected and replaced by one reference component.

   Components that do not have corresponding components (i.e., similar components) in other family members are member-specific and are transformed directly into a reference component. Such components are connected with a constraint indicating the conditions under which the component becomes a component of a new family member.

3. **Create the reference architecture.** A human expert forms the reference architecture from the reference components. The architectures of the family members represent the implementation architectures of a system. The reference architecture represents the conceptual architecture of a system.

When different family members are being compared, three outcomes are possible:

1. **Full match.** Full-match components provide and require the same services in all product members. The similarities of the components are so strong that the components can be replaced directly by one reference component that becomes part of the reference architecture (that is, full-match components can be transformed directly into a reference component).

2. **No match.** No-match components have no properties similar to those of any other component of the other product families. No-match components provide

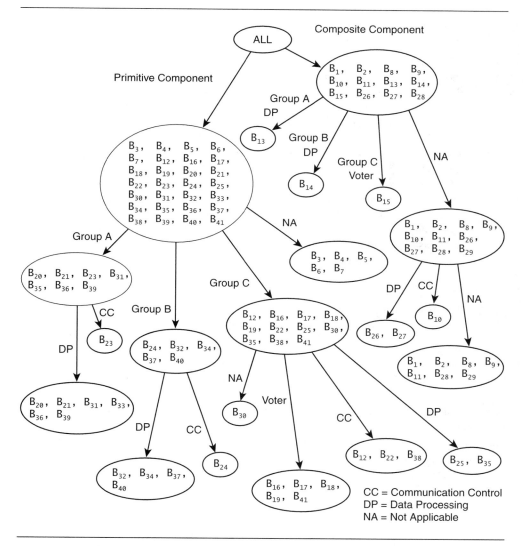

FIGURE 7.5   Selection Tree of the Bilbao Member of the TCS Case Study

services that are specific for one product family member. These components are candidates for transformation to reference components. An expert, however, might exclude no-match components because they do not conform to the reference architecture requirements, which are developed in close cooperation with system engineers. The engineers try to anticipate future changes and extensions and document this information in the reference architecture requirements. Transformed no-match components are annotated with a constraint indicating the conditions under which the component should be derived for new family members.

3. **Partial match.** Partial-match components are components from different family members that share some similarity in their properties but are not full-match components. An example is a component in family member A that provides services similar to those provided by two components in family member B. The direct transformation to a reference architecture component is not possible, and an expert, in most cases together with the system architect, must decide what should happen to these components. Partial-match components can be combined to form one component, or they can be divided into multiple components. The resulting components must conform to the reference architecture requirements. About 75 percent of all components in our case study were partial-match components. The transformation step in the TCS case study thus requires special attention from both the expert who is redesigning the architecture and the system architect.

7.4.1 Architecture As Is versus Architecture As It Should Be

The recovered architectural descriptions represent the implementation architecture of the case study system (i.e., the architecture of the system as is). The reference architecture represents a conceptual architecture of system (i.e., what the architecture should be) that will not be instantiated but will be used for deriving the initial architectures of new family members.

The handling of the partial-match components indicates that the commonality analysis process is not purely a process of redesigning the architecture but is also influenced by software architecture design and forward engineering. The resulting reference architecture does not have a direct relation to the as-is architectures of the existing family members because of the transformations of partial-match components. Therefore, before we move on to the reference architecture, we must carefully validate the implementation architecture.

7.5   Description of Architectures

As described in Chapter 4, the recovered architectural elements must be represented in an appropriate form. We used architectural description languages for this purpose. ADLs (see Chapter 2) are formal tools for representing system architectures (Clements 1996). Several ADLs have been developed for particular domains and as general-purpose architectural description languages. The current ADLs have not been used in real-world applications (Bass, Clements, and Kazman 1998). One of our goals in this experiment was to evaluate ADLs in our large case study.

The subsections that follow present our experiences in describing the architecture of the case study system in three different ADLs. Darwin was the first language we used. To remedy some of the shortcomings of Darwin, we created a new ADL called ASDL (Architecture Structure Description Language) based on the concepts of architectural properties presented in Chapter 4. We also used a third language, UML (Unified Modeling Language), because of its expected acceptance in the future as a widely used and standardized language.

7.5.1 Darwin

Darwin (Ng, Kramer, and Magee 1996) and its supporting tool the Software Architect's Assistant (SAA) were described in Chapter 2. In Darwin, software architectures can be represented in terms of components and interfaces, separately from other aspects of the system, such as computation and communication. Darwin has a graphical and a textual syntax. SAA allows conversion of the graphical representation to the textual representation, which can then be used for conversion to other representations.

Views

Darwin provides two main views: the structural view and the service view. Other views, such as behavior and performance views, can be attached to the basic structural view. The *structural view* visualizes components and interfaces. A Darwin interface represents the services provided and required by that component. Each service within the interface is in turn represented by a portal. Hence a component interface is made up of a collection of portals. Portal names refer to actions in a specification or functions in an implementation. In the *service view,* a portal can be specified as either a service provided or a service required by that component. The service view leads toward an implementation by providing CORBA connection. Interfaces can be specified in CORBA IDL (interface definition language), and primitive (i.e., noncompound) components can be implemented as CORBA objects. The structural and service views contain complementary information. The service view is a refinement of the structural view. Together they describe the static structure of an architecture.

Darwin descriptions provide a compact structural view of the case study architectures. The structural view visualizes components, including their interfaces and connectors. It is easy to understand and is an excellent communication tool. It shows not only services provided by components but also the services they require. Few description languages provide this information. It is not possible, however, to represent additional information—e.g., safety-critical aspects, rationale, or component roles—graphically.

The browsing capability of the tool gives the user different views of the system. This ability makes SAA a powerful communication tool, allowing system stakeholders to talk about a system from a highly abstract level to a very detailed level.

Components

In Darwin, a component can be either composite or primitive. *Composite components* are constructed hierarchically from other composite or primitive components. *Primitive components* form the leaves of the system hierarchy and are not further decomposed. Primitive components represent computational elements. The interface of a component is defined in terms of services that the component provides and requires. It gives no further information about the functionality of the component. SAA checks that bindings are made only between services of compatible types. Darwin supports the concept of component *types* as distinct from *instances*. In the TCS case study there was only one instance of each component type. The description of components as component types and component instances was therefore not exploited in the recovery process. In a subsequent forward engineering process, this distinction could be advantageous.

A useful feature in Darwin is the support for partial component types. This feature allows new component types to be derived from a more general component by fixing the values of some or all of its parameters. This capability is useful in the development of product families because it provides a simple mechanism for deriving many different, more specialized family instances from a generic family description. A special requirement in the TCS case study is the need for diversified (A and B) components. Both components have the same input data (the B component works on inverted data to ensure a fail-safe condition) and produce the same output data (nonidentical output data indicates that an internal error has occurred in the component). The components can be seen as instances of the same type because they provide and require the same services. The implementation of the A and B components is different, however, because they are designed by different development groups. In the TCS case study, both instances of diversified components belong to the same type.

Component roles (e.g., client, server) cannot be directly described in Darwin. Services (e.g., require, provide) implicitly describe the consumer and producer roles. Component roles could be described using the tag mechanism in Darwin that allows arbitrary information or attributes to be associated with individual Darwin objects. There are, however, two problems with this approach: (1) Components in our system may have more than one role, and (2) tag information is not fully supported by SAA. The communication of component role information between software architectures is therefore reduced. Components are described in Darwin by description of the interface. Darwin does not provide concepts for detailed functional descriptions of the component itself.

Connectors

Unlike other ADLs, Darwin cannot be used to decompose connectors. If processing or filtering needs to take place along a connector, an extra component must be introduced to perform this task, such as the connector component between components A and B. This connector component can be further elaborated with the help of an additional language if it is a primitive component, or Darwin subcomponents if it is a composite component.

Darwin provides no construct to define the connector type—for example, shared memory or function call. Additional information can be defined in the Darwin source code. This information is called tag information.

Darwin does not support the definition of control flow explicitly. There is just the general concept of information flow, which can represent data flow, control flow, or both. All additional information, such as the type of information flow (e.g., synchronous or asynchronous, protocols, hardware information) would be recorded with the help of the Darwin tag mechanism.

Darwin has concepts similar to those of data flow diagrams. The connectors can have direction and are used to transport data—characteristics that make them similar to the arrows of data flow diagrams. The components of a Darwin diagram can be seen as data stores or as actors. The advantage of Darwin over data flow diagrams is that there is a clearly defined language in Darwin.

In Darwin, as mentioned already, connectors can have direction and are used only to transport data. The language definition says nothing about whether this data transport represents data flow, control flow, or even both. Information about protocols that may be implemented by the connector cannot be visualized.

Experiences with Darwin

Not all of the architectural information of the TCS case study can be described with the basic Darwin language. However, Darwin offers the possibility of attaching extra information or attributes to components or connectors by use of the tag mechanism. Thus it is an easily extensible language. A tag can contain any textual information (e.g., comments, formal specification, resource usage) and is not processed by SAA or the Darwin compiler. The tag information is therefore not visible on the graphical model of the case study.

Tags are intended to be used by special-purpose, external tools that will be able to access them through either the SAA or the file system. Tags are useful for expressing and recording special attributes of the ATP system.

Darwin provides no concept for stating that components are executed on different hardware platforms or that components are realized in hardware instead of software. The only possibility for giving this information is to use the tag concept.

Given that Darwin is purely a structuring language, the dynamic behavior of a system cannot be described within the language alone. For this purpose, additional formalisms have to be used that can be attached to the basic Darwin architecture via the tag mechanism.

The timing of a component or a connector cannot be properly described with the Darwin language. The timing of components is especially important to express for real-time systems. In Darwin, the timing of a component or a connector can be recorded only using the tag mechanism.

For documentation and maintenance purposes, documenting the reasons for specific design decisions (the rationale) is of critical importance. The TCS case study software is divided into two hardware platforms for historical reasons. This rationale should be part of the architectural description to give designers of future members of the product family comprehensive information. Rationales cannot be described in Darwin without the use of tags.

There is no way to describe the roles of a component in Darwin. The require and provide services are similar to consumer and producer roles, respectively, but there is no way to describe client and server roles. Again we could use the tag information, but the components in our system have different roles depending on what other components are involved.

For description of the family architecture, Darwin offers some useful features: the support for partial component types, generic types, and conditions. *Partial component types* allow the architect to define new component types to be derived from a more general component by fixing the value of some or all of its parameters. *Generic types* are placeholders for component types, portal classes, and predefined types. A *condition* offers the possibility to show different versions of how a system can be built from a component set. An example of a condition could be the required *hardware platform*. If the condition indicates *single hardware platform*, then the construction of the system component will be different from the condition *multiple hardware platforms*. The prototype version of the SAA tool that we used, however, did not support these features of the Darwin syntax. The parameterization of the components gives the user a good overview of the system and its potential variant configurations. With the use of parameters, it is possible to generate different internal structures of a component at build time.

The SAA tool supports a hierarchical composition and decomposition of the components. We used this feature to define several abstraction levels of the case study system, thereby creating the useful possibility of navigating from a high abstraction level to a low one. SAA supports such navigation.

SAA is a prototype tool, and Darwin is not widely used in industry. Both of these aspects are important disadvantages for the industrial use of the language and the tool.

7.5.2   UML

The Unified Modeling Language (UML) (Fowler and Scott 1997) is an object-oriented analysis and design method that unifies the methods of Booch, Rumbaugh (OMT), and Jacobson. UML was standardized by the Object Management Group (OMG) at the end of 1997.

UML offers several kinds of diagrams, each of which captures a different view of the system. The following UML diagrams were of special interest for modeling the architectures of our case study system:

- **Class diagram** showing the important abstractions in a system and how they relate to each other.

- **Use case diagram** giving a step-by-step description of how the system reacts to input stimuli.

- **Interaction diagram** representing the interactions among system entities. UML provides three interaction diagrams: sequence diagrams, collaboration diagrams, and scenarios.

- **State diagram** representing the behavior of one object or class.

- **Component diagram** used to model the development view of the system components and their relationships representing the mapping between a logical element in the model to an implementation artifact.

- **Deployment diagram** showing processors and devices, and connections between them.

Experiences with UML

For describing the static view, we used the UML class diagram. In UML, information about class operations is visible, but it is not clear which services are provided to another component and which services are required from other components. Darwin diagrams give a much better view of the static architecture of a system than the UML class diagram does. Darwin shows the most vital information—for example, the components, the connectors, and the services provided and required. The UML class diagram forces the designer to think about design and not about architectural design. Classes represent data structures and operations, which are clearly design information. In the architectural design phase, the architect is interested not in data structures and operations but in the overall structure of the system.

While we were describing the case study with the different UML diagrams, it was unclear how the different UML views should be integrated. Thus one of the problems we faced in the use of UML during the TCS case study was the lack of comprehensive information about how to use UML in real-time systems.

Constructs that support the representation of specific architectural information—for example, timing, rationales, and several architectural styles—are currently missing in UML. One way of expressing such information is to insert notes in the diagrams consisting of plain text. This approach is unsatisfying, however, because the information notation is not part of the language and cannot be analyzed by a tool.

7.5.3 Architecture Structure Description Language (ASDL)

Darwin and other ADLs support the description of the structural model consisting of the architectural elements: components, interfaces, and connectors. For completely describing the TCS case study, it was necessary to describe the architectural elements in more detail. The detailed description supports architectural understanding, architectural assessment, and product line recovery.

To describe architectural elements of the case studies in more detail, we incrementally developed the Architecture Structure Description Language (ASDL) on the basis of our architecture recovery process. ASDL (Eixelsberger and Gall 1998) represents important properties, such as the type of information exchange used between component interfaces, in a compact form. Details—for example, interface behavior—are not represented in the language. Such information overloads the system architect with unnecessary details. ASDL supports the architect in making typical architectural decisions such as architectural partitioning or global error-handling policy. ASDL is also meant as a communication medium for distributing architectural decisions to system stakeholders. Domain-specific aspects such as safety or fault tolerance are described in a simple yet powerful way.

ASDL describes an architecture as a set of components that provide at least one interface to the environment and that are interrelated with connectors. It describes not only the basic attributes of the architectural elements but also additional attributes, called architectural properties.

ASDL is a flexible language that may be adapted to different domains. The language is divided into the structure base and the property base. The *structure base* describes the structural elements of an architecture and usually is not changed once it is defined. The *property base* describes additional architectural concepts and can be changed according to the needs of the domain.

The ASDL Structure Base

Architectural elements—components, interfaces, connectors—are defined in the structure base.

- **Components.** The component base concept consists of the component identifier, the component name, and the component description in plain text.

- **Interfaces.** The interface base concept consists of the interface name and the interface description.

- **Connectors.** The connector base concept consists of the connector name, the connector description, and the connecting components (represented by the corresponding identifiers).

The ASDL Property Base

Information other than architectural elements is defined in the property base. The property base supports the communication of architectural information to system stakeholders and the recovery process of the reference architecture. Property values in most cases can be selected from a predefined list of values. The number of property values is therefore rather small and supports analysis of the architectures. Commonality analysis for identifying the reference architecture can be based on the property base elements.

- **Component properties.** Components are either primitive or composite. Composite components consist of at least one composite or primitive component. Primitive components are on the lowest level of the component hierarchy and do not contain any other components; they are elementary entities. The property describing this information is called the *structure*.

  The system in our case study is a safety-critical system in which *n*-version programming is used for failure detection. Two versions of software for the same functionality have been developed by two different teams. At run time, both versions (called A and B) are executed, and the results are compared by a software voter (called C). Components are designated either as A, B, or C or as non-safety-critical components. This property is called *component group*.

  Each component provides a set of services that can be summarized by the main characteristics or type of the component. Components can be characterized as data-processing components, data store components, or other types of components. The property describing this information is the *type*.

- **Interface properties.** Interfaces are a part of components. Components play different roles depending on their relationships to other components. Component A can play the role of server to component B, while at the same time playing the role of producer to component C. The role of a component, therefore, cannot be related directly to a component; rather it must be related to the component interface. The property *interface role* provides the relevant information.

The interface can provide a service, require a service, or both. The services can be implemented as a signal exchange or a procedure call, or by other communication techniques. The properties *interface type* and *interface service* provide information about the interface services.

- **Connector properties.** Connectors link two interfaces of two components together. The property *connecting components* provides information about the two components. The property *communication type* provides information about how information is exchanged between two services. This information includes the direction of the data flow, the nature of the control flow (synchronous, asynchronous), and whether or not the flow is continuous.

The block of code that follows represents part of Figure 7.3 in ASDL. The DEC and RECEIVE components, together with the relating connector and the corresponding interfaces (dcom_data_p, dcom_data_c), are represented.

```
comp_begin comp_id F2
      comp_name DEC
      comp_desc The DEC subsystem ...
      comp_group n_a
      comp_ role composite_comp
      child_desc child_of F1
      comp_type n_a
      safety_critical yes
      intf_name dcom_data_p
      intf_desc The dcom_data_p ...
      intf_role producer
      intf_role_desc data_transmit (decoded transp info data, cf22)
comp_end btm
comp_begin comp_id F4
      comp_name RECEIVE
      comp_desc The driver ...
      comp_group n_a
      comp_role primitive_comp
      c_child_of child_of F1
      comp_type n_a
      safety_critical yes
      intf_name dcom_data_c
      intf_desc The dcom_data_c ...
      intf_role consumer
      intf_role_desc data_receive (decoded transponder information, cf22)
comp_end RECEIVE
conn_name dcom_data
conn_desc The dcom_data connector ...
```

```
conn_intf (dcom_data_p - dcom_data_c)
communication type
        data_flow unidirectional(intf dcom_data_p to intf dcom_data_c)
        control_flow unidirectional(intf dcom_data_p to intf dcom_data_c)
        transfer asyn
info_exch discontinuous
```

The ASDL description was transformed from the Darwin diagrams representing the case study architectures. Basic information about components, interfaces, and connectors could be transformed directly. The architectural elements were then described in more detail with ASDL. Each component, interface, and connector was analyzed carefully. For the detailed description of the interfaces, the identification of the interface roles required an exact inspection of the source code to enable description of which data are processed by the interface.

7.6   Final Remarks

This chapter has described our experiences of applying the architecture recovery framework of Chapter 4 to an industrial case study at ABB. Recovery of architectural information is a promising approach for gaining control over the evolution of existing software systems. The recovery of a reference architecture for a product family allows reasoning about the quality of systems and will lead to reduced development and maintenance costs.

The system under consideration influences the architecture recovery process. Depending on the system domain, different architectural properties are of interest, different architectural descriptions are required, and the system information to recover the software architecture varies. From our experience with the TCS case study, we conclude that no single method is best suited for the recovery of all architectural properties. Furthermore, an architecture recovery method may be appropriate and well suited for one system, but not for another system. By focusing on architectural properties, the recovery process benefits from separation of concerns: Architectural properties are manageable units for architectural reasoning; it is easier to recover the software architecture of a system in parts; and different views and recovery methods can be used depending on the property to be recovered.

For the recovery of a reference architecture, we developed a commonality analysis method that identifies the reference architecture on the basis of the architectural descriptions of family members. The input to this analysis method consists of the individually recovered members of the product family.

The recovery process is done manually and must be supported by a systems expert. In the TCS case study the reference architecture was recovered from the architectural descriptions of three family members. For this rather small number of members the process was manageable. For a larger number of members or more complex structures, however, tool support and modified methods are necessary.

We also developed the flexible and extensible architectural description language ASDL to describe structural aspects of software architectures and their properties. ASDL provides concepts for comprehensive architectural description of a software system and consists of a structure base and a property base. Although ASDL was developed in the architecture recovery process of an embedded real-time system, it is adaptable to other domains. ASDL can be integrated in the company-specific software development process. Representation of the reference architecture of a product family can be supported by ASDL, together with the commonality analysis process.

We found that, in general, the exploitable results of the ARES project were techniques and experiences that directly influence the software engineering process, such as the recovery methods and the description languages. Direct results are better handling of early design decisions, increased communication among system stakeholders, transferable system abstractions, and increased application maintainability.

8

Looking Back and Looking Ahead

Mehdi Jazayeri

This book has attempted to present some of what we learned about software architecture for product families during the three years of the ARES project. It would be nice if we could look back and summarize in a cogent way the experiences of all the people involved. It would be even nicer if we could all agree on a consistent set of lessons learned. We could then come up with a checklist of dos and don'ts to be used by every software architect. Every experienced software engineer, however, knows this is not possible.

Technology transfer is notoriously difficult in software engineering precisely because of this problem of summarizing, or "packaging," experience. Yet we hope that the earlier chapters of the book do communicate some of the major lessons we have learned. What is more difficult, perhaps impossible, is to integrate the many different lessons we have learned in just a few pages. Often complex trade-offs rule out any simple conclusions. Whether a lesson learned by one group applies to another project by another group depends very much on the contexts of the projects.

This context dependency is precisely the reason that the ARES project took the industry-as-laboratory approach of evaluating research results in industrial settings. For the same reason, we have presented each industrial partner's experience separately in its own chapter, describing the complete experience. In this way the reader can see the context of the experiment and decide to what degree it applies in his or her own context.

In this chapter we review in a more general way than the previous chapters have some of the experiences of the project, lessons learned, and difficulties encountered. Some of these issues apply to any such project that involves partners from different institutions, and in particular from both industry and academia. We also discuss some of the issues and difficulties involved in packaging and exporting such experience for others to use and in technology transfer in general.

8.1   Why This Book?

The ARES project started in December 1995 and was completed in February 1999. During this time many people from all the partners worked on the project. The focus of the project was to produce results that could be exploited immediately by the partners. For example, we at the Technical University of Vienna started a software architecture course that relies heavily on the case studies from the ARES project. At Philips, engineers developed new tools for documenting software architectures and automatically generating code for module interconnection. At Nokia, engineers developed Web-based tools for organizing the documentation of complex systems. At ABB, the results of some of the ARES work drove the design of a new family architecture for train control systems. At Imperial College, the feedback from engineers in the three companies led to improvements in the Darwin tool set.

Although such results of the ARES project were useful to the partners, the goal of the project was much larger. As partners in a research project, we wanted to communicate our results to the larger research and industrial community. This we did through many publications in conferences and journals. The goal of this book is to integrate the different results into a bigger picture based on more than three years of experience. This book is our attempt to communicate what we learned in the project to the larger community of software engineers.

8.2   Some Things That Worked

We might ask how well our industry-as-laboratory approach worked. Did we make advances in the software architecture area by having researchers and practitioners work closely together? Indeed, there were many unforeseen successes. In this section we review some examples of these. Reading the chapters of the book individually may not make the links among the different components of the project clear. Each chapter tries to discuss only the subject of that chapter. Here we show a few examples of how the different parts of the project influenced one another.

One of the best examples of the interaction of research and practice had to do with architecture description. After many discussions among all the partners, the engineers at Philips said they were convinced that high-level documentation of architectures was useful and they were willing to give it a try, but they wanted a tool to help them get started. After some discussion, the colleagues at Imperial College completed the Darwin tool set and delivered it to Philips. After months of experimentation the engineers decided they could not use the tool because it was too fragile; after all, it was only a prototype tool, constantly under development. They were convinced, however, of the usefulness of certain concepts in Darwin—in particular the way in which component interfaces are defined in terms of `provides` and `requires` interfaces. They did not want to use the whole language, but they wanted to use some of the ideas.

Thus the Philips engineers developed their own language and tool, Koala, which implemented the ideas from Darwin but customized them for C and the Philips environment. The transfer of technology from research to practice was very clear and rapid in this case. The feedback from the engineers to the Darwin developers was also invaluable in refining both the Darwin language and its tool set. Publications have described both Darwin and Koala, but perhaps the harmonious working of research and practice does not come through clearly in these publications.

The use of Darwin at Asea Brown Boveri had a different result. There the engineers decided that Darwin's support for commonality analysis was severely limited. As a result, they developed their own language (ASDL), which was specifically designed for analyzing and identifying common modules in different members of a product family. Still, using Darwin helped the engineers discover the importance of commonality analysis support as a requirement for an architectural description language

An example in which tools were indeed transferred was the use of the Relational Calculator developed at the Philips laboratories. The researchers at the Technical University of Vienna, who were working with the engineers of ABB on architecture recovery, discovered that no single reverse engineering tool was sufficient for the task. Each one has strengths in some areas and produces its own kind of output or view of the system. Often we can derive high-level architectural information by combining the different views produced by reverse engineering tools. In many cases this combination involves combining several relations, such as which functions are used by which modules, or which functions are not used by any module (these are interrupt routines). It turned out that Philips had already developed a tool (the Relational Calculator) for another application that made it possible to compute such relations easily. This calculator ended up being adopted as part of the recovery tool set.

The case study approach in the ARES project provided a firm ground for experimentation. The case studies also provided the researchers with a great source of practical examples in their work. For example, though it did not start out this way, the software architecture course at the Technical University of Vienna is now based on these case studies. The instructors recognized that the case studies add a level of realism to the course that was previously lacking.

8.3   Some Problems We Encountered

The industry-as-laboratory approach to research and technology transfer is appealing, but it is not without problems. Indeed, researchers and practitioners have their own individual goals, and those goals are not always compatible. The problems encountered seem mundane, sometimes silly, but they are real. Here are two examples of such problems we faced that are classic catch-22 situations.

In one project, the source code of an industrial partner's product could not be released to the researchers because of the proprietary value of the product. It was the most important product of that particular partner, and the partner did not want to jeopardize its privacy.

Instead the industrial partner offered the source code for an older product whose protection was not as critical. Released to the researchers after two months of negotiations and many signatures, this source code was used for many experiments, and the researchers were quite pleased with the results they achieved: They were able to point out many significant ways in which this product, in particular its architecture, could be improved. Unfortunately, because the product was already old, the industrial partner that had developed it did not really care about the results. After all, that was the reason the code could be released to the researchers in the first place! This type of catch-22 situation often works to the detriment of both researchers and practitioners.

Another interesting episode involved the insistence of practitioners on having tools before they would consider using a particular method or technique. If researchers provide prototype tools, the main focus of the discussion turns toward features of the implementation rather than the method. Often the researchers are not really motivated to produce professional-quality tools, and the practitioners are not interested in using prototype tools. Any widespread experience with a significant method, such as a new architectural description language, necessarily requires high-quality, well-supported tools. This requirement limits the ability of researchers to transfer their technology unless they are willing to expend significant effort on tool development, which is often outside the area of their research. Even if they do invest time in producing high-quality tools, the next hurdle for researchers is to answer the question, Is your method standard?

8.4   Putting Research into Practice

This section presents some of the issues relating to the interaction of research and practice. These are some of the lessons we learned in trying to put research results into practice.

The first lesson is that any software technology must be adapted to the environment and experience of the practitioners who are considering the technology. In some cases, we had engineers who were already using the language SDL. They were not willing to learn and experiment with anything that was significantly different from SDL. SDL, after all, was a standard and "everybody" was using it. In another case, something as mundane as the direction of an arrow in a notation—whether it pointed toward or away from a box—was considered significant by the practitioners and required changing by the researchers. Such issues have nothing to do with research, but they do affect whether the results are accepted by practitioners.

A large part of the need for adapting technology could often be avoided if researchers used standard notations and techniques rather than inventing their own. Fortunately we now have a number of official and de facto standards in software engineering. Unfortunately, the introduction of standards has also become somewhat of a marketing ploy. It is not unusual these days to see a company introduce their de facto standard and take the next few years to complete it. Standards take years to mature. Typically, research proceeds years ahead of standards. The industry-as-laboratory approach cannot depend exclusively on the use of standards, but the use of nonstandard notations asks for significant commitment from practitioners.

Such nonstandard notations are often resisted, even when existing standard notations are known to be deficient. In the ARES project, we sometimes expended a lot of effort showing why standards did not meet our requirements. For example, no CORBA implementation met real-time requirements of a certain application. Clearly such assertions about the capabilities of implementations are time-dependent and apply only to the version of the standard being used. Standards and implementations evolve to meet expanding requirements. Researchers are therefore always pressed to compare their contributions to the best current standards. Half-finished or poorly defined standards force the practitioner to choose between waiting until the standard is finished or risking the adoption of a nonstandard solution.

Standards are particularly important for description tools. A standard notation for architecture description would facilitate communication not only among project members but also among different projects. Such notation could even be taught at the university. Unfortunately, standards often do not meet all the requirements of cutting-edge projects. What we found was that practitioners in such projects do not hesitate to extend standards when necessary. They are, however, not as accepting of extensions proposed by researchers. Indeed, we found many nonstandard tools and notations in use by the industrial partners, but nonstandard notations proposed by researchers were met with strong—perhaps healthy—skepticism.

One of the advantages of using a standard notation is the general availability of supporting tools from commercial vendors. The importance of tools in such cooperative efforts between research and industry cannot be overemphasized. Indeed, even though the ARES project specifically did not have the development of tools as a goal, we found that the best way to communicate ideas to our partners was through the use of tools, even tools with limited functionality. The best approach was to demonstrate the use of the tool on a problem posed by the practitioner. Sometimes the practitioners developed the tools themselves, if they were convinced of the usefulness of the idea or method. A tool, even if it was a simple program, served as the embodiment of a research idea and was the most effective vehicle for technology transfer.

In a project such as ARES, when researchers and practitioners work together, when we see that a method works (or doesn't work), that is only half the battle. For some practitioners, this may be enough. But for others, and certainly for the researcher, the next difficulty is to generalize the findings into widely applicable results. This task is notoriously difficult in software-engineering projects, and there are different theories about how to accomplish such generalization. For years, Basili (1995) and his group have been working on the idea of the *experience factory*—an organizational structure that captures and packages exeriences from software projects in such a way that they can be tailored and applied to different projects. We faced many situations in which we could have used such a factory. An interesting recent article by Pfleeger (1999) offers some ideas about how to do "empirical software engineering" research. In a very real sense, the ARES project was involved in empirical software engineering, and we hope others will try to replicate our results so that they can be generalized further.

Empirical software engineering, in the way we did it with case studies from real applications, taxes the patience and time of the researcher. A serious problem with such efforts is the enormous amount of detail and tedium in practical applications. For example, although we would like to work with high-level abstractions and principles that we assume are language-independent, real applications are very much language-dependent. In the architecture recovery case study, the application consisted of three different programming languages, at least one specification language, and some assembly language. Any tools we built to demonstrate or evaluate our methodologies had to deal with the intricacies of all these languages. The assembly language, in particular, was a source of serious problems: Any high-level analysis (such as data flow analysis) was defeated when data was communicated among modules through assembly language. Incidentally, none of the commercial tools we examined was able to deal with assembly language. We had to write our own tools for assembly language analysis.

In another case study, there were over a thousand C language `#ifdef` statements. No simplifying assumptions can eliminate this tedium. Being forced to deal with such details slows the pace of research. But attacking this tedium ensures that the techniques are validated with cases of real interest and have a higher chance of being accepted by practitioners. It is the first step in addressing the problem of technology transfer.

Another issue we faced in seriously applying our industry-as-laboratory approach to research was that the researchers needed to gain a tremendous amount of understanding about the application domain. Architects of real systems have a deep understanding of both the application domain and the system architecture. This understanding is the result of years of experience. How can this understanding be passed on to a researcher in software architecture? Without an appropriate understanding of the domain on the part of the researcher, the results produced by the researcher may be overly general and run the risk of being irrelevant to the application domain. As Jackson (1995) points out, software researchers tend to jump quickly to system issues without adequately understanding the domain.

Our solution to this problem was to form teams that included software researchers and domain experts who frequently reviewed the intermediate results. In one case the domain model that was produced in one of these meetings proved to be an invaluable documentation for the practitioners. This was the first time that the project had had such a concise documentation of its domain requirements. In the past this information had always been communicated informally. The domain model could not have been produced by the software researchers (who lacked understanding of the domain) or the domain experts (who lacked knowledge of domain description notation) alone. Perhaps advances and acceptance of software architecture will lead to better documentation of application domains, and thus to better communication between software engineers and domain experts.

8.5   Education of a Software Architect

The ARES project brought together researchers and engineers who were interested in applying recent research results to practical situations. Outside of the context of such a project, it is rare for practitioners to have either the time for or the benefit of close collaboration with researchers; similarly, researchers do not have the benefit of receptive practitioners. In this larger context, how do we transfer knowledge between practitioners and researchers in such a rapidly moving field as software engineering?

The problem is that the application and problem domains are evolving so rapidly that they often overtake the research problems being studied at universities. Without paying careful attention to problems of current interest to industry, researchers run the risk of working on irrelevant problems. On the other hand, because of time-to-market pressures, practitioners often are forced to ignore solutions already well known in academia.

The need for close contact between academia and industry—or research and practice—is especially acute in the area of software architecture because software architecture is relevant only for large systems and families of systems that are developed in industry. It is difficult to replicate realistic architectural problems in research situations or student projects.

On the basis of these analyses, we can make the following observations about education, research, and industry enterprises involved in software architecture:

- **Education.** There is certainly enough known now in the area of software architecture to warrant university courses on software architecture. Indeed, industry needs graduating software engineers to be well versed in models and methods of software architecture. With the increasing reliance on system integration out of existing components, and the growing importance of distributed heterogeneous systems, software architecture will become even more critical. Few universities offer such courses now, and fewer still require them. Our experience has shown us that such courses must be complemented by realistic case studies. Better still, they could be enhanced by short-term stints in industrial projects. In any event, studying models, notations, and formalisms is not enough. Software architecture must necessarily deal with real systems. Careful selection of case studies can go a long way toward demonstrating real architectural problems to students.

- **Continuing education.** Standard university courses for students are not enough. The pace of change in software technology and software architecture ensures that practicing engineers must seek new training periodically if they are to stay current. Such retraining is currently difficult because we lack a comprehensive picture of software architecture. That picture, and what we can teach about it, is evolving as new studies are performed. Perhaps a solution is to have a permanent industry-academia consortium that assists the transfer of knowledge in both directions. It could work on packaging case studies based on industrial needs for use by researchers, and it could develop training courses based on these case studies for practicing engineers.

The implications for industry and research are clear: They must work closely together. Research must start with industrially relevant problems, and industry must apply the best available results. Close collaboration will benefit both.

8.6   State of the Practice and Future Outlook

ARES is one of several projects started in the last five years that have focused strictly on software architecture. Software architecture has become of central importance to many companies as a way to control growing complexity. Fortunately, numerous workshops and conferences are now held regularly to enable communication between software architecture researchers and practitioners to discuss problems and solutions of mutual interest. At least two of these workshops are specifically on system family or product lines. Furthermore, the International Federation for Information Processing (IFIP) has formed a special study group on software architecture. These developments promise further and rapid advances in the area of software architecture.

One of the most important outcomes from these workshops is discussion of realistic case studies, including the problem statement, the solutions tried, and what worked and didn't work. Such descriptions of case studies enable the comparison of approaches in different companies and therefore an evaluation of the generality of the approaches. The description of the problems also helps explore the terrain of software architecture problems.

Some of the projects described in the workshops have also published complete books on their experiences. We hope to see many more such books. The state of the art is such that there are many areas of the field that need to be covered—and from various angles—before we have a complete understanding of all the issues in software architecture. Eventually, maybe in a few years, consensus about the essential elements and principles in software architecture will allow a textbook on the subject to be written. In the meantime we have to be satisfied with many different books. We hope that this book provides a small step to a better understanding of software architecture—in this case for product families.

Bibliography

Abowd, G. D., R. Allen, and D. Garlan. 1995. Formalizing style to understand descriptions of software architecture. *ACM Transactions on Software Engineering and Methodology* 4: 319–64.

Abowd, G., L. Bass, P. Clements, R. Kazman, L. Northrop, and A. Zaremski. 1997. *Recommended best industrial practice for software architecture evaluation.* Technical Report SEI 96–TR-025. Pittsburgh, Pa.: Carnegie Mellon University.

Adler, R. M. 1995. Emerging standards for component software. *IEEE Computer* 28(3): 68–77.

Allan, R., and D. Garlan. 1994. Formalizing architectural connection. In *Proceedings of the 16th International Conference on Software Engineering (ICSE '94),* pp. 71–80. Los Alamitos, Calif.: IEEE Computer Society Press.

Alonso, A., M. G. Valls, and J. A. de la Puente. 1999. Time response analysis of complex systems. In F. De Paoli and I. M. MacLeod (eds.), *Distributed computer control systems, 1998,* pp. 99–104. Oxford, England: Pergamon.

Awad, M., J. Kuusela, and J. Ziegler. 1996. *Object technology for real-time systems: A practical approach using OMT and fusion.* Englewood Cliffs, N.J.: Prentice-Hall.

Barbacci, M., M. H. Klein, T. H. Longstaff, and C. B. Weinstock. 1995. *Quality attributes.* Technical Report 95–TR-021. Pittsburgh, Pa,: Carnegie Mellon University/Software Engineering Institute.

Basili, V. R. 1995. The experience factory and its relationship to other quality approaches. *Advances in Computers* 41: 65–82.

Bass, L., P. Clements, and R. Kazman. 1998. *Software architecture in practice.* Reading, Mass.: Addison-Wesley.

Batory, D., and S. O'Malley. 1992. The design and implementation of hierarchical software systems with reusable components. *ACM Transactions on Software Engineering and Methodology* 1: 355–98.

Bellay, B., and H. Gall.. 1997. *The hot-spots technique to scavenge for architectural elements.* Technical Report TUV-1841–97–11. Vienna: Distributed Systems Group, Technical University of Vienna.

———. 1998a. An evaluation of reverse engineering tool capabilities. *Journal of Software Maintenance: Research and Practice* 10: 305–32.

———. 1998b. Reverse engineering to recover and describe a system's architecture. In F. van der Linden (ed.), *Proceedings of 2nd International Workshop on Development and Evolution of Software Architectures for Product Families,* pp. 115–22. Lecture Notes in Computer Science, 1429. Berlin: Springer.

Bergstra, J. A., and L. M. G. Feijs. 1991. *Algebraic methods: Theory, tools and applications,* Part II. Lecture Notes in Computer Science, 490. Berlin: Springer.

Bieman, J. M., and L. M. Ott. 1994. Measuring functional cohesion. *IEEE Transactions on Software Engineering* 20: 644–57.

Biggerstaff, T. J. 1989. Design recovery for maintenance and reuse. *IEEE Computer* 22(7): 36–49.

Biggerstaff, T. J., B. G. Mitbander, and D. E. Webster. 1994. Program understanding and the concept assignment problem. *Communications of the ACM* 37(5): 72–83.

Boehm, B., D. Port, A. Egyed, and M. Abi-Anton. 1999. The MBASE life cycle architecture milestone package. In *Proceedings of 1st IFIP Conference on Software Architecture (WICSA 1),* pp. 511–28. Boston: Kluwer Academic.

Booch, G. 1994. *Object-oriented analysis and design with applications.* 2nd ed. Reading, Mass.: Addison-Wesley.

Braek, R., and O. Haugen. 1993. *Engineering real time systems.* Englewood Cliffs, N.J.: Prentice-Hall.

Briand, L., S. Morasca, and V. R. Basili. 1994. *Defining and validating high-level design metrics.* Technical Report CS-TR-3301. College Park, Md.: University of Maryland.

Burns, A. 1994. Preemptive priority based scheduling: An appropriate engineering approach. In S. H. Son (ed.), *Advances in Real-Time Systems,* pp. 225–48. Englewood Cliffs, N.J.: Prentice-Hall.

Cheong, Y. C., A. L. Ananda, and S. Jarzabeck. 1998. Handling variant requirements in software architectural perspective. In F. van der Linden (ed.), *Proceedings of 2nd International Workshop on Development and Evolution of Software Architectures for Product Families,* pp. 188–96. Lecture Notes in Computer Science, 1429. Berlin: Springer.

Clements, P. C. 1996. A survey of architecture description languages. In *Proceedings of the Eighth International Workshop on Software Specification and Design (IWSSD-8),* pp. 16–25. Los Alamitos, Calif.: IEEE Computer Society Press.

DeBaud, J. M., and J. F. Girard. 1998. The relation between the product line development entry points and reengineering. In F. van der Linden (ed.), *Proceedings of 2nd International Workshop on Development and Evolution of Software Architectures for Product Families,* pp. 132–9. Lecture Notes in Computer Science, 1429. Berlin: Springer.

Design/CPN occurrence graph manual, version 3.0. 1996. Aarhus, Denmark: Computer Science Department of Aarhus University.

Design/CPN reference manual. 1993. Cambridge, Mass.: Computer Science Department of Aarhus University and Metasoftware Corporation.

Diefenbuch, M. 1997a. *Quest user manual, v 1.0.* Technical Report. Essen, Germany: Department of Mathematics and Computer Science, University of Essen. (http://www.cs. uni-essen.de/Fachgebiete/SysMod/Forschung/QUEST/)

———. 1997b. *Queueing SDL: A language for the functional and quantitative specification of distributed systems.* Essen, Germany: University of Essen. (http://www.cs. uni-essen.de/Fachgebiete/SysMod/Forschung/QUAFOS/TechRep/Q1/Q1.html).

Dikel, D., D. Kane, S. Ornburn, W. Loftus, and J. Wilson. 1997. Applying software product-line architecture. *IEEE Computer* 30(8): 49–55.

Douglass, B. P. 1997. *Real-time UML—Developing efficient objects for embedded systems.* Reading, Mass.: Addison-Wesley.

Dueñas, J. C., W. L. de Oliviera, and J. A. de la Puente. 1998. A software architecture evaluation model. In F. van der Linden (ed.), *Proceedings of 2nd International Workshop on Development and Evolution of Software Architectures for Product Families,* pp. 148–57. Lecture Notes in Computer Science, 1429. Berlin: Springer.

Eixelsberger, W., and H. Gall. 1998. Describing software architectures by system structure and properties. In *Proceedings of the 22nd Computer Software and Applications Conference (COMPSAC '98),* pp. 106–11. Los Alamitos, Calif.: IEEE Computer Society Press.

Eixelsberger, W., M. Kalan, M. Ogris, H. Beckman, B. Bellay, and H. Gall. 1998. Recovery of architectural structure: A case study. In F. van der Linden (ed.), *Proceedings of 2nd International Workshop on Development and Evolution of Software Architectures for Product Families,* pp. 89–96. Lecture Notes in Computer Science, 1429. Berlin: Springer.

Eixelsberger, W., M. Ogris, H. Gall, and B. Bellay. 1998. Software architecture recovery of a program family. In *Proceedings of the 20th International Conference on Software Engineering (ICSE '98) Lessons and Status Reports,* pp. 508–11. Los Alamitos, Calif.: IEEE Computer Society Press.

Eixelsberger, W., L. Warholm, R. Klösch, and H. Gall. 1997. Software architecture recovery of embedded software. In *Proceedings of the 19th International Software Engineering Conference (ICSE '97), Lessons in Organizations,* pp. 558–9. New York, N.Y.: Association for Computing Machinery.

Ellis, J. R. 1994. *Objectifying real-time systems.* New York: SIGS Books.

Feijs, L. M. G. 1993. *A formalisation of design methods.* Ellis Horwood Series in Computers and Their Applications. Chichester, England: Ellis Horwood.

Feijs, L. M. G., and H. B. M. Jonkers. 1992. *Formal specification and design.* Cambridge Tracts in Theoretical Computer Science, 35. Cambridge: Cambridge University Press.

Feijs, L. M. G., and R. van Ommering. 1996. Architecture visualisation and analysis. Paper presented at 1st ARES Workshop on Development and Evolution of Software Architectures for Product Families.

Feijs, L. M. G., H. B. M. Jonkers, and C. A. Middelburg. 1994. *Notations for software design.* Berlin: Springer.

Fenton, N. E., and S. L. Pfleeger. 1997. *Software metrics: A rigorous & practical approach.* 2nd ed. London: International Thompson Computer Press.

Fowler, M., and K. Scott. 1997. *UML distilled—Applying the standard object modeling language.* Object Technology Series. Reading, Mass.: Addison-Wesley.

Gaffney, J. E., Jr., and R. D. Cruickshank. 1992. A general economic model of software reuse. In *Proceedings of the Fourteenth International Conference on Software Engineering (ICSE '92),* pp. 327–37. New York: ACM Press.

Gamma, E., R. Helm, R. Johnson, and J. Vlissides. 1994. *Design patterns.* Reading, Mass.: Addison-Wesley.

Garlan, D. 1995. *An introduction to the Aesop system.* Pittsburgh, Pa.: School of Computer Science, Carnegie Mellon University.

Garlan, D., R. Allen, and J. Ockerbloom. 1994. Exploiting style in architectural design environments. *Software Engineering Notes* 19(5): 175–88.

Garlan, D., and D. Perry. 1994. Software architecture: Practice, potential and pitfalls (panel introduction). In *Proceedings of the 16th International Conference on Software Engineering (ICSE '94)*, pp. 354–63. Los Alamitos, Calif.: IEEE Computer Society Press.

———. 1995. Introduction to the special issue on software architecture. *IEEE Transactions on Software Engineering* 21: 269–74.

Garlan, D., and M. Shaw. 1993. An introduction to software architecture. In V. Ambriola and G. Tortora (eds.), *Advances in software engineering and knowledge engineering,* Vol. 2, pp. 1–39. Singapore: World Scientific.

Gomaa, H. 1993. *Software design methods for concurrent and real-time systems.* Reading, Mass.: Addison-Wesley.

Gomaa, H., L. Kerschberg, V. Sugumaran, C. Bosch, and I. Tavakoli. 1994. A prototype domain modeling environment for reusable software architecture. In *Proceedings of the Third International Conference on Software Reuse,* pp. 74–83. Los Alamitos, Calif.: IEEE Computer Society Press.

Graves, H. 1992. Lockheed environment for automatic programming. *IEEE Expert* 7(6): 15–25.

Harel, D. 1987. Statecharts: A visual formalism for complex systems. *Science of Computer Programming* 8: 231–74.

IEEE Std 982.1. IEEE Standard dictionary of measures to produce reliable software. IEEE Software Engineering Standards Collection, 1988 ed. New York: IEEE.

ISO-9126. Software product evaluation: Quality characteristics and guidelines for their use. 1991. Technical Report ISO/IEC 9126. Geneva, Switzerland: ISO.

ITU Message Sequence Chart (MSC). 1993. Technical Report ITU-T Recommendation Z.120. Geneva, Switzerland: International Telecommunication Union.

ITU Specification and Description Language (SDL). 1993. Technical Report ITU-T Recommendation Z.100. Geneva, Switzerland: International Telecommunication Union.

Jackson, K. and M. Boasson. 1995. The benefits of good architectural style in the engineering of computer based systems. In B. Melhart and J. Rozenblit (eds.), *Proceedings of the International Symposium and Workshop on Systems Engineering of Computer Based Systems,* pp. 103–13. Los Alamitos, Calif.: IEEE Computer Society Press.

Jackson, M. 1995. *Software requirements & specifications.* Reading, Mass.: Addison-Wesley.

Jacobson, I., M. Griss, and P. Jonsson. 1997. *Software reuse.* Reading, Mass.: Addison-Wesley.

Jerding, D. F., J. T. Stasko, and T. Ball. 1997. Visualizing interactions in program executions. In *Proceedings of the 19th International Conference on Software Engineering (ICSE '97)*, pp. 360–70. Los Alamitos, Calif.: IEEE Computer Society Press.

Johnson, B., S. Ornburn, and S. Rugaber. 1992. A quick tools strategy for program analysis and software maintenance. In *Proceedings of the International Conference on Software Maintenance (ICSM)*, pp. 206–13. Los Alamitos, Calif.: IEEE Computer Society Press.

Jonkers, H. B. M. 1991. Upgrading the pre- and postcondition technique. In *VDM '91,* pp. 428–56. Berlin: Springer.

———. 1993. An overview of the SPRINT method. In J. C. P. Woodcock and P. G. Larsen (eds.), *Proceedings of FME '93,* pp. 403–27. Berlin: Springer.

Kazman, R., L. Bass, G. Abowd, and M. Webb. 1994. SAAM: A method for analyzing the properties of software architectures. In *Proceedings of the 16th International Conference on Software Engineering,* pp. 81–90. Los Alamitos, Calif.: IEEE Computer Society Press.

Klein, M. H., T. Ralya, B. Pollak, R. Obenza, and M. González-Harbour. 1993. *A practitioner's handbook for real-time analysis: Guide to rate monotonic analysis for real-time systems.* Boston: Kluwer Academic.

Knor, R. 1997. *Converting data structures and algorithms from C to C++ applying the Standard Template Library.* Technical Report TUV-1841–97–16. Vienna: Distributed Systems Group, Technical University of Vienna.

Knor, R., G. Trausmuth, and J. Weidl. 1998. Reengineering C/C++ source code by transforming state machines. In F. van der Linden (ed.), *Proceedings of 2nd International Workshop on Development and Evolution of Software Architectures for Product Families,* pp. 97–105. Lecture Notes in Computer Science, 1429. Berlin: Springer.

Kogut, P., and P. Clements. 1994. The software architecture renaissance. *Crosstalk—The Journal of Defense Software Engineering* 7(11): 1–5.

Kozaczynski, W. (V.), and Ning, J. Q. 1996. Concern-driven design for a specification language supporting component-based software engineering. In *Proceedings of the Eighth International Workshop on Software Specification and Design (IWSSD-8).* Los Alamitos, Calif.: IEEE Computer Society Press.

Kramer, J. 1990. Configuration programming—A framework for the development of distributable systems. In *IEEE International Conference on Computer Systems and Software Engineering (CompEuro '90),* pp. 374–84. Los Alamitos, Calif.: IEEE Computer Society Press.

Kramer, J., and J. Magee. 1985. Dynamic configuration for distributed systems. *IEEE Transactions on Software Engineering* 11: 424–36.

Kramer, J., J. Magee, and M. Sloman. 1992. Configuring distributed systems. In *Proceedings of the 5th ACM SIGOPSEuropean Workshop,* pp. 1–5. New York: ACM.

Kruchten, P. B. 1995. The 4+1 View Model of architecture. *IEEE Software* 12(6): 42–50.

Leary, J. L. 1995. An architectural basis for evolving software systems. *Journal of Systems and Software* 30: 27–43.

Lindqvist, M., E. Routhula, E. Kettunen, and H. Tuominen. 1995. *The TNSDL book.* 3rd ed. Helsinki, Finland: Nokia Telecommunications.

Magee, J., N. Dulay, S. Eisenbach, and J. Kramer. 1995. Specifying distributed software architectures. In *Proceedings of the 5th European Software Engineering Conference,* pp. 137–53. Lecture Notes in Computer Science, 989. Berlin: Springer.

Magee, J., N. Dulay, and J. Kramer. 1994a. A constructive development environment for parallel and distributed programs. In *Proceedings of the 2nd International Workshop on Configurable Distributed Systems (IWCDS-2),* pp. 4–14. Los Alamitos, Calif.: IEEE Computer Society Press.

———. 1994b. Regis: A constructive development environment for distributed programs. *Distributed Systems Engineering Journal* 1: 304–12.

———. 1997. Analysing the behaviour of distributed software architectures: A case study. In *Proceedings of the 5th IEEE Workshop on Future Trends in Distributed*

Computing Systems (FTDCS '97), pp. 240–7. Los Alamitos, Calif.: IEEE Computer Society Press.

Magee, J., J. Kramer, and D. Giannakopoulou. 1998. Software architecture directed behaviour analysis. In *Proceedings of the 9th International Workshop on Software Specification and Design (IWSSD-9),* pp. 144–6. Los Alamitos, Calif.: IEEE Computer Society Press

———. 1999. Behaviour analysis of software architectures. In *Proceedings of the 1st IFIP Conference on Software Architecture (WICSA 1),* pp. 35–50. Boston: Kluwer Academic.

Magee, J., J. Kramer, and M. Sloman. 1989. Constructing distributed systems in Conic. *IEEE Transactions on Software Engineering* 15: 663–75.

Miguel, M. Á. de, J. C. Dueñas, Á. Rendón, J. A. de la Puente, A. Alonso, and G. León. 1996. Early validation of real-time systems by model execution. In *Proceedings of the 13th World Congress of the International Federation of Automatic Control,* pp. 315–20. San Francisco, Calif.: Pergamon Press.

Monroe, R. T., A. Kompanek, R. Melton, and D. Garlan. 1997. Architectural styles, design patterns, and objects. *IEEE Software* 14(1): 43–52.

Ng, K., J. Kramer, and J. Magee. 1996. A CASE tool for software architecture design. *Journal of Automated Software Engineering* 3: 261–84.

Object Management Group. 1991. *The common object request broker: Architecture and specification.* Framingham, Mass.: OMG.

Olsen, A., O. Færgemand, B. Møller-Pedersen, R. Reed, and J. R. W. Smith. 1994. *Systems engineering using SDL-92.* Amsterdam: Elsevier Science.

Parnas, D. L. 1976. On the design and development of program families. *IEEE Transactions on Software Engineering* 2: 1–9.

Parnas, D. L., P. Clements, and D. Weiss. 1985. The modular structure of complex systems. *IEEE Transactions on Software Engineering* 11: 259–66.

Perry, D. E., and A. L. Wolf. 1992. Foundations for the study of software architecture. *ACM SIGSOFT Software Engineering Notes* 17(4): 40–52.

Pfleeger, S. L. 1999. Albert Einstein and empirical software engineering. *IEEE Computer* 32(11): 32–7.

Ran, A. 1996. MOODS: Models for object-oriented design with state. In J. M. Vlissides, J. O. Coplien, and N. L. Kerth (eds.), *Pattern languages of program design 2,* pp. 119–42. Reading, Mass.: Addison-Wesley.

Ran, A., and J. Kuusela. 1996a. Design decision trees. In *Proceedings of the Eighth International Workshop on Software Specification and Design (IWSSD-8),* pp. 172–5. Los Alamitos, Calif.: IEEE Computer Society Press.

———. 1996b. Selected issues in architecture of software intensive products. In *Proceedings of the Second International Software Architecture Workshop (ISAW-2),* pp. 147–151. New York: ACM.

Rechtin, E., and M. W. Maier. 1997. *The art of systems architecting.* Systems Engineering Series. Boca Raton, Fla.: CRC Press.

Redl, S., M. Weber, and M. Oliphant. 1995. *An introduction to GSM.* Boston: Artech House.

Reenskaug, T., P. Wold, and O. A. Lehne. 1996. *Working with objects: The OOram software engineering method.* Greenwich, Conn.: Manning Publications.

Rumbaugh, J., M. Blaha, W. Premerlani, F. Eddy, and W. Lorensen. 1991. *Object-oriented modeling and design.* Englewood Cliffs, N.J.: Prentice-Hall.

Rushby, J. 1994. Critical systems properties: Survey and taxonomy. *Reliability Engineering and System Safety* 43: 189–219.

Schwanke, R. W., V. A. Strack, and T. Werthmann-Auzinger. 1996. Industrial architecture with gestalt. In *Proceedings of the Eighth International Workshop on Software Specification and Design (IWSSD-8),* pp. 176–80. Los Alamitos, Calif.: IEEE Computer Society Press.

Selic, B., P. T. Ward, and G. Gullekson. 1994. *Real-time object-oriented modelling.* New York: Wiley.

Shaw, M. 1995. Comparing architectural design styles. *IEEE Software* 12(6): 27–41.

Shaw, M., and D. garlan. 1995. Formulations and formalisms in software architecture. In J. van Leeuwen (ed.), *Computer science today. Recent trends and developments,* pp. 307–23. Lecture Notes in Computer Science, 1000. Berlin: Springer.

———. 1996. *Software architecture—Perspectives on an emerging discipline.* Englewood Cliffs, N.J.: Prentice-Hall.

Shaw, M., R. DeLine, D. V. Klein, T. L. Ross, D. M. Young, and G. Zelesnik. 1995. Abstractions for software architecture and tools to support them. *IEEE Transactions on Software Engineering* 21: 314–35.

Smith, C., and L. Williams. 1993. Software performance engineering: A case study including performance comparison with design alternatives. *IEEE Transactions on Software Engineering* 19: 720–41.

Sommerville, I., and G. Dean. 1994. PCL: A configuration language for modelling evolving system architectures. Technical Report SE/8/94. Lancaster, England: Lancaster University. (Available at ftp://ftp.comp.lancs.ac.uk/pub/reports/1994/SE.8.94.ps.Z.).

Soni, D., R. L. Nord, and C. Hofmeister. 1995. Software architecture in industrial applications. In *Proceedings of the 17th International Conference on Software Engineering (ICSE '95),* pp. 196–207. Los Alamitos, Calif.: IEEE Computer Society Press.

Szyperski, C. 1997. *Component software—Beyond object-oriented programming.* Reading, Mass.: Addison-Wesley.

Turner, K. J. (ed.). 1993. Using formal description techniques—An introduction to Estelle, LOTOS and SDL. New York: Wiley.

van der Hamer, P., F. van der Linden, A. Saunders, and H. Sligte. 1998. An integral hierarchy and diversity model for describing product family architectures. In F. van der Linden (ed.), *Proceedings of 2nd International Workshop on Development and Evolution of Software Architectures for Product Families,* pp. 66–86. Lecture Notes in Computer Science, 1429. Berlin: Springer.

van der Linden, F., and J. Müller. 1995a. Composing product families from reusable components. In B. Melhart and J. Rozenblit (eds.), *Proceedings 1995 IEEE International Symposium and Workshop on Systems Engineering of Computer Based Systems,* pp. 35–40. Los Alamitos, Calif.: IEEE Computer Society Press.

———. 1995b. Creating architectures with building blocks. *IEEE Software* 12(6): 51–60.

van Ommering, R. 1998. Koala, a component model for consumer electronics product software. In F. van der Linden (ed.), *Proceedings of 2nd International Workshop on*

Development and Evolution of Software Architectures for Product Families, pp. 76–86. Lecture Notes in Computer Science, 1429. Berlin: Springer.

van Vlijmen, S. F. M., and J. J. Wamel. 1993. *A semantic approach to protocol using process algebra.* Technical Report P9311. Amsterdam: Programming Research Group, University of Amsterdam.

Wirsing, M., and J. A. Bergstra. 1989. *Algebraic methods: Theory, tools and applications.* Lecture Notes in Computer Science, 394. Berlin: Springer.

Witt, D. I., F. T. Baker, and E. W. Merritt. 1994. *Software architecture and design—Principles, models, and methods.* Amsterdam: Van Nostrand Reinhold.

Index